MARVEL KNIG

DAREDEVIL

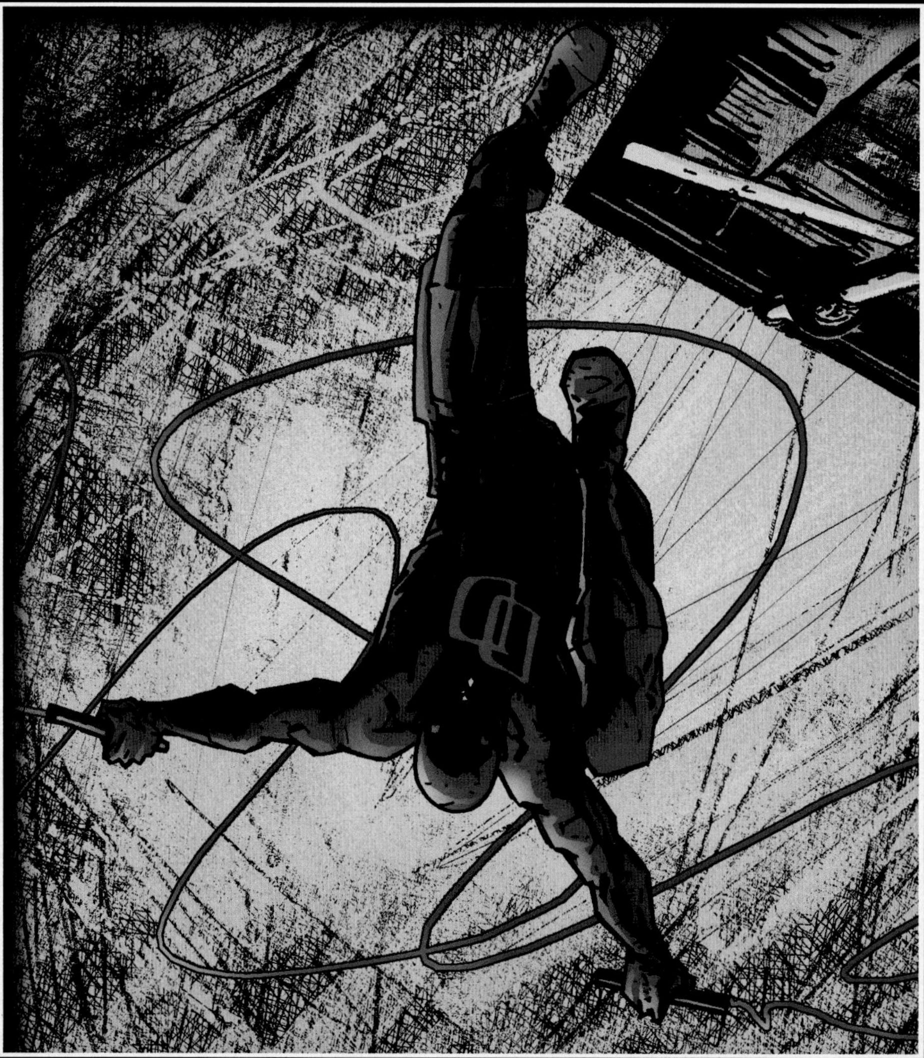

UNDERBOSS

MARVEL KNIGHTS

DAREDEVIL
UNDERBOSS

BRIAN MICHAEL BENDIS
Writer

ALEX MALEEV
Artist

MATT HOLLINGSWORTH
Colorist

RICHARD STARKINGS & COMICRAFT'S **WES ABBOTT**
Letterer

STUART MOORE
Editor

KELLY LAMY
Associate Managing Editor

NANCI DAKESIAN
Managing Editor

Collection Editor **JENNIFER GRÜNWALD**
Assistant Editor **CAITLIN O'CONNELL**
Associate Managing Editor **KATERI WOODY**
Associate Manager, Digital Assets **JOE HOCHSTEIN**

Editor, Special Projects **MARK D. BEAZLEY**
VP Production & Special Projects **JEFF YOUNGQUIST**
Book Designer **ADAM DEL RE**
SVP Print, Sales & Marketing **DAVID GABRIEL**

Editor In Chief **C.B. CEBULSKI**
Chief Creative Officer **JOE QUESADA**
President **DAN BUCKLEY**
Executive Producer **ALAN FINE**

MARVEL KNIGHTS DAREDEVIL BY BENDIS & MALEEV: UNDERBOSS. Contains material originally published in magazine form as DAREDEVIL #26-31. First printing 2018. ISBN 978-1-302-91403-5. Published by MARVEL WORLDWIDE, INC., a subsidiary of MARVEL ENTERTAINMENT, LLC. OFFICE OF PUBLICATION: 135 West 50th Street, New York, NY 10020.

Printed in the U.S.A. DAN BUCKLEY, President, Marvel Entertainment; JOHN NEE, Publisher; JOE QUESADA, Chief Creative Officer; TOM BREVOORT, SVP of Publishing; DAVID BOGART, SVP of Business Affairs & Operations, Publishing & Partnership; DAVID GABRIEL, SVP of Sales & Marketing, Publishing; JEFF YOUNGQUIST, VP of Production & Special Projects; DAN CARR, Executive Director of Publishing Technology; ALEX MORALES, Director of Publishing Operations; DAN EDINGTON, Managing Editor; SUSAN CRESPI, Production Manager; STAN LEE, Chairman Emeritus. For information regarding advertising in Marvel Comics or on Marvel.com, please contact Vit DeBellis, Custom Solutions & Integrated Advertising Manager, at vdebellis@marvel.com. For Marvel subscription inquiries, please call 888-511-5480. **Manufactured between 8/24/2018 and 9/25/2018 by LSC COMMUNICATIONS INC., KENDALLVILLE, IN, USA.**

10 9 8 7 6 5 4 3 2 1

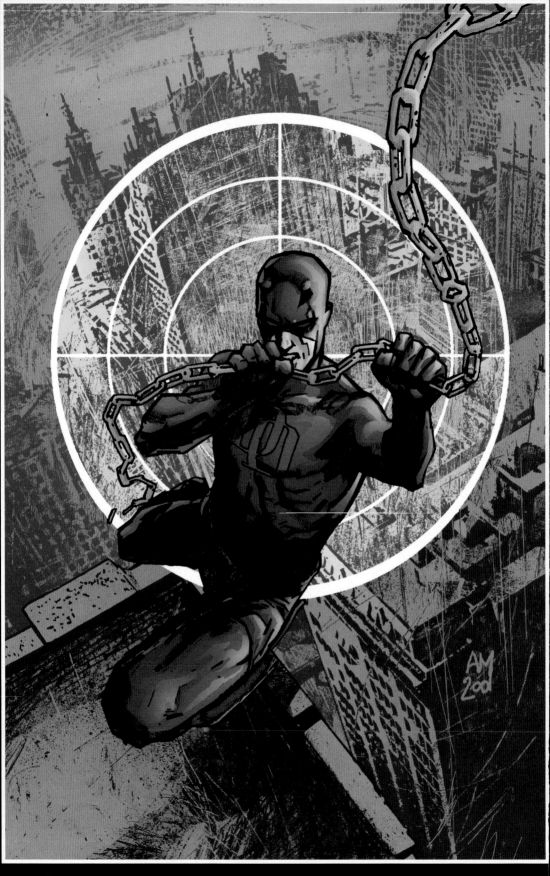

I DON'T KNOW IF I EVER TOLD YOU THIS --

BUT BACK IN THE DAY -- I DON'T KNOW -- BACK BEFORE I HAD HAIR ON MY CHIN -- MY UNCLE OWED A GUY SOME MONEY AT A STREET RATE.

YOU KNOW, TO A SHARK. THE NEIGHBORHOOD GUY EVERYBODY WENT TO.

MY UNCLE? ENDS UP HE COULDN'T PAY.

AND YOU KNOW WHAT HAPPENS NEXT -- OLDEST STORY EVER TOLD --

POP. BLAMMO!

DEAD.

THAT'S IT. HE'S GONE.

FACE DOWN IN HIS CORNFLAKES.

AND MAN, I REMEMBER -- THE WHOLE NEIGHBORHOOD WENT INTO SOMETHING THAT CAN ONLY BE DESCRIBED AS A COMA.

SEE? BACK IN THE DAY -- ONE BULLET.

SIMPLE. CLEAN. RIGHT TO THE HEAD.

ONE BULLET AND *EVERYONE* FROM THE BRONX TO ORLANDO -- *EVERYONE!* -- KNOWS IT WAS A HIT.

EVERYONE KNOWS WHO DID IT. AND EVERYONE KNOWS WHY.

BUSINESS TAKEN CARE OF. MESSAGE RECEIVED.

AND THE MESSAGE SAYS: YOU-DO-NOT-SCREW-WITH-THE-SHARK.

THOSE DAYS ARE LONG SINCE PAST, SILKE.

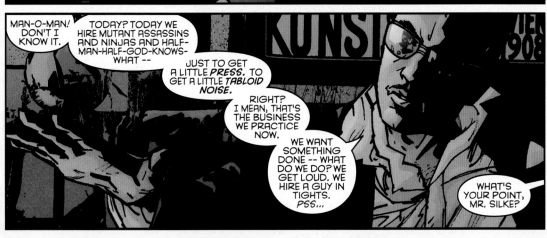

MAN-O-MAN! DON'T I KNOW IT.

TODAY? TODAY WE HIRE MUTANT ASSASSINS AND NINJAS AND HALF-MAN-HALF-GOD-KNOWS-WHAT --

JUST TO GET A LITTLE *PRESS.* TO GET A LITTLE *TABLOID NOISE.*

RIGHT? I MEAN, THAT'S THE BUSINESS WE PRACTICE NOW.

WE WANT SOMETHING DONE -- WHAT DO WE DO? WE GET LOUD. WE HIRE A GUY IN TIGHTS. *PSS...*

WHAT'S YOUR POINT, MR. SILKE?

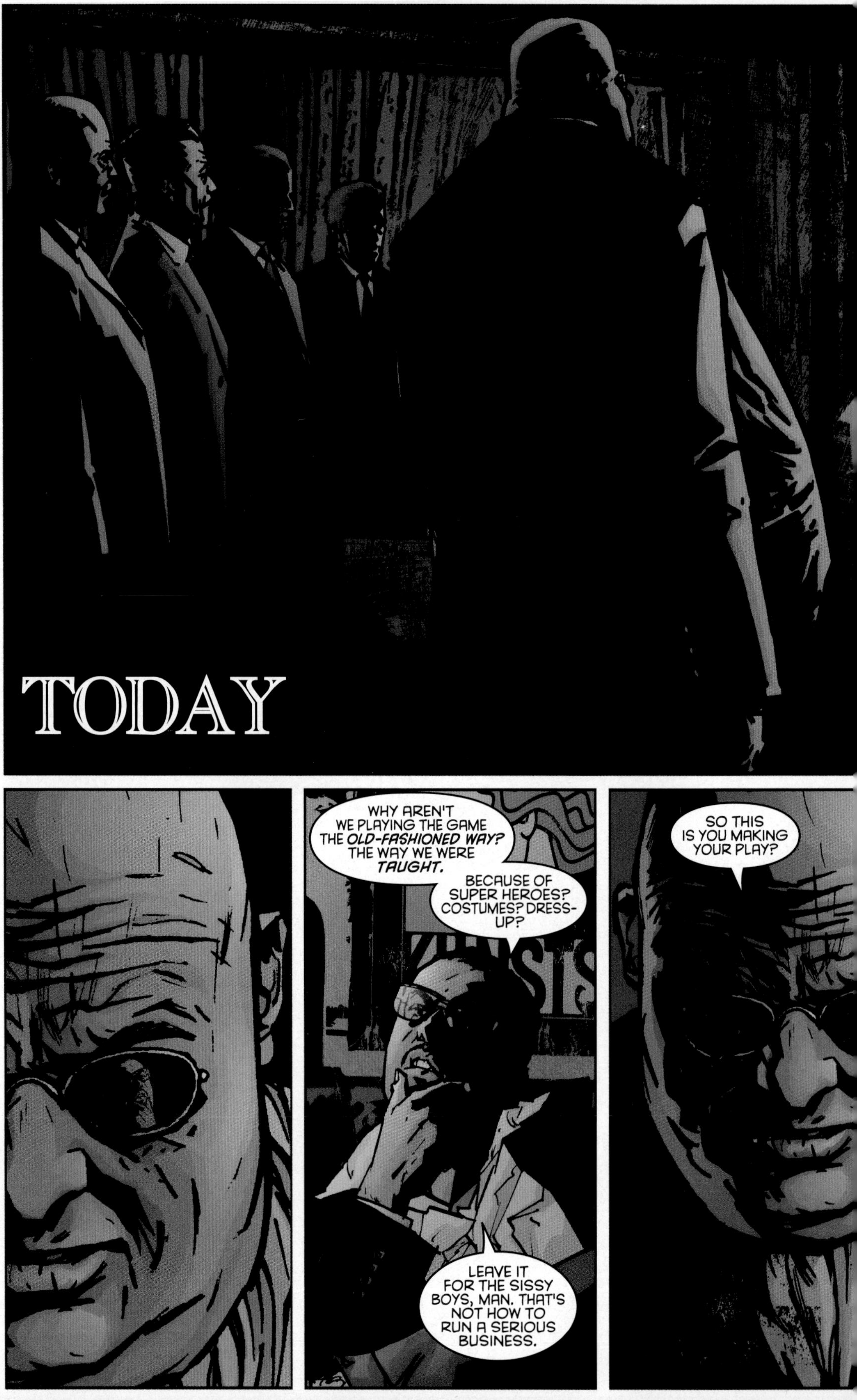
TODAY
WHY AREN'T WE PLAYING THE GAME THE *OLD-FASHIONED WAY?* THE WAY WE WERE ***TAUGHT.***
BECAUSE OF SUPER HEROES? COSTUMES? DRESS-UP?
LEAVE IT FOR THE SISSY BOYS, MAN. THAT'S NOT HOW TO RUN A SERIOUS BUSINESS.
SO THIS IS YOU MAKING YOUR PLAY?

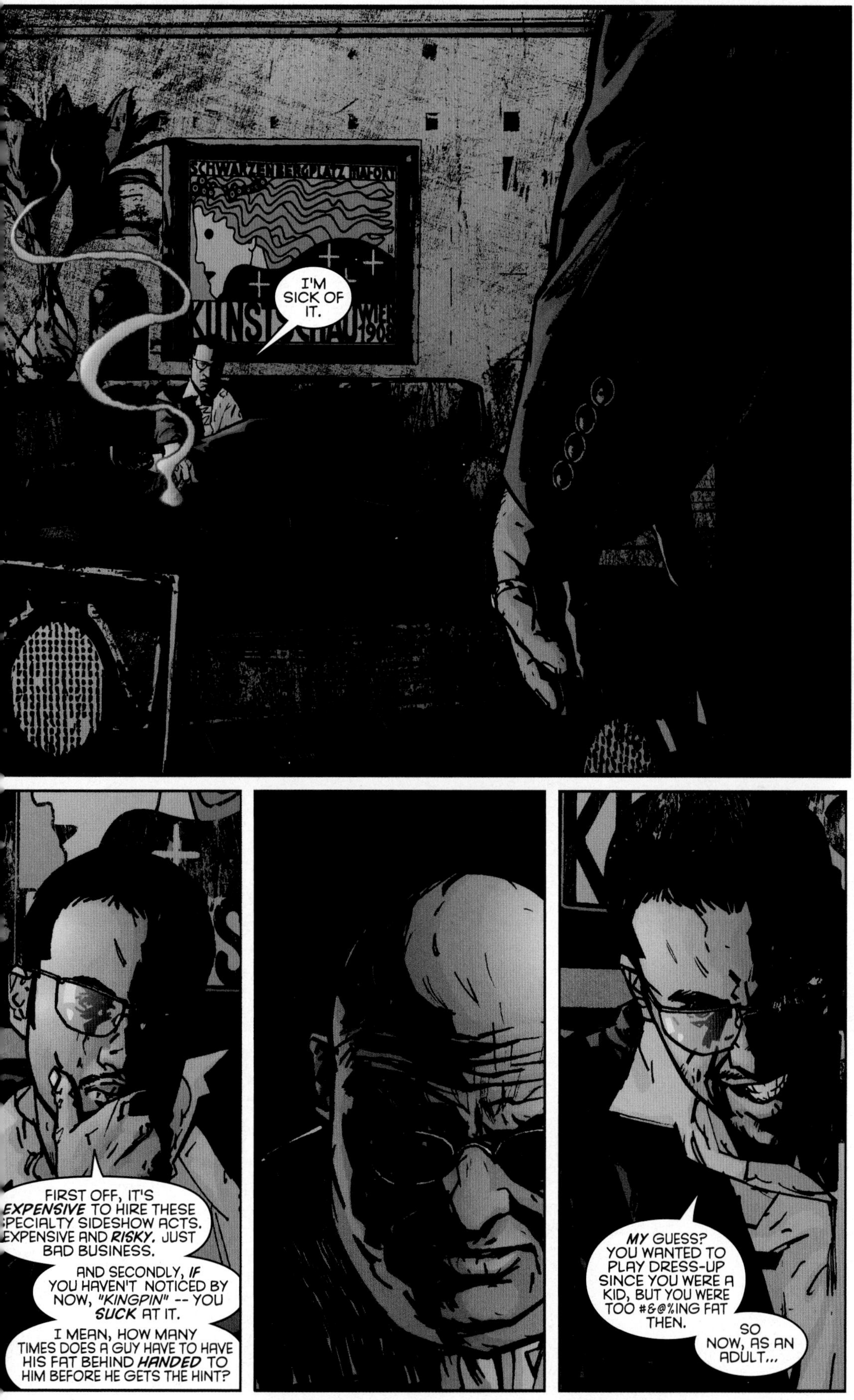
I'M SICK OF IT.
FIRST OFF, IT'S ***EXPENSIVE*** TO HIRE THESE SPECIALTY SIDESHOW ACTS. EXPENSIVE AND ***RISKY.*** JUST BAD BUSINESS.
AND SECONDLY, ***IF*** YOU HAVEN'T NOTICED BY NOW, ***"KINGPIN"*** -- YOU ***SUCK*** AT IT.
I MEAN, HOW MANY TIMES DOES A GUY HAVE TO HAVE HIS FAT BEHIND ***HANDED*** TO HIM BEFORE HE GETS THE HINT?
MY GUESS? YOU WANTED TO PLAY DRESS-UP SINCE YOU WERE A KID, BUT YOU WERE TOO #&@%ING FAT THEN.
SO NOW, AS AN ADULT...

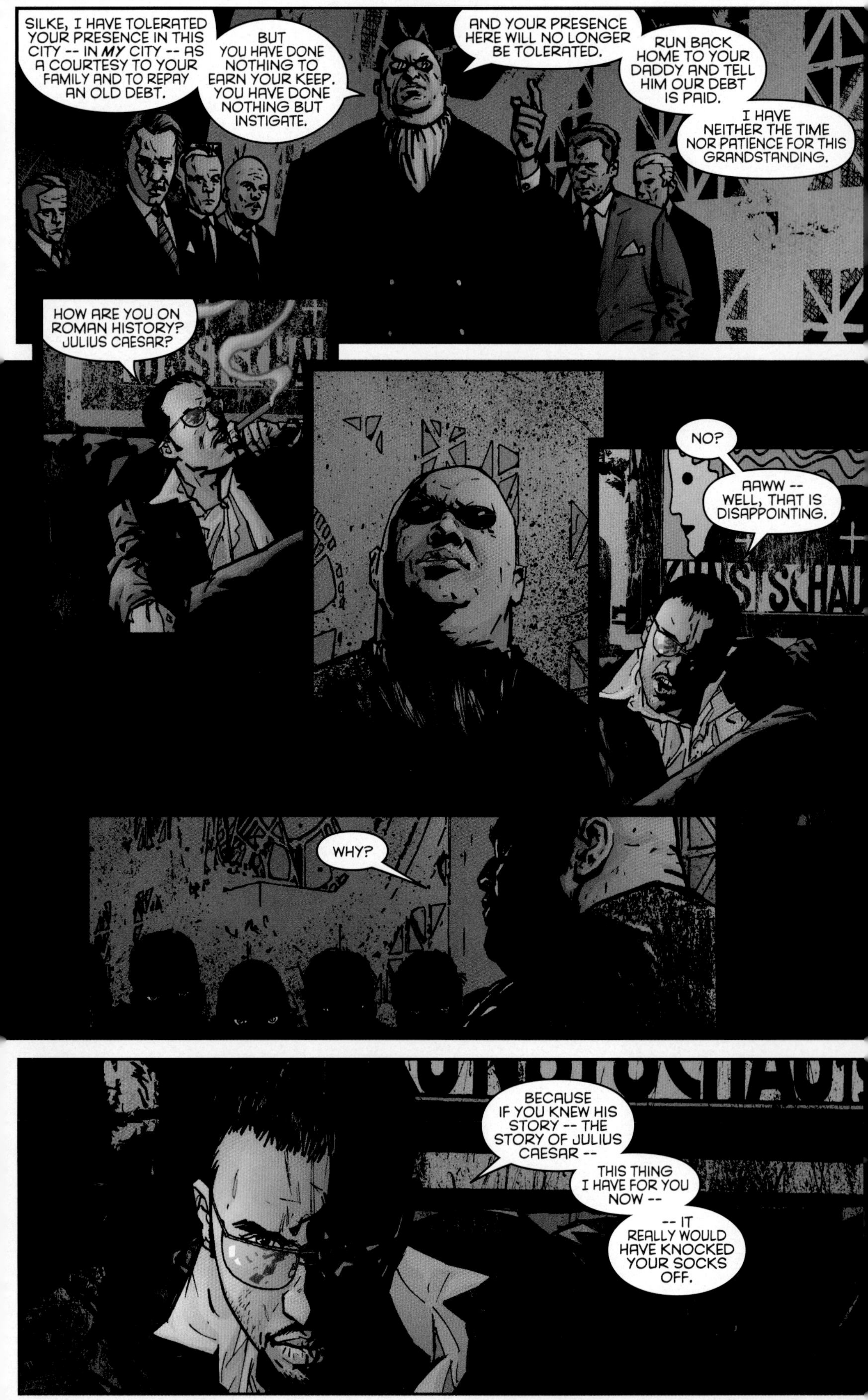
SILKE, I HAVE TOLERATED YOUR PRESENCE IN THIS CITY -- IN *MY* CITY -- AS A COURTESY TO YOUR FAMILY AND TO REPAY AN OLD DEBT.
BUT YOU HAVE DONE NOTHING TO EARN YOUR KEEP. YOU HAVE DONE NOTHING BUT INSTIGATE.
AND YOUR PRESENCE HERE WILL NO LONGER BE TOLERATED.
RUN BACK HOME TO YOUR DADDY AND TELL HIM OUR DEBT IS PAID.
I HAVE NEITHER THE TIME NOR PATIENCE FOR THIS GRANDSTANDING.
HOW ARE YOU ON ROMAN HISTORY? JULIUS CAESAR?
NO?
AAWW -- WELL, THAT IS DISAPPOINTING.
KUNSTSCHAU
WHY?
BECAUSE IF YOU KNEW HIS STORY -- THE STORY OF JULIUS CAESAR --
THIS THING I HAVE FOR YOU NOW --
-- IT REALLY WOULD HAVE KNOCKED YOUR SOCKS OFF.

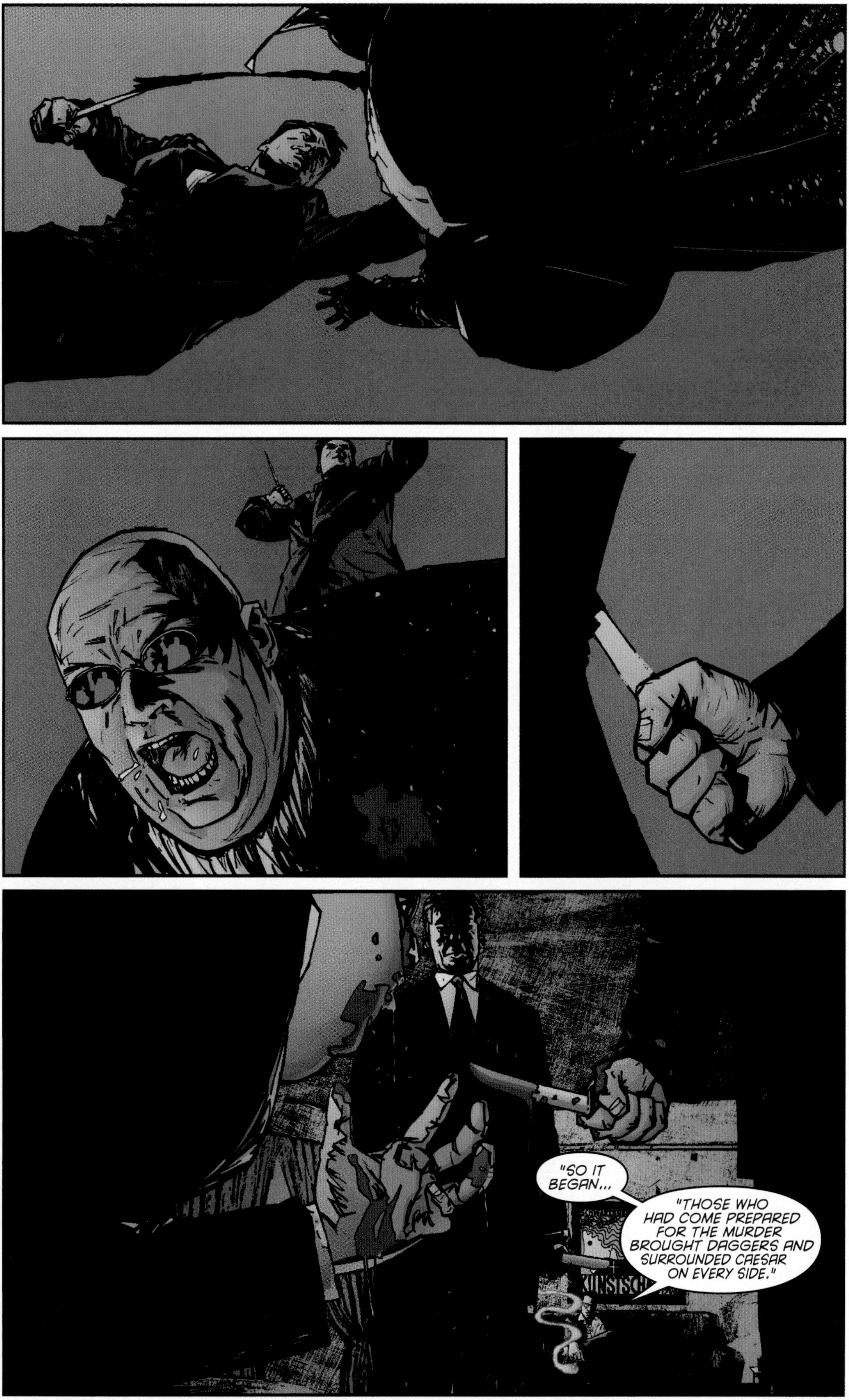
"SO IT BEGAN...
"THOSE WHO HAD COME PREPARED FOR THE MURDER BROUGHT DAGGERS AND SURROUNDED CAESAR ON EVERY SIDE."
KUNSTSCH

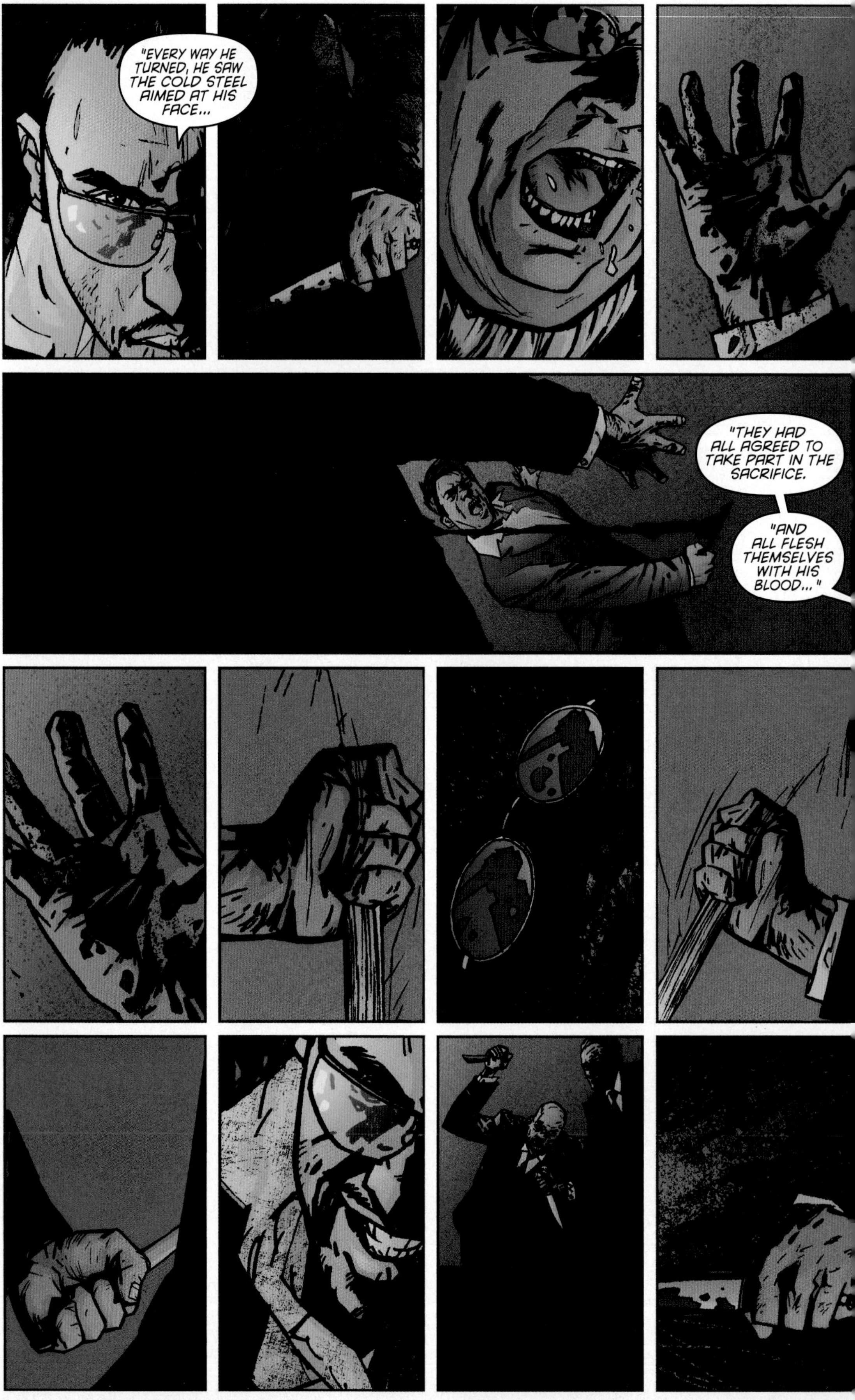
"EVERY WAY HE TURNED, HE SAW THE COLD STEEL AIMED AT HIS FACE...
"THEY HAD ALL AGREED TO TAKE PART IN THE SACRIFICE.
"AND ALL FLESH THEMSELVES WITH HIS BLOOD..."

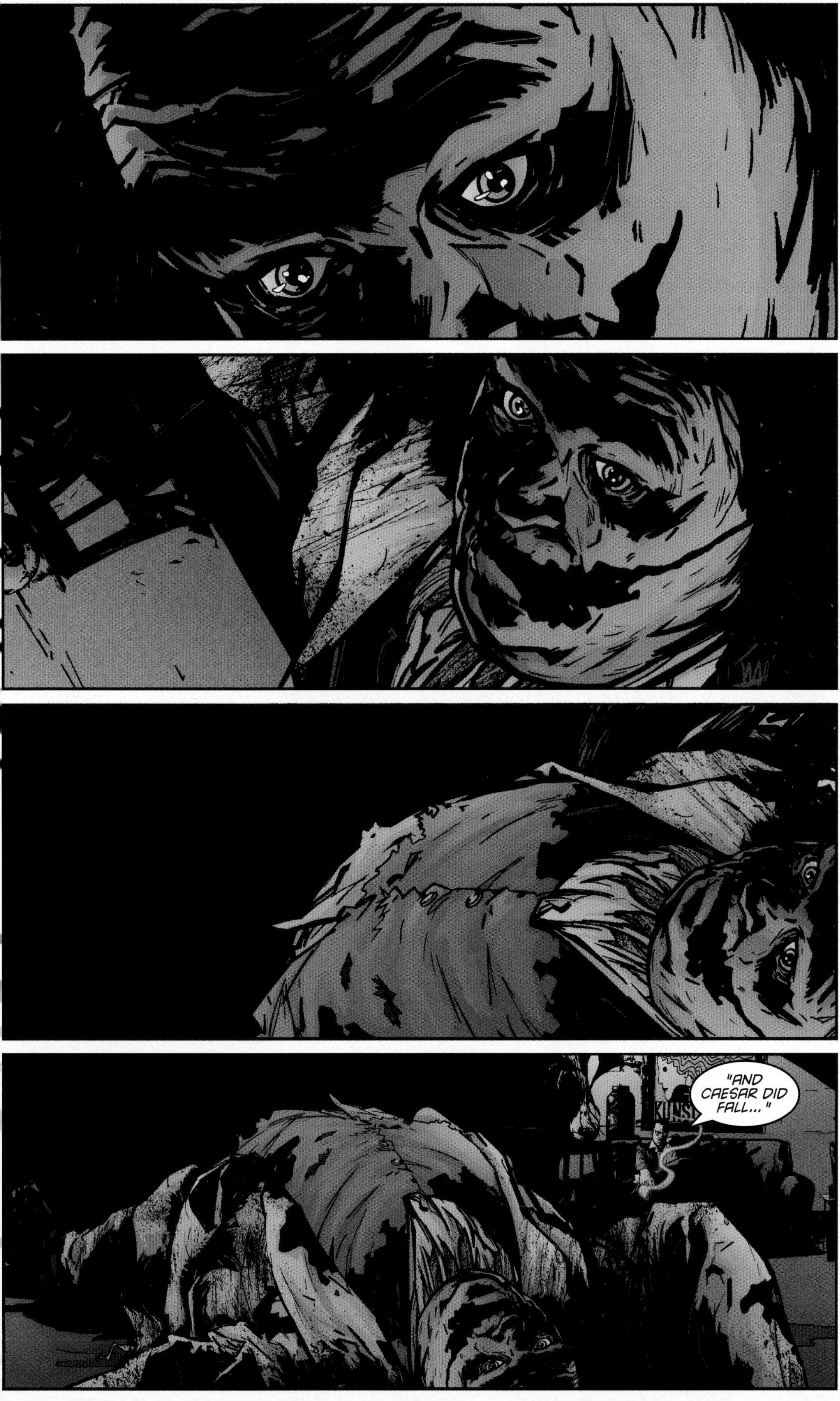
"AND CAESAR DID FALL..."

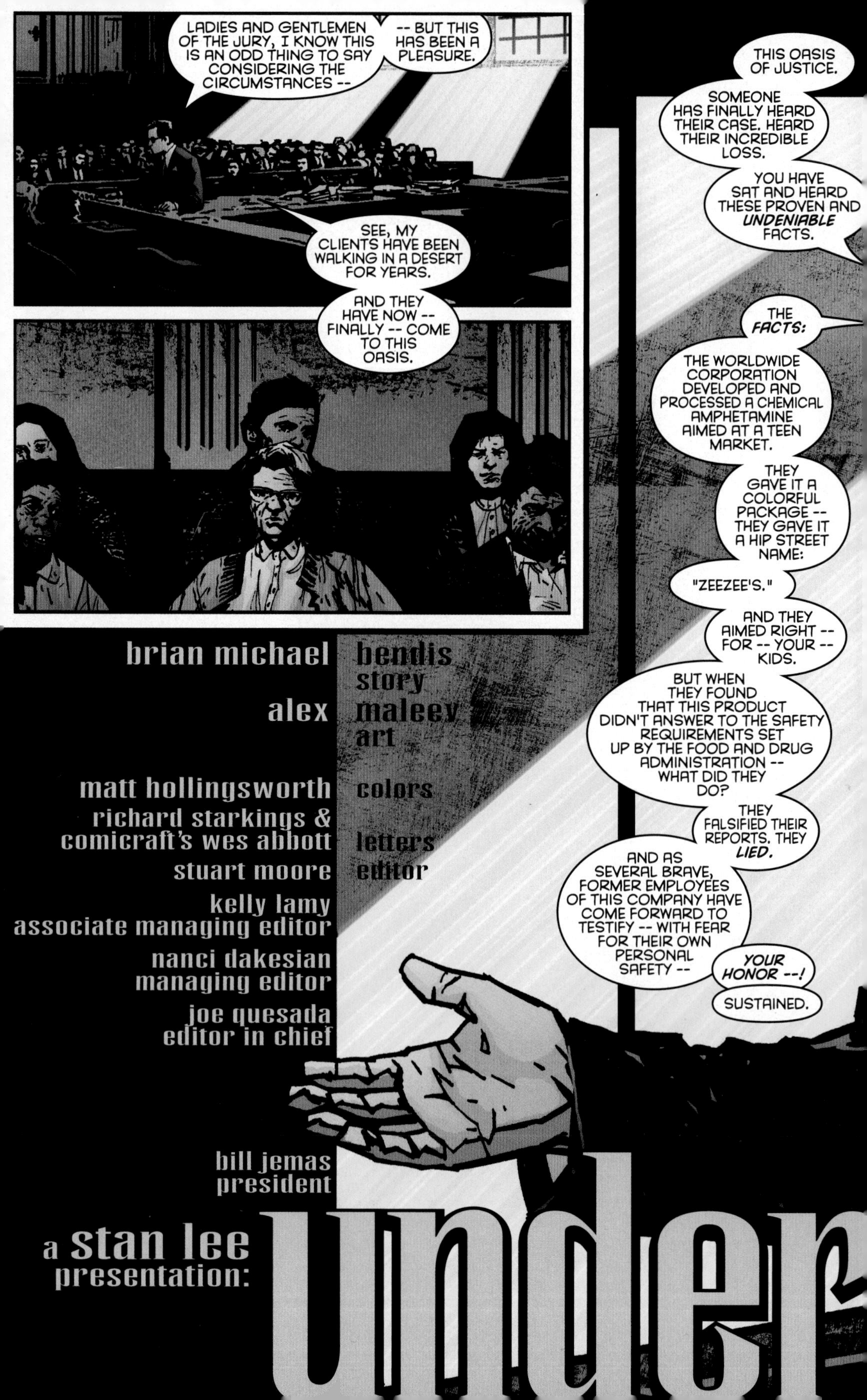
LADIES AND GENTLEMEN OF THE JURY, I KNOW THIS IS AN ODD THING TO SAY CONSIDERING THE CIRCUMSTANCES --
-- BUT THIS HAS BEEN A PLEASURE.
SEE, MY CLIENTS HAVE BEEN WALKING IN A DESERT FOR YEARS.
AND THEY HAVE NOW -- FINALLY -- COME TO THIS OASIS.
THIS OASIS OF JUSTICE.
SOMEONE HAS FINALLY HEARD THEIR CASE. HEARD THEIR INCREDIBLE LOSS.
YOU HAVE SAT AND HEARD THESE PROVEN AND *UNDENIABLE* FACTS.
THE *FACTS:*
THE WORLDWIDE CORPORATION DEVELOPED AND PROCESSED A CHEMICAL AMPHETAMINE AIMED AT A TEEN MARKET.
THEY GAVE IT A COLORFUL PACKAGE -- THEY GAVE IT A HIP STREET NAME:
"ZEEZEE'S."
AND THEY AIMED RIGHT -- FOR -- YOUR -- KIDS.
BUT WHEN THEY FOUND THAT THIS PRODUCT DIDN'T ANSWER TO THE SAFETY REQUIREMENTS SET UP BY THE FOOD AND DRUG ADMINISTRATION -- WHAT DID THEY DO?
THEY FALSIFIED THEIR REPORTS. THEY *LIED.*
AND AS SEVERAL BRAVE, FORMER EMPLOYEES OF THIS COMPANY HAVE COME FORWARD TO TESTIFY -- WITH FEAR FOR THEIR OWN PERSONAL SAFETY --
YOUR HONOR --!
SUSTAINED.
brian michael bendis story
alex maleev art
matt hollingsworth colors
richard starkings & comicraft's wes abbott letters
stuart moore editor
kelly lamy associate managing editor
nanci dakesian managing editor
joe quesada editor in chief
bill jemas president
a stan lee presentation:
under

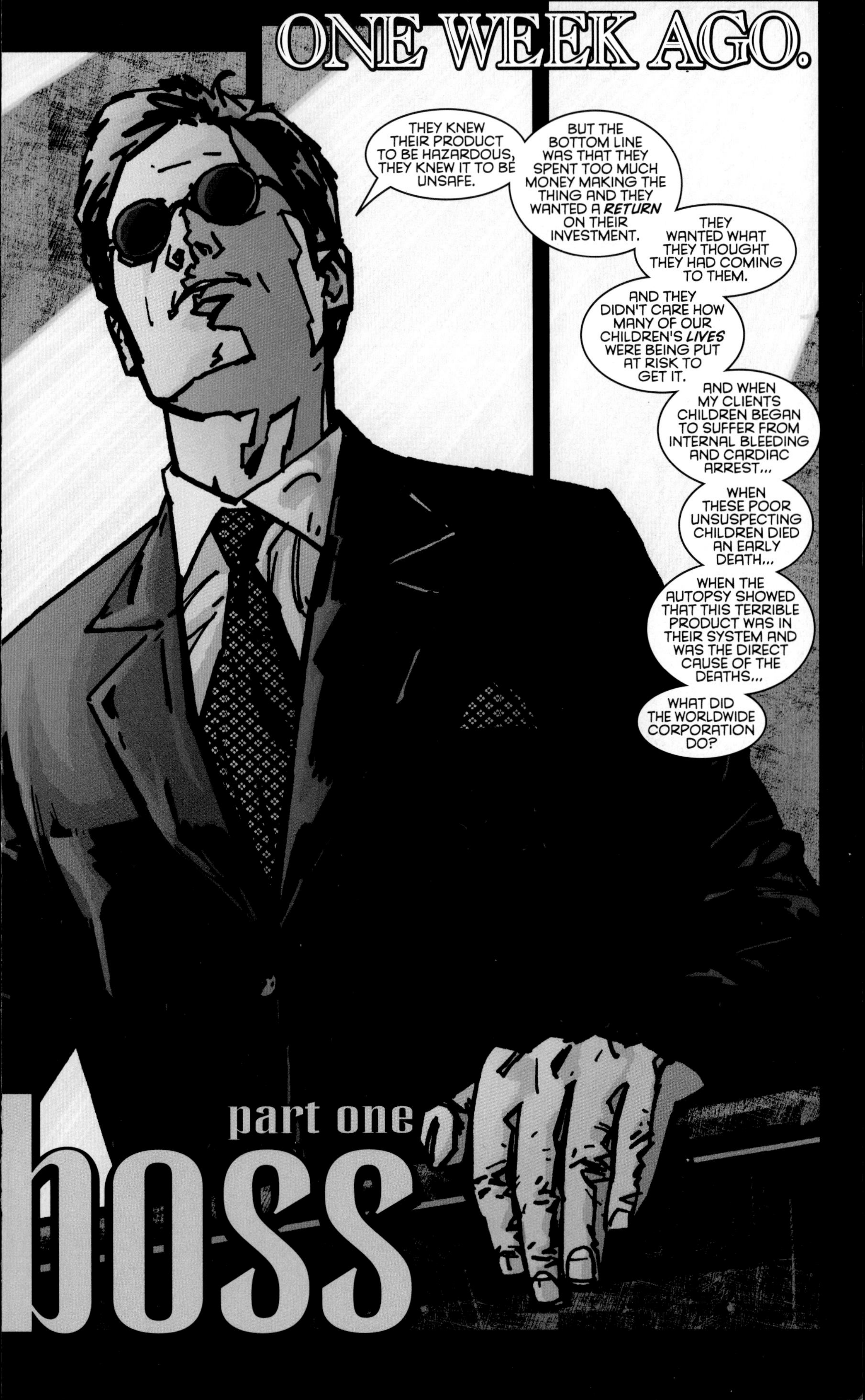
ONE WEEK AGO.
THEY KNEW THEIR PRODUCT TO BE HAZARDOUS, THEY KNEW IT TO BE UNSAFE.
BUT THE BOTTOM LINE WAS THAT THEY SPENT TOO MUCH MONEY MAKING THE THING AND THEY WANTED A *RETURN* ON THEIR INVESTMENT.
THEY WANTED WHAT THEY THOUGHT THEY HAD COMING TO THEM.
AND THEY DIDN'T CARE HOW MANY OF OUR CHILDREN'S *LIVES* WERE BEING PUT AT RISK TO GET IT.
AND WHEN MY CLIENTS CHILDREN BEGAN TO SUFFER FROM INTERNAL BLEEDING AND CARDIAC ARREST...
WHEN THESE POOR UNSUSPECTING CHILDREN DIED AN EARLY DEATH...
WHEN THE AUTOPSY SHOWED THAT THIS TERRIBLE PRODUCT WAS IN THEIR SYSTEM AND WAS THE DIRECT CAUSE OF THE DEATHS...
WHAT DID THE WORLDWIDE CORPORATION DO?
part one
boss

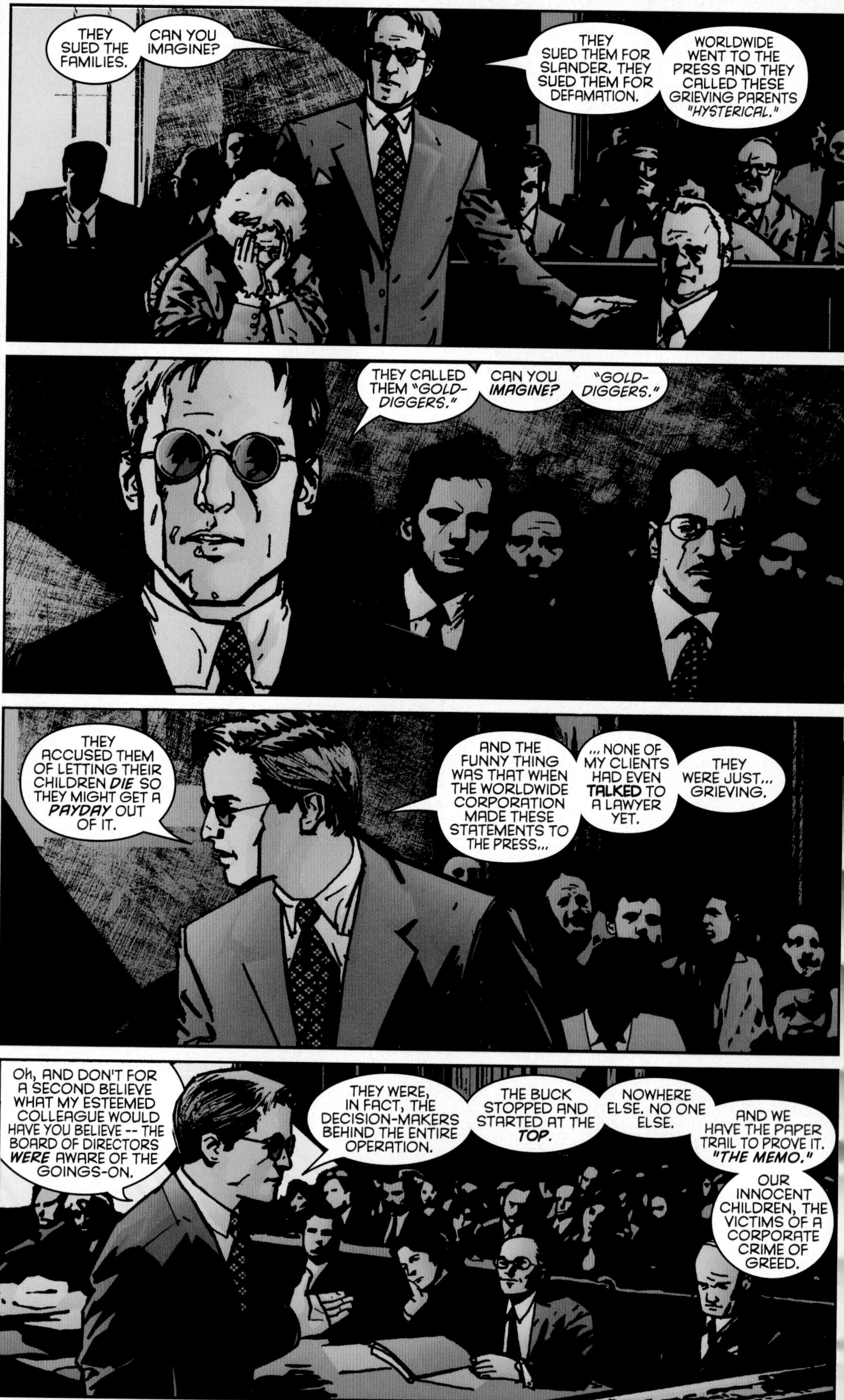
THEY SUED THE FAMILIES.
CAN YOU IMAGINE?
THEY SUED THEM FOR SLANDER. THEY SUED THEM FOR DEFAMATION.
WORLDWIDE WENT TO THE PRESS AND THEY CALLED THESE GRIEVING PARENTS "HYSTERICAL."
THEY CALLED THEM "GOLD-DIGGERS."
CAN YOU IMAGINE?
"GOLD-DIGGERS."
THEY ACCUSED THEM OF LETTING THEIR CHILDREN DIE SO THEY MIGHT GET A PAYDAY OUT OF IT.
AND THE FUNNY THING WAS THAT WHEN THE WORLDWIDE CORPORATION MADE THESE STATEMENTS TO THE PRESS...
...NONE OF MY CLIENTS HAD EVEN TALKED TO A LAWYER YET.
THEY WERE JUST... GRIEVING.
Oh, AND DON'T FOR A SECOND BELIEVE WHAT MY ESTEEMED COLLEAGUE WOULD HAVE YOU BELIEVE -- THE BOARD OF DIRECTORS WERE AWARE OF THE GOINGS-ON.
THEY WERE, IN FACT, THE DECISION-MAKERS BEHIND THE ENTIRE OPERATION.
THE BUCK STOPPED AND STARTED AT THE TOP.
NOWHERE ELSE. NO ONE ELSE.
AND WE HAVE THE PAPER TRAIL TO PROVE IT. "THE MEMO."
OUR INNOCENT CHILDREN, THE VICTIMS OF A CORPORATE CRIME OF GREED.

BUT I KNOW WHAT YOU'RE THINKING: IT'S A TRAGEDY, SURE...

BUT WHAT WILL MONEY DO?

WILL MONEY BRING BACK THE DEAD?

THE JURY THINKS THAT THEY SIT SILENT FOR ME AS I TALK.

THEY DON'T. THEY JUST THINK THEY DO.

I CAN HEAR THEIR HEARTS BEATING IN THEIR CHESTS. I CAN HEAR THEIR CLOTHES RUSTLING FROM THE SLIGHTEST SHIFT.

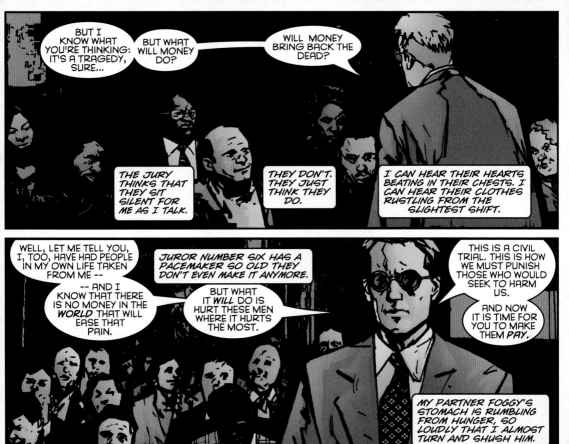

WELL, LET ME TELL YOU, I, TOO, HAVE HAD PEOPLE IN MY OWN LIFE TAKEN FROM ME --

-- AND I KNOW THAT THERE IS NO MONEY IN THE WORLD THAT WILL EASE THAT PAIN.

JUROR NUMBER SIX HAS A PACEMAKER SO OLD THEY DON'T EVEN MAKE IT ANYMORE.

BUT WHAT IT WILL DO IS HURT THESE MEN WHERE IT HURTS THE MOST.

THIS IS A CIVIL TRIAL. THIS IS HOW WE MUST PUNISH THOSE WHO WOULD SEEK TO HARM US.

AND NOW IT IS TIME FOR YOU TO MAKE THEM PAY.

MY PARTNER FOGGY'S STOMACH IS RUMBLING FROM HUNGER, SO LOUDLY THAT I ALMOST TURN AND SHUSH HIM.

THESE ARE THE FACTS OF THIS CASE.

WHEN I WAS A CHILD -- I WAS IN AN ACCIDENT THAT BLINDED ME FOR LIFE -- BUT MADE MY OTHER SENSES SUPER-HUMAN -- OTHERWORLDLY --

AND I KNOW THAT YOU WILL DO WHAT IS RIGHT -- BEFORE THE EYES OF GOD.

I CAN TASTE -- SMELL -- HEAR -- IN WAYS PEOPLE COULDN'T EVEN IMAGINE.

THEY ALSO COULDN'T IMAGINE THAT UNDER THIS TWO-THOUSAND-DOLLAR SUIT IS THE UNIFORM OF A MAN THE CITY KNOWS AS DAREDEVIL -- THE MAN WITHOUT FEAR.

THANK YOU.

AND BECAUSE OF THESE ABILITIES, I KNOW HOW THEY WILL VOTE BEFORE IT EVEN HAPPENS.

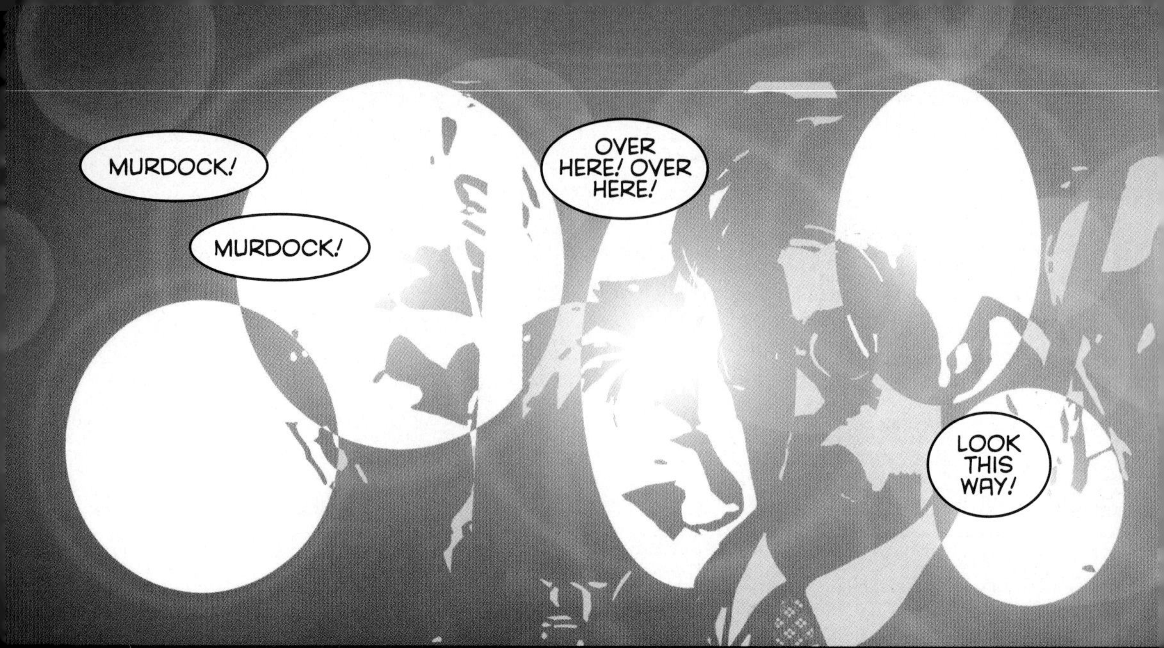
MURDOCK!
MURDOCK!
OVER HERE! OVER HERE!
LOOK THIS WAY!

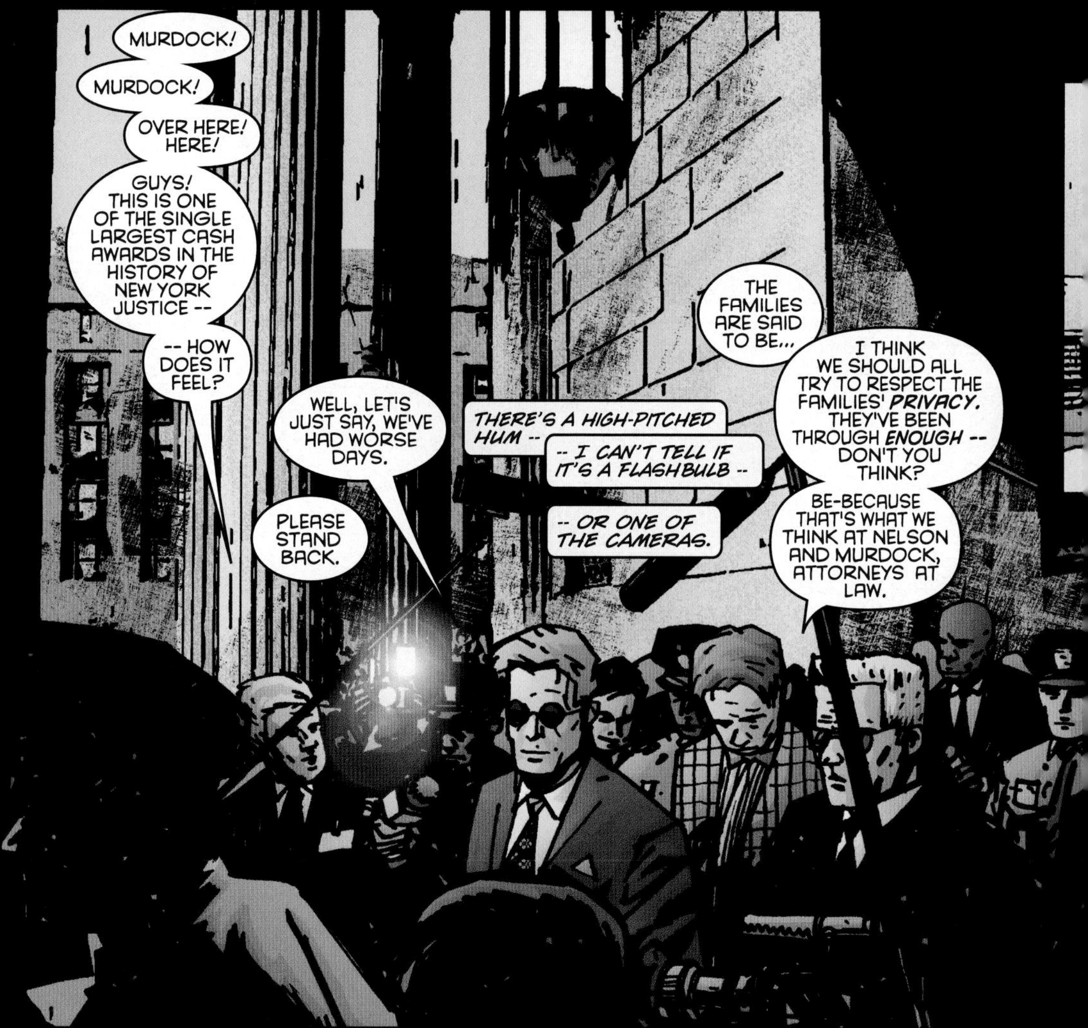
MURDOCK!
MURDOCK!
OVER HERE! HERE!
GUYS! THIS IS ONE OF THE SINGLE LARGEST CASH AWARDS IN THE HISTORY OF NEW YORK JUSTICE --
-- HOW DOES IT FEEL?
PLEASE STAND BACK.
WELL, LET'S JUST SAY, WE'VE HAD WORSE DAYS.
THERE'S A HIGH-PITCHED HUM --
-- I CAN'T TELL IF IT'S A FLASHBULB --
-- OR ONE OF THE CAMERAS.
THE FAMILIES ARE SAID TO BE...
I THINK WE SHOULD ALL TRY TO RESPECT THE FAMILIES' PRIVACY. THEY'VE BEEN THROUGH ENOUGH -- DON'T YOU THINK?
BE-BECAUSE THAT'S WHAT WE THINK AT NELSON AND MURDOCK, ATTORNEYS AT LAW.

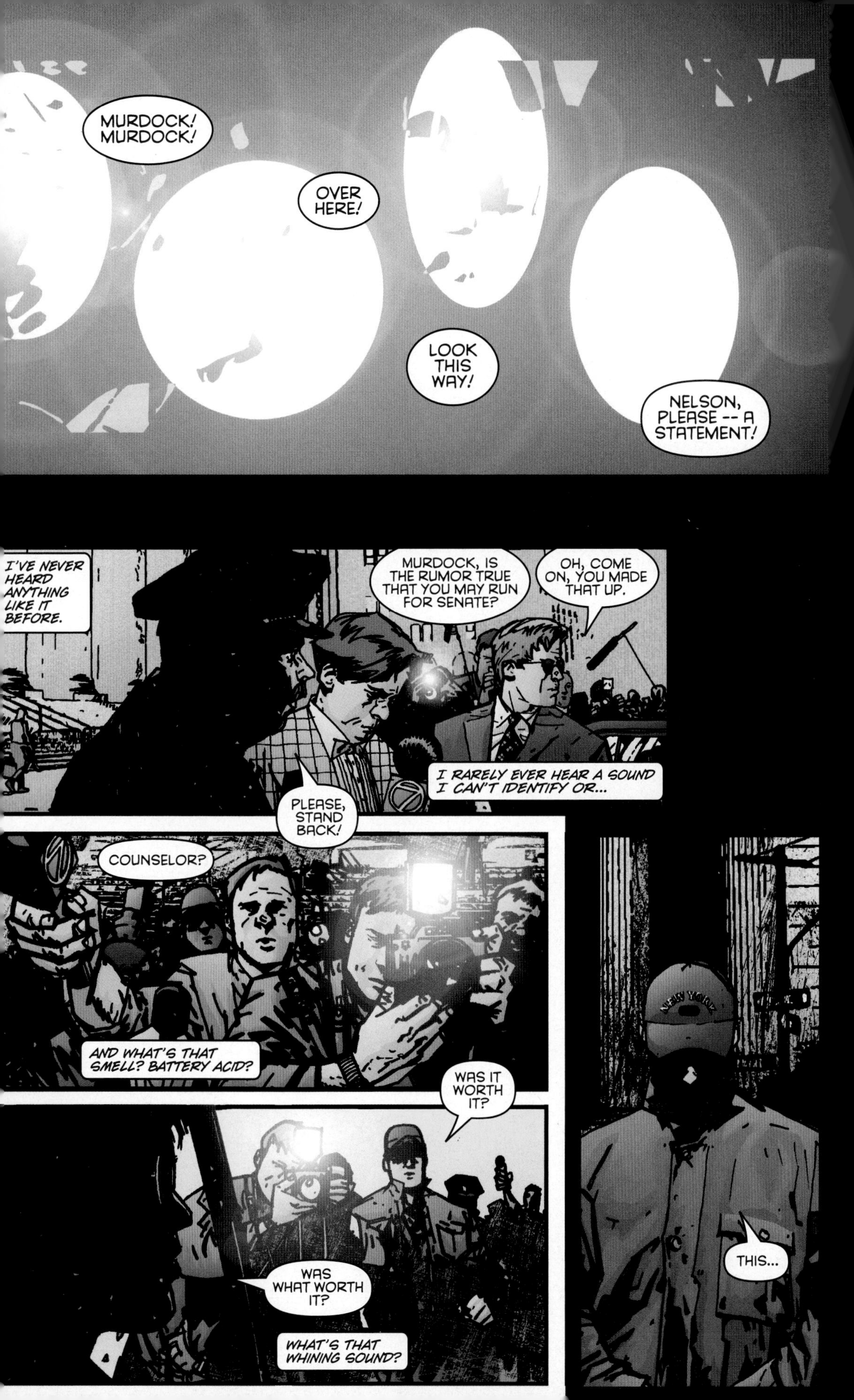

MURDOCK! MURDOCK!
OVER HERE!
LOOK THIS WAY!
NELSON, PLEASE -- A STATEMENT!
I'VE NEVER HEARD ANYTHING LIKE IT BEFORE.
MURDOCK, IS THE RUMOR TRUE THAT YOU MAY RUN FOR SENATE?
OH, COME ON, YOU MADE THAT UP.
I RARELY EVER HEAR A SOUND I CAN'T IDENTIFY OR...
PLEASE, STAND BACK!
COUNSELOR?
AND WHAT'S THAT SMELL? BATTERY ACID?
WAS IT WORTH IT?
WAS WHAT WORTH IT?
WHAT'S THAT WHINING SOUND?
THIS...

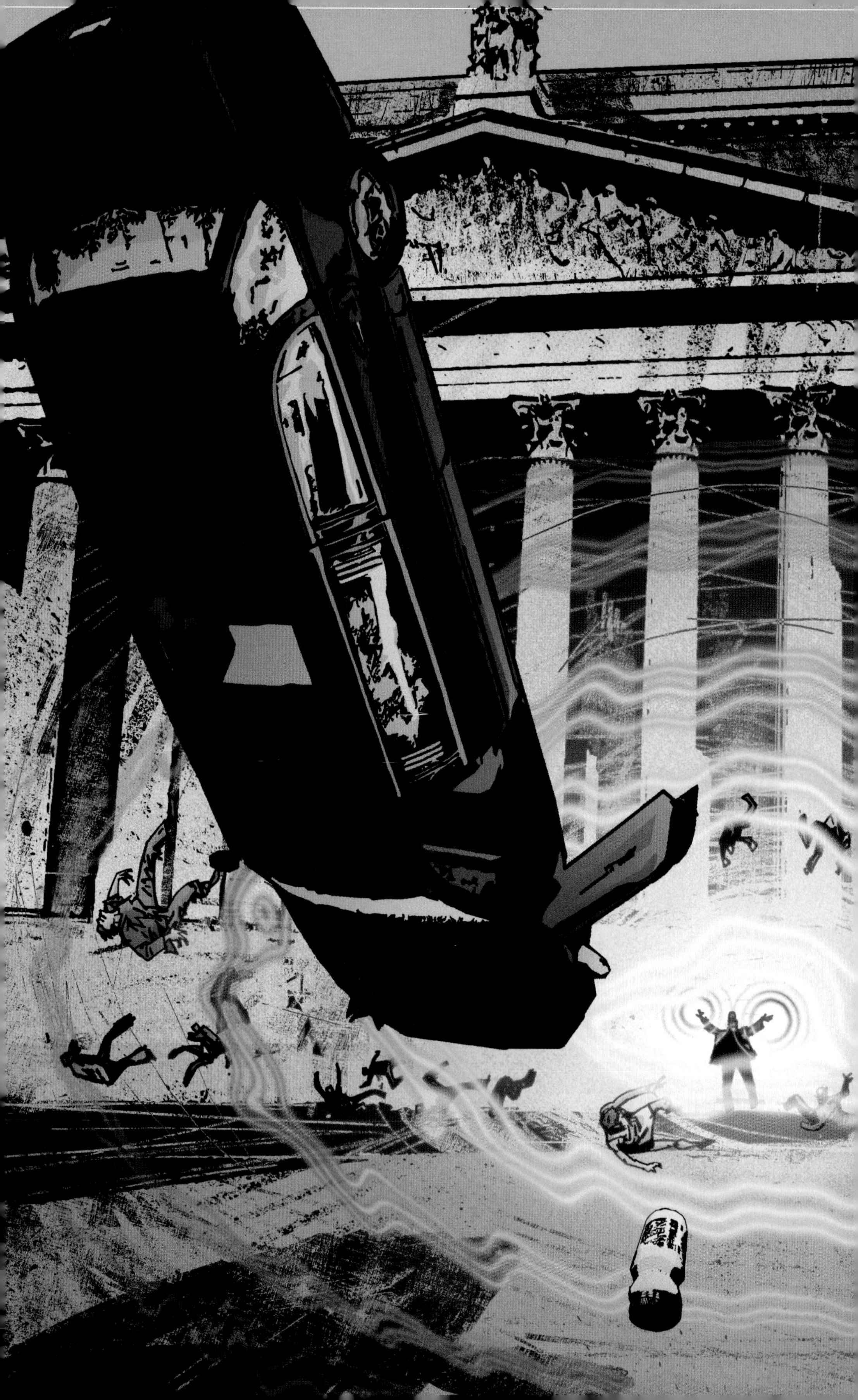

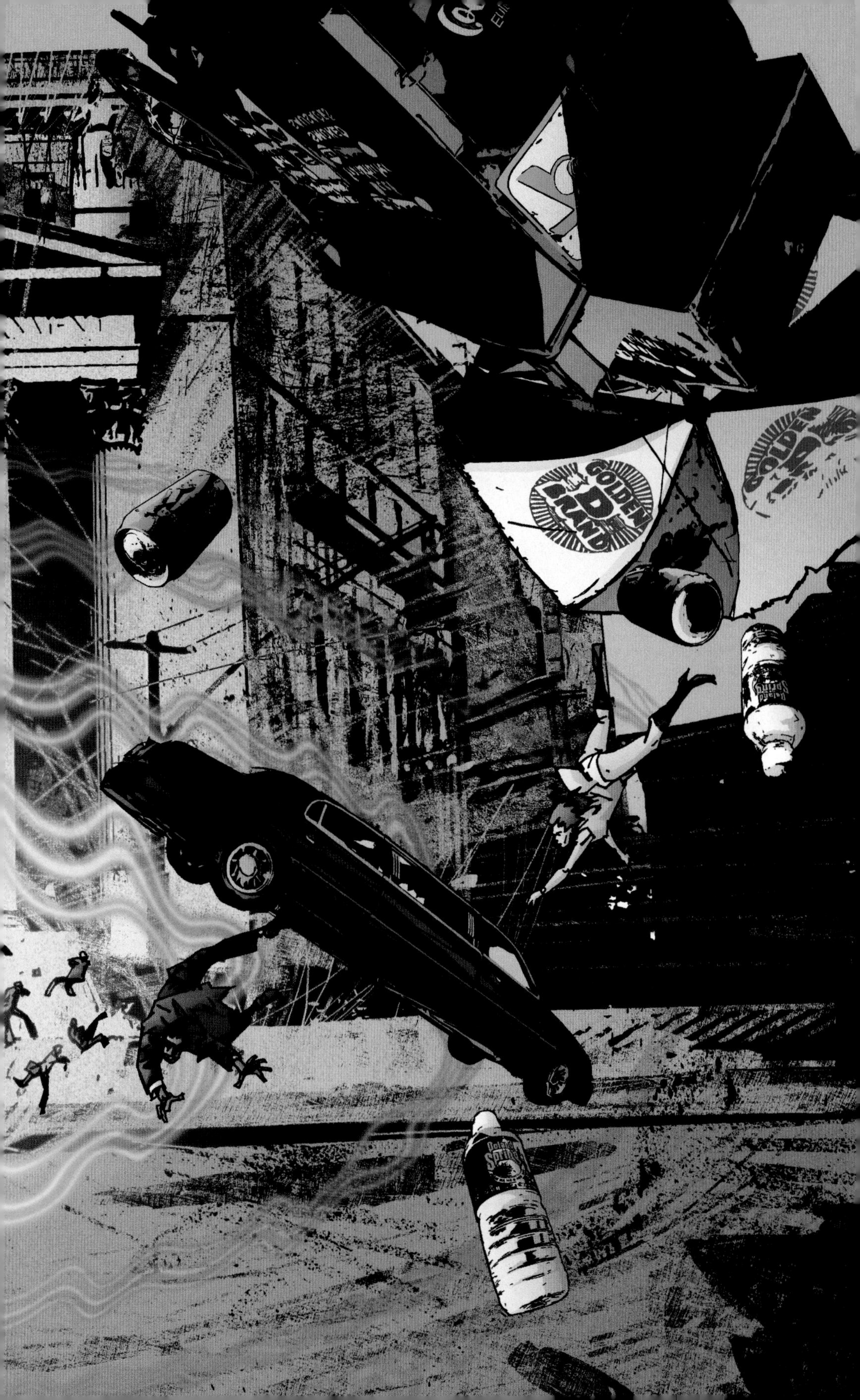
GOLDEN D BRAND

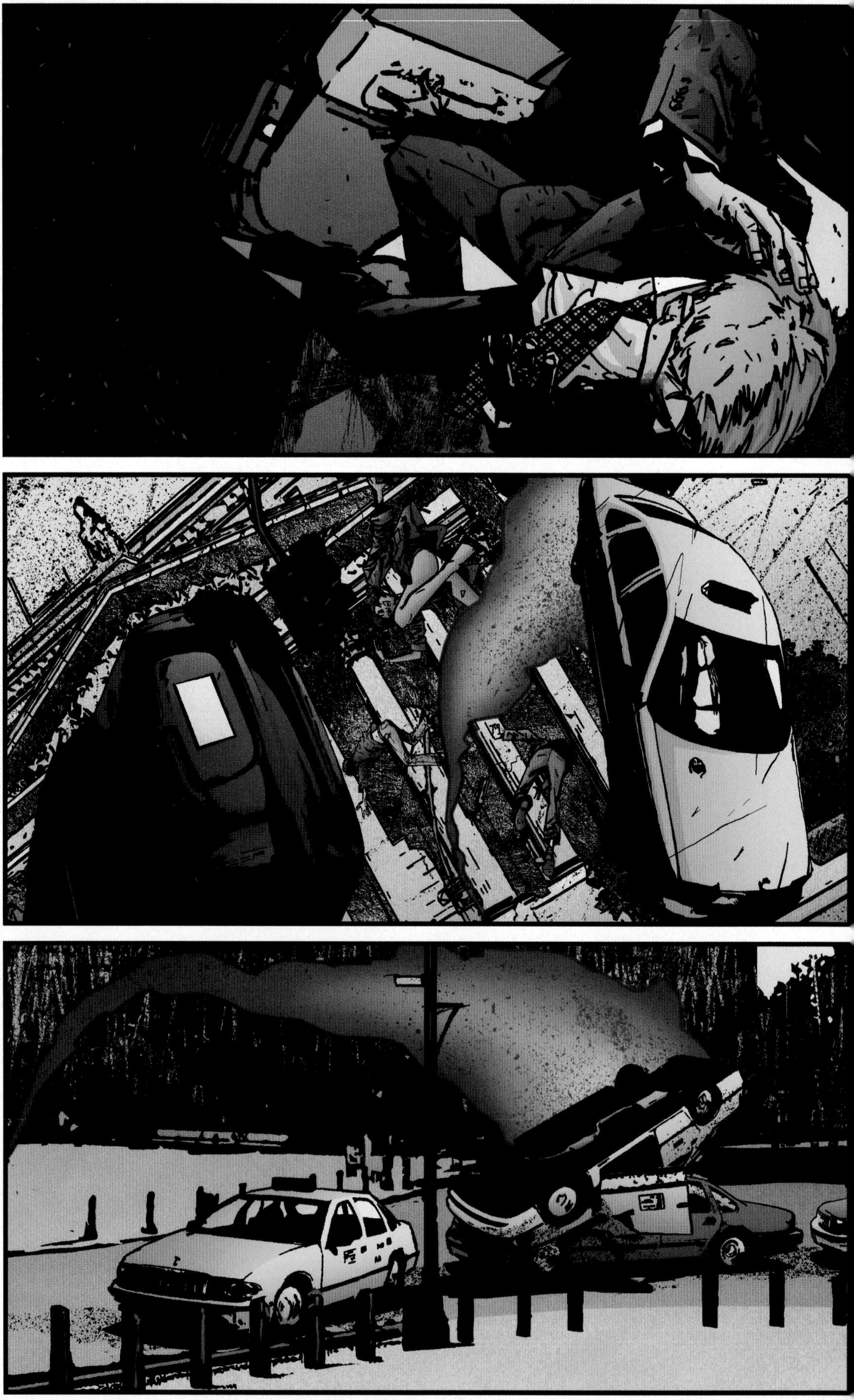

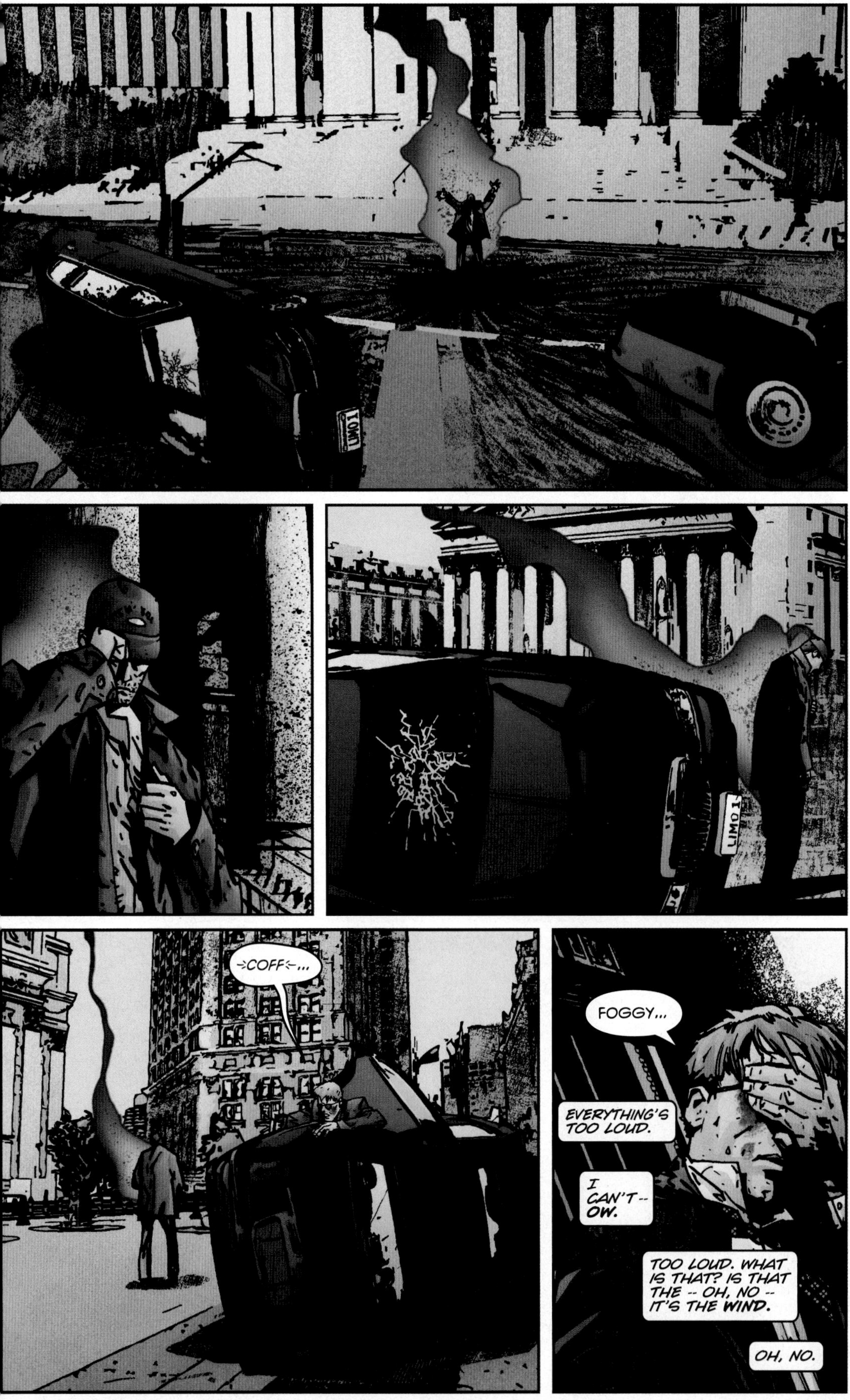

LIMO 1
LIMO 1
=COFF=...
FOGGY...
EVERYTHING'S TOO LOUD.
I CAN'T-- OW.
TOO LOUD. WHAT IS THAT? IS THAT THE -- OH, NO -- IT'S THE WIND.
OH, NO.

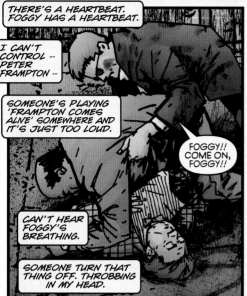

THERE'S A HEARTBEAT. FOGGY HAS A HEARTBEAT.

I CAN'T CONTROL -- PETER FRAMPTON --

SOMEONE'S PLAYING 'FRAMPTON COMES ALIVE' SOMEWHERE AND IT'S JUST TOO LOUD.

FOGGY!! COME ON, FOGGY!!

CAN'T HEAR FOGGY'S BREATHING.

SOMEONE TURN THAT THING OFF. THROBBING IN MY HEAD.

WILL SOMEBODY PLEASE HELP? HELP!!

TOO LOUD. BABY I LOVE YOUR WAY.

I HATE THAT SONG. HATE THAT ENTIRE ALBUM. WIND IS --

THE WIND IS TOO STRONG. IT'S A -- IT'S A --

NO -- JUST THE SOUND OF IT. IT'S JUST THE SOUND. HAVE TO CONTROL IT. CONTROL MY SENSES.

WHAT THE HELL WAS THAT? OW...

DON'T MOVE. YOUR ARM SOUNDS FUNNY.

MY STOMACH. PEOPLE ARE HURT. FOCUS. FOCUS ON THE -- BLAS SCREWED UP MY HEAD

UGH -- GOD -- HORRIBL THERE'S VOMIT ON TH GROUND SOMEWHERE

SOMEONE VOMITED -- HATE FRAMPTON AND SPRINGSTEEN. LUNGS ARE ON FIRE.

ENTIRE BODY SMELLS LIKE MILDEW.

STARCH. BRUCE. MY NOSE IS BLEEDING.

WHAT ARE YOU DOING, MATT?

-COFF- PUT ON -- AHH --

PUT ON YOUR UNIFORM AND TAKE CARE OF THIS.

NO, NO I HAVE TO HELP.

THESE PEOPLE -- IT'S HORRIBLE -- I --

SOMEONE'S TYPING. STOP TYPING!! STOP IT!!

YOU'RE KILLING ME.

IS THERE BLOOD ON MY FACE?

MATT!

PUT ON YOUR UNIFORM AND -- AHUH --

-- THE GUY MIGHT DO THIS AGAIN.

I'LL MAKE SURE THE EMERGENCY TEAMS GET TO THE PEOPLE HERE.

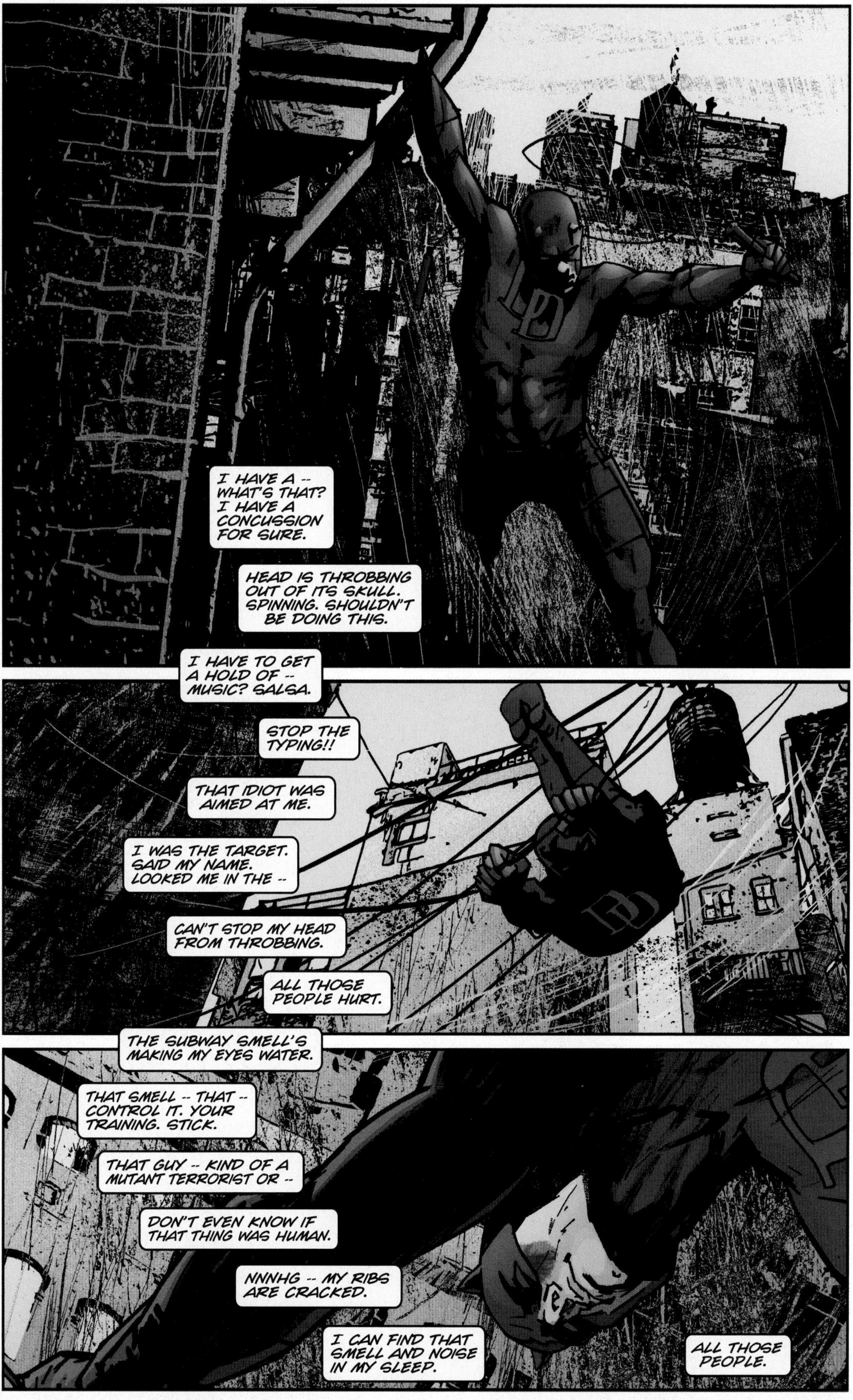

I HAVE A -- WHAT'S THAT? I HAVE A CONCUSSION FOR SURE.
HEAD IS THROBBING OUT OF ITS SKULL. SPINNING. SHOULDN'T BE DOING THIS.
I HAVE TO GET A HOLD OF -- MUSIC? SALSA.
STOP THE TYPING!!
THAT IDIOT WAS AIMED AT ME.
I WAS THE TARGET. SAID MY NAME. LOOKED ME IN THE --
CAN'T STOP MY HEAD FROM THROBBING.
ALL THOSE PEOPLE HURT.
THE SUBWAY SMELL'S MAKING MY EYES WATER.
THAT SMELL -- THAT -- CONTROL IT. YOUR TRAINING. STICK.
THAT GUY -- KIND OF A MUTANT TERRORIST OR --
DON'T EVEN KNOW IF THAT THING WAS HUMAN.
NNNHG -- MY RIBS ARE CRACKED.
I CAN FIND THAT SMELL AND NOISE IN MY SLEEP.
ALL THOSE PEOPLE.

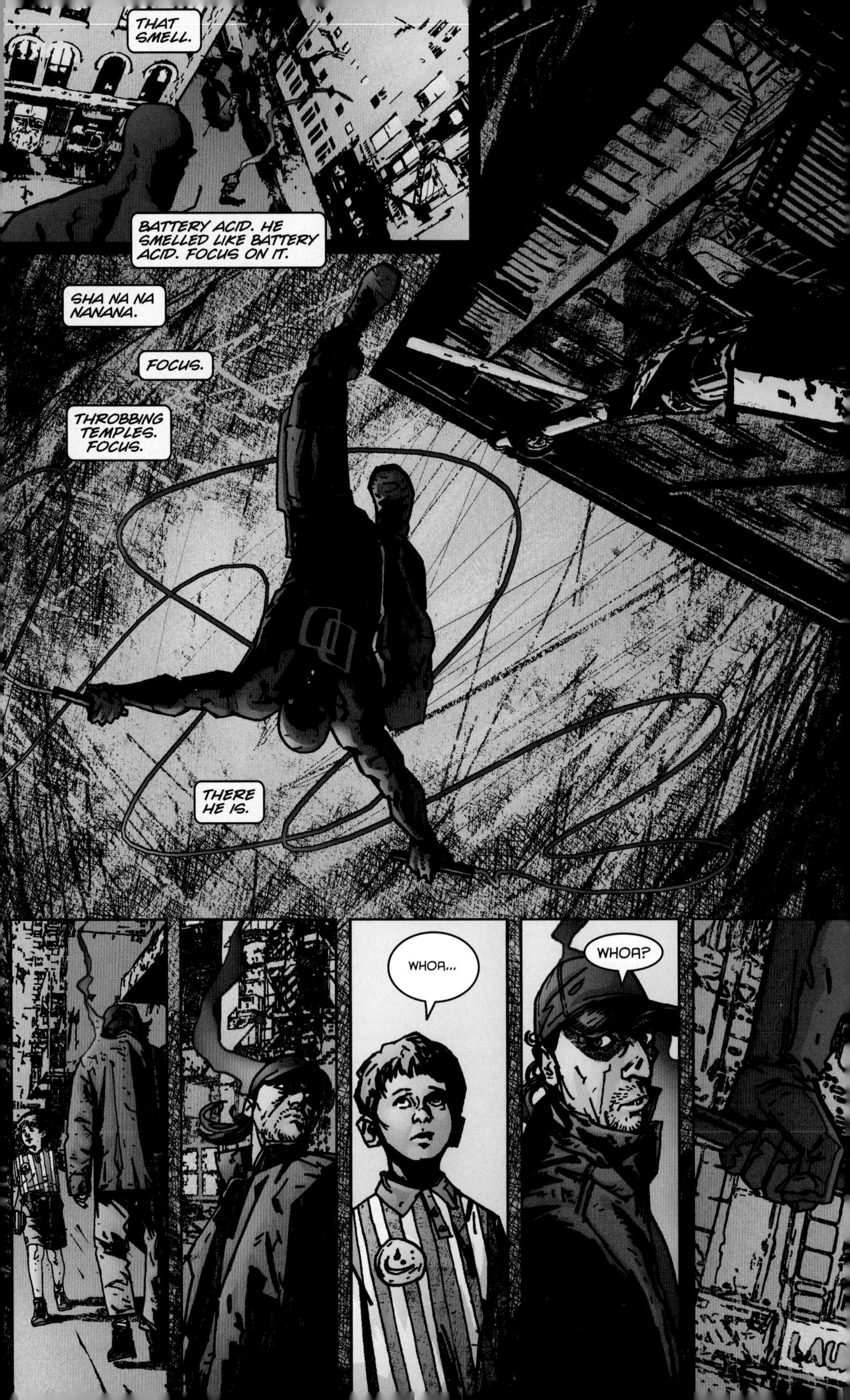
THAT SMELL.
BATTERY ACID. HE SMELLED LIKE BATTERY ACID. FOCUS ON IT.
SHA NA NA NANANA.
FOCUS.
THROBBING TEMPLES. FOCUS.
THERE HE IS.
WHOA...
WHOA?

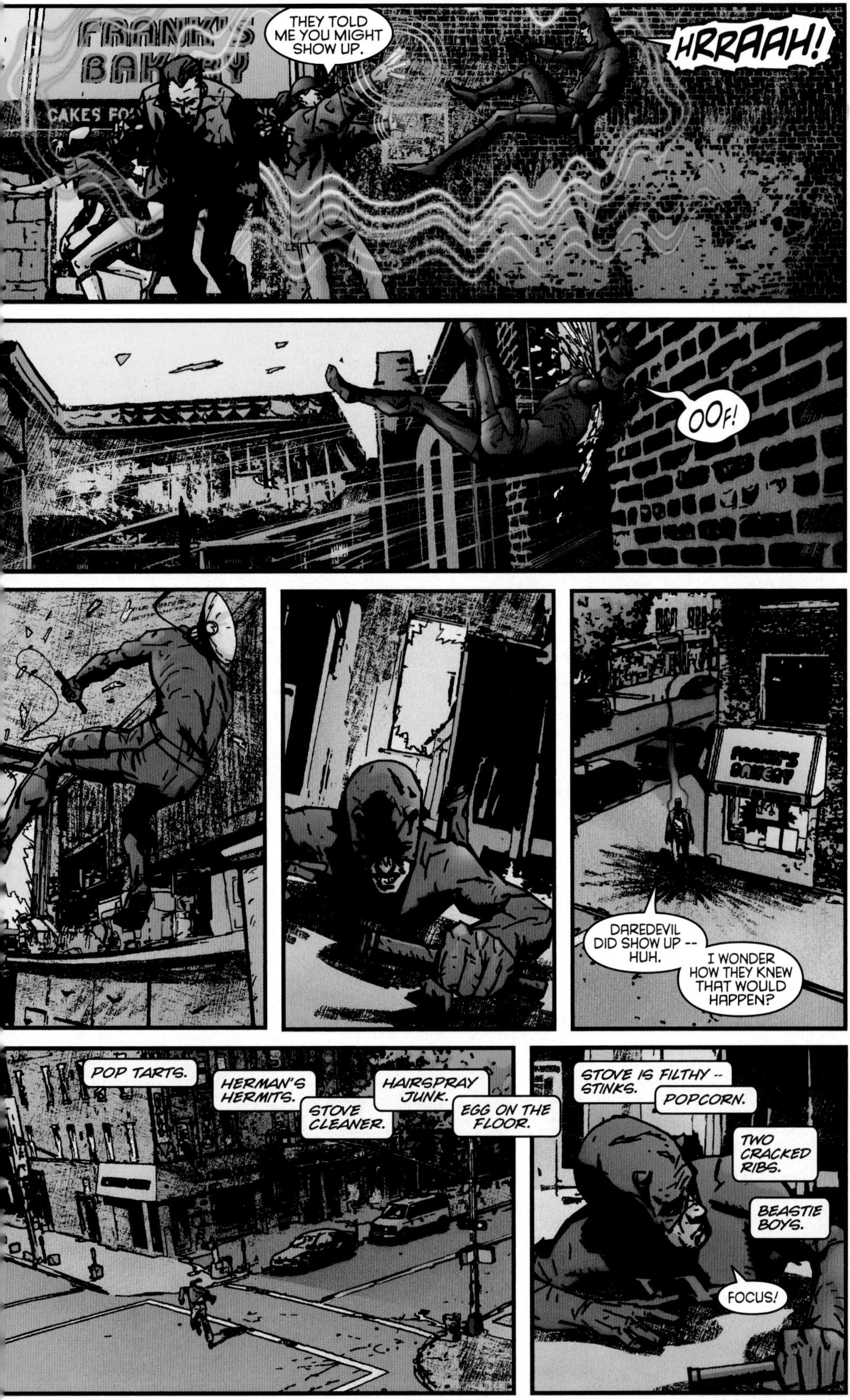
FRANK'S BAKERY
CAKES FO
THEY TOLD ME YOU MIGHT SHOW UP.
HRRAAH!
OOF!
FRANK'S BAKERY
DAREDEVIL DID SHOW UP -- HUH.
I WONDER HOW THEY KNEW THAT WOULD HAPPEN?
POP TARTS.
HERMAN'S HERMITS.
STOVE CLEANER.
HAIRSPRAY JUNK.
EGG ON THE FLOOR.
STOVE IS FILTHY -- STINKS.
POPCORN.
TWO CRACKED RIBS.
BEASTIE BOYS.
FOCUS!

HUH HUH HUH -- FREAKIN' DAREDEVIL --

HUH HUH -- HOW DID THEY KNOW?

THIS IS A MUNI METER PARKING FACILITY

WHACK

--GOAAHH!

TRY TO DO THAT LITTLE MAGIC TRICK OF YOURS AGAIN!!

TRY ME AGAIN AND SEE WHAT HAPPENS!!

NO, NO -- OW!!

SHA NA NA NANANA LIVE FOR TODAY!

THROBBING TEMPLES.

LIKE BATTERY ACID ON MY TONGUE.

OPIE AND ANTHONY WILL BE --

TIRES. SIRENS.

POP TARTS.

HURTING!

INNOCENT!!

NO, NO, PFFTTT!

SKIN SCRAPE

HELICOPTER NEWS 'COPTER.

HERMAN'S HERMITS.

SMACK

CRACKI SCRAPING.

BEASTIE BOYS. BLOOD IN M

THE WIND SCRAPE SCRAPE

IT TAKES A COUPLE -- PFFTT -- MINUTES TO RECHARGE! I CAN'T DO IT AGAIN!

I GIVE! I GIVE!

WHO ARE YOU?

WHO SENT YOU?

BLOOD B.O. BODY ODOR

HELICOPTER FOGGY.

BODY ODOR

NEWS 'COPT

CRAC RIBS.

FOGGY.

TELL ME, OR I SWEAR TO GOD, YOU DIE RIGHT NOW!

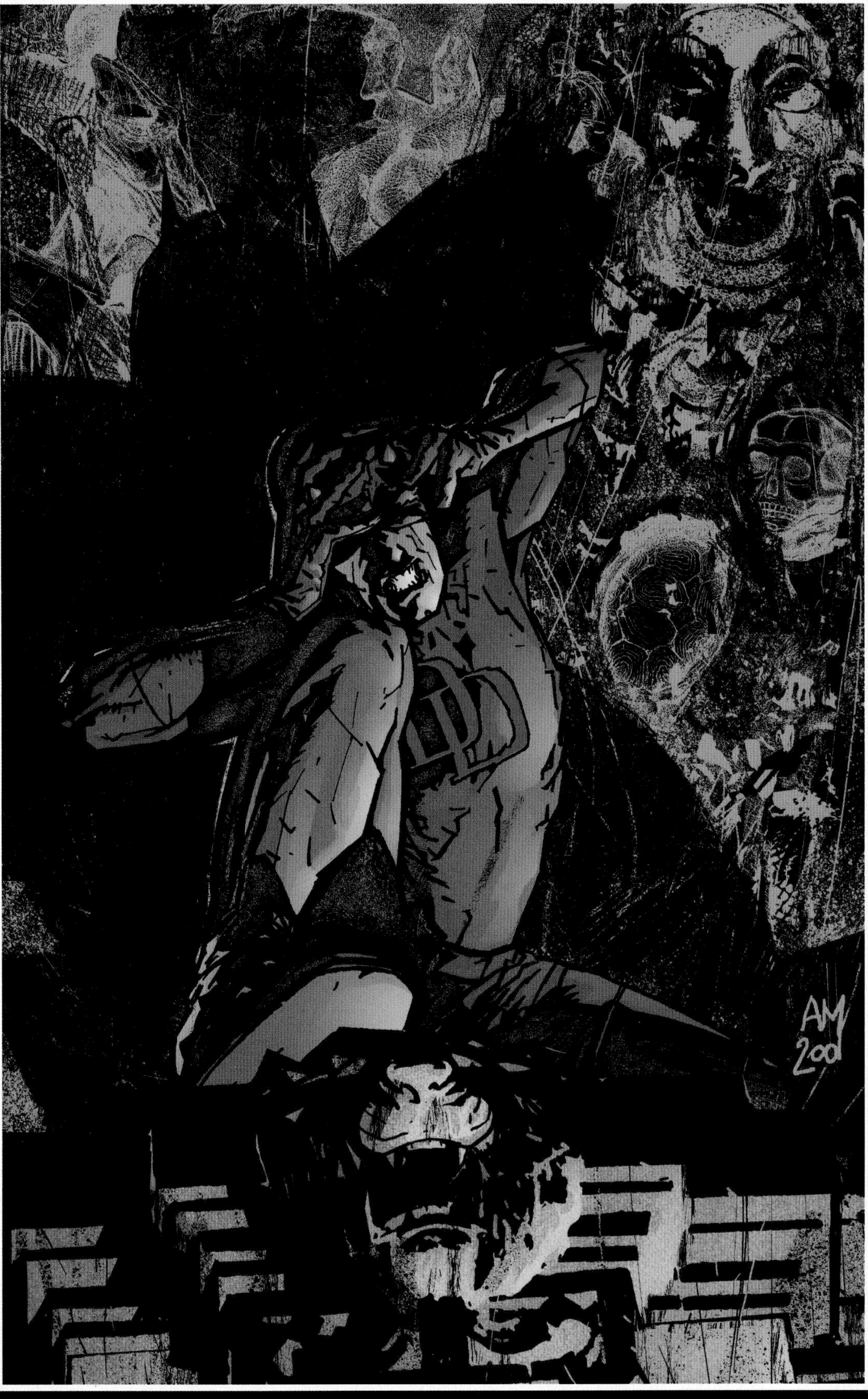

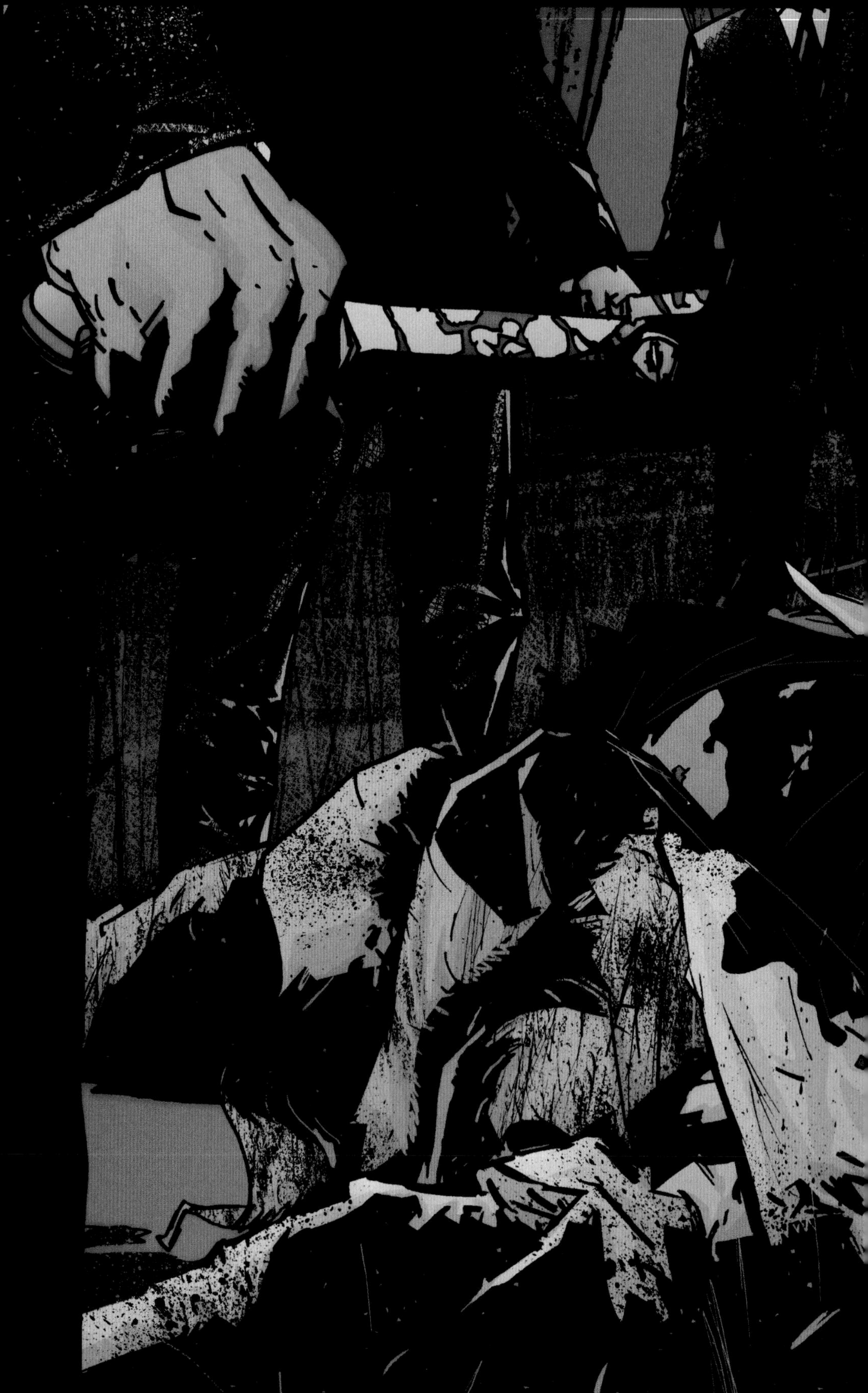

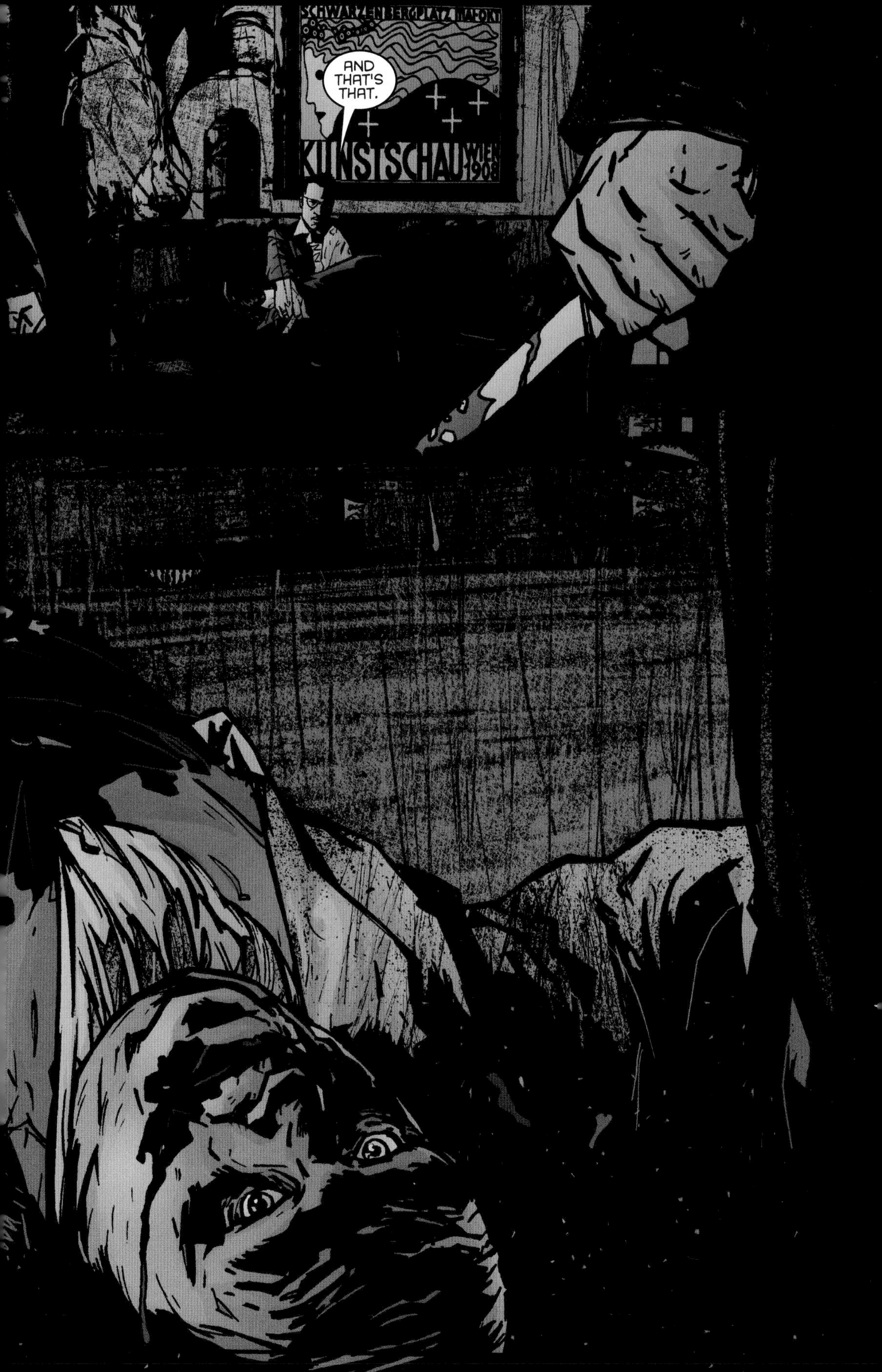
SCHWARZENBERGPLATZ MAI-OKT
AND THAT'S THAT.
KUNSTSCHAU WIEN 1908

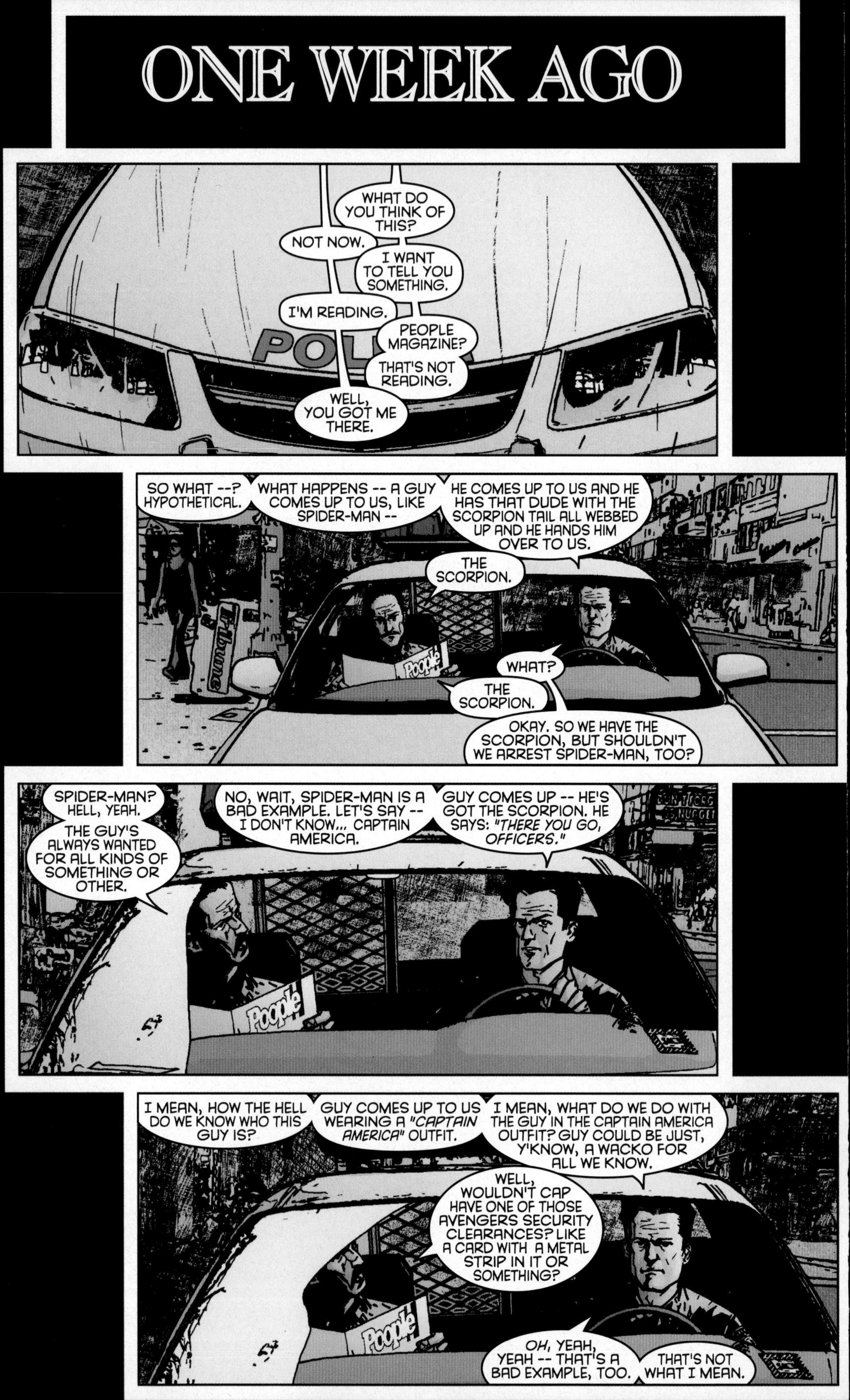
ONE WEEK AGO
WHAT DO YOU THINK OF THIS?
NOT NOW.
I WANT TO TELL YOU SOMETHING.
I'M READING.
PEOPLE MAGAZINE?
THAT'S NOT READING.
WELL, YOU GOT ME THERE.
POL
SO WHAT --? HYPOTHETICAL.
WHAT HAPPENS -- A GUY COMES UP TO US, LIKE SPIDER-MAN --
HE COMES UP TO US AND HE HAS THAT DUDE WITH THE SCORPION TAIL ALL WEBBED UP AND HE HANDS HIM OVER TO US.
THE SCORPION.
WHAT?
THE SCORPION.
OKAY. SO WE HAVE THE SCORPION, BUT SHOULDN'T WE ARREST SPIDER-MAN, TOO?
Tribune
People
SPIDER-MAN? HELL, YEAH.
THE GUY'S ALWAYS WANTED FOR ALL KINDS OF SOMETHING OR OTHER.
NO, WAIT, SPIDER-MAN IS A BAD EXAMPLE. LET'S SAY -- I DON'T KNOW... CAPTAIN AMERICA.
GUY COMES UP -- HE'S GOT THE SCORPION. HE SAYS: "THERE YOU GO, OFFICERS."
People
I MEAN, HOW THE HELL DO WE KNOW WHO THIS GUY IS?
GUY COMES UP TO US WEARING A "CAPTAIN AMERICA" OUTFIT.
I MEAN, WHAT DO WE DO WITH THE GUY IN THE CAPTAIN AMERICA OUTFIT? GUY COULD BE JUST, Y'KNOW, A WACKO FOR ALL WE KNOW.
WELL, WOULDN'T CAP HAVE ONE OF THOSE AVENGERS SECURITY CLEARANCES? LIKE A CARD WITH A METAL STRIP IN IT OR SOMETHING?
OH, YEAH, YEAH -- THAT'S A BAD EXAMPLE, TOO.
THAT'S NOT WHAT I MEAN.
People

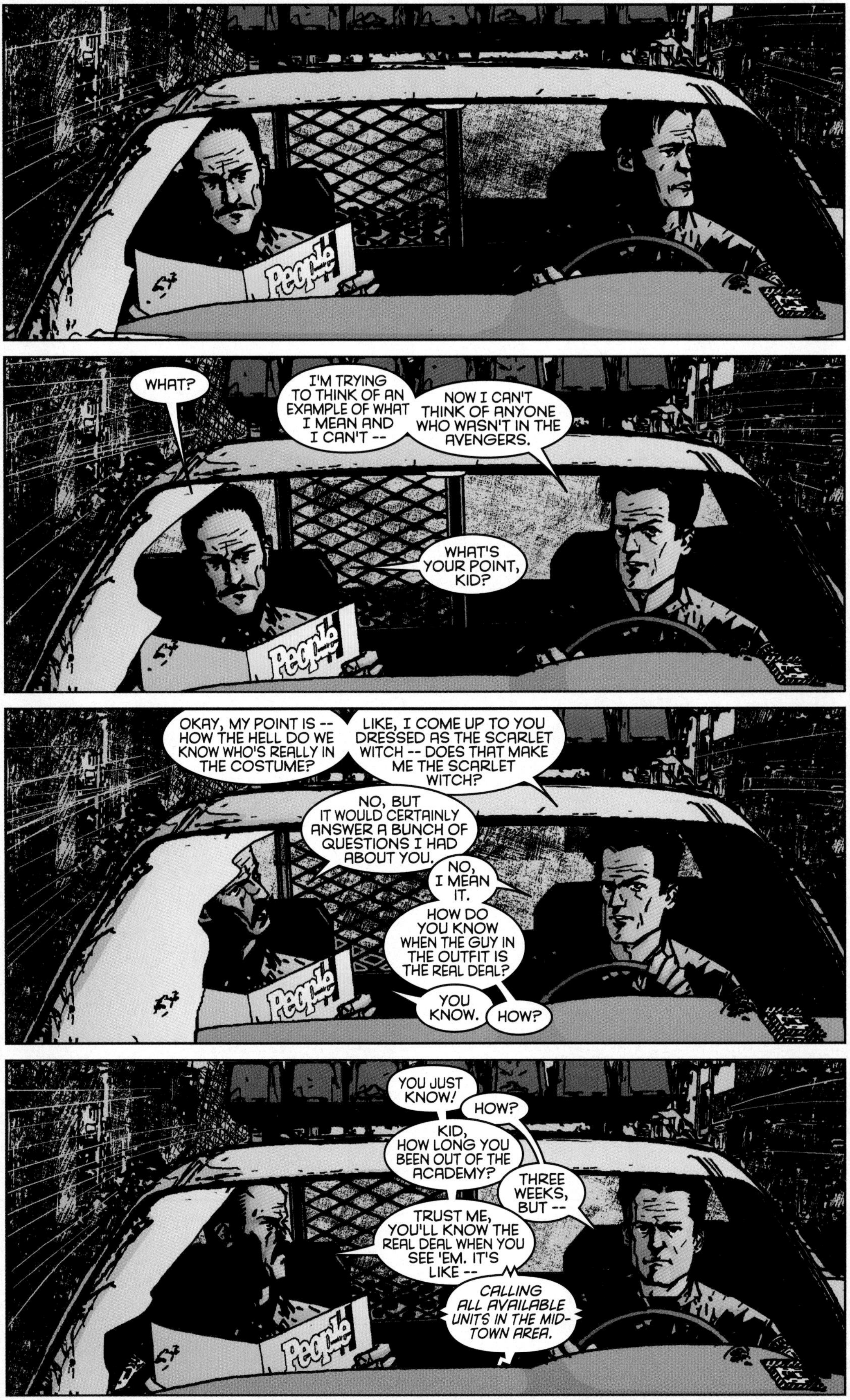
WHAT?
I'M TRYING TO THINK OF AN EXAMPLE OF WHAT I MEAN AND I CAN'T --
NOW I CAN'T THINK OF ANYONE WHO WASN'T IN THE AVENGERS.
WHAT'S YOUR POINT, KID?
OKAY, MY POINT IS -- HOW THE HELL DO WE KNOW WHO'S REALLY IN THE COSTUME?
LIKE, I COME UP TO YOU DRESSED AS THE SCARLET WITCH -- DOES THAT MAKE ME THE SCARLET WITCH?
NO, BUT IT WOULD CERTAINLY ANSWER A BUNCH OF QUESTIONS I HAD ABOUT YOU.
NO, I MEAN IT.
HOW DO YOU KNOW WHEN THE GUY IN THE OUTFIT IS THE REAL DEAL?
YOU KNOW.
HOW?
YOU JUST KNOW!
HOW?
KID, HOW LONG YOU BEEN OUT OF THE ACADEMY?
THREE WEEKS, BUT --
TRUST ME, YOU'LL KNOW THE REAL DEAL WHEN YOU SEE 'EM. IT'S LIKE --
CALLING ALL AVAILABLE UNITS IN THE MID-TOWN AREA.

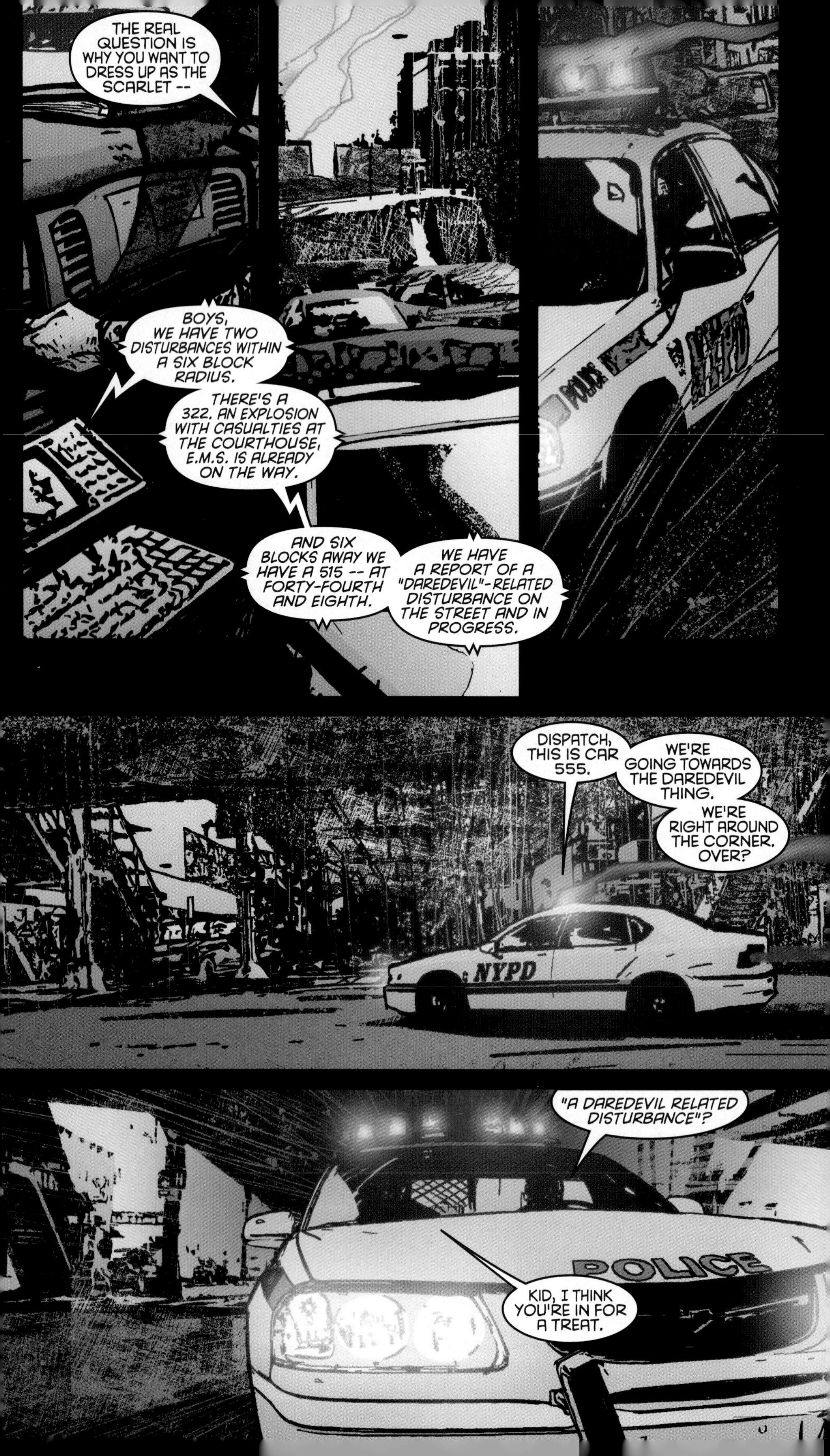
THE REAL QUESTION IS WHY YOU WANT TO DRESS UP AS THE SCARLET --
BOYS, WE HAVE TWO DISTURBANCES WITHIN A SIX BLOCK RADIUS.
THERE'S A 322. AN EXPLOSION WITH CASUALTIES AT THE COURTHOUSE, E.M.S. IS ALREADY ON THE WAY.
AND SIX BLOCKS AWAY WE HAVE A 515 -- AT FORTY-FOURTH AND EIGHTH.
WE HAVE A REPORT OF A "DAREDEVIL"-RELATED DISTURBANCE ON THE STREET AND IN PROGRESS.
POLICE
NYPD
DISPATCH, THIS IS CAR 555.
WE'RE GOING TOWARDS THE DAREDEVIL THING.
WE'RE RIGHT AROUND THE CORNER. OVER?
NYPD
"A DAREDEVIL RELATED DISTURBANCE"?
POLICE
KID, I THINK YOU'RE IN FOR A TREAT.

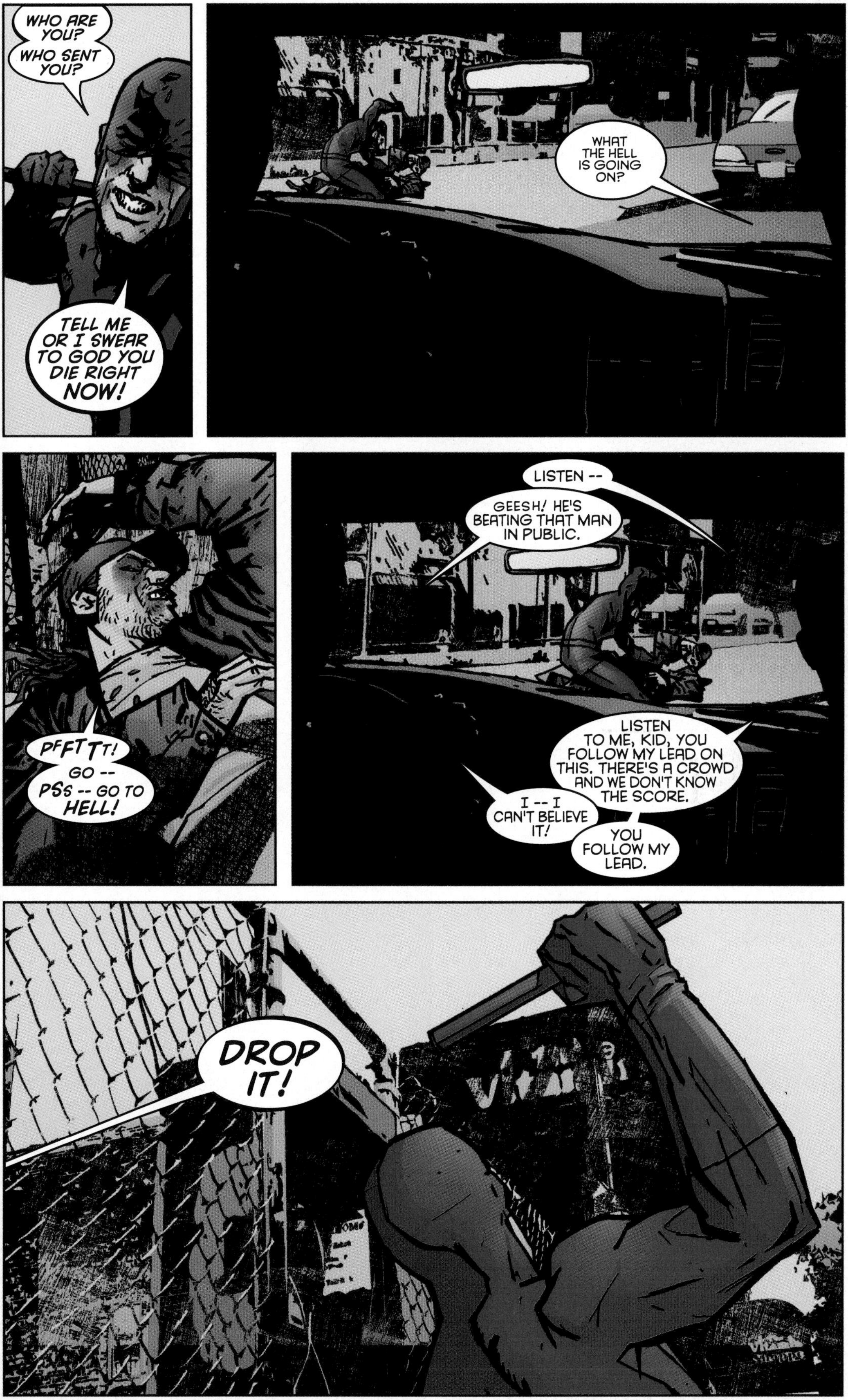
WHO ARE YOU? WHO SENT YOU?
TELL ME OR I SWEAR TO GOD YOU DIE RIGHT NOW!
WHAT THE HELL IS GOING ON?
PFFTTT! GO -- PSS -- GO TO HELL!
LISTEN --
GEESH! HE'S BEATING THAT MAN IN PUBLIC.
LISTEN TO ME, KID, YOU FOLLOW MY LEAD ON THIS. THERE'S A CROWD AND WE DON'T KNOW THE SCORE.
I -- I CAN'T BELIEVE IT!
YOU FOLLOW MY LEAD.
DROP IT!

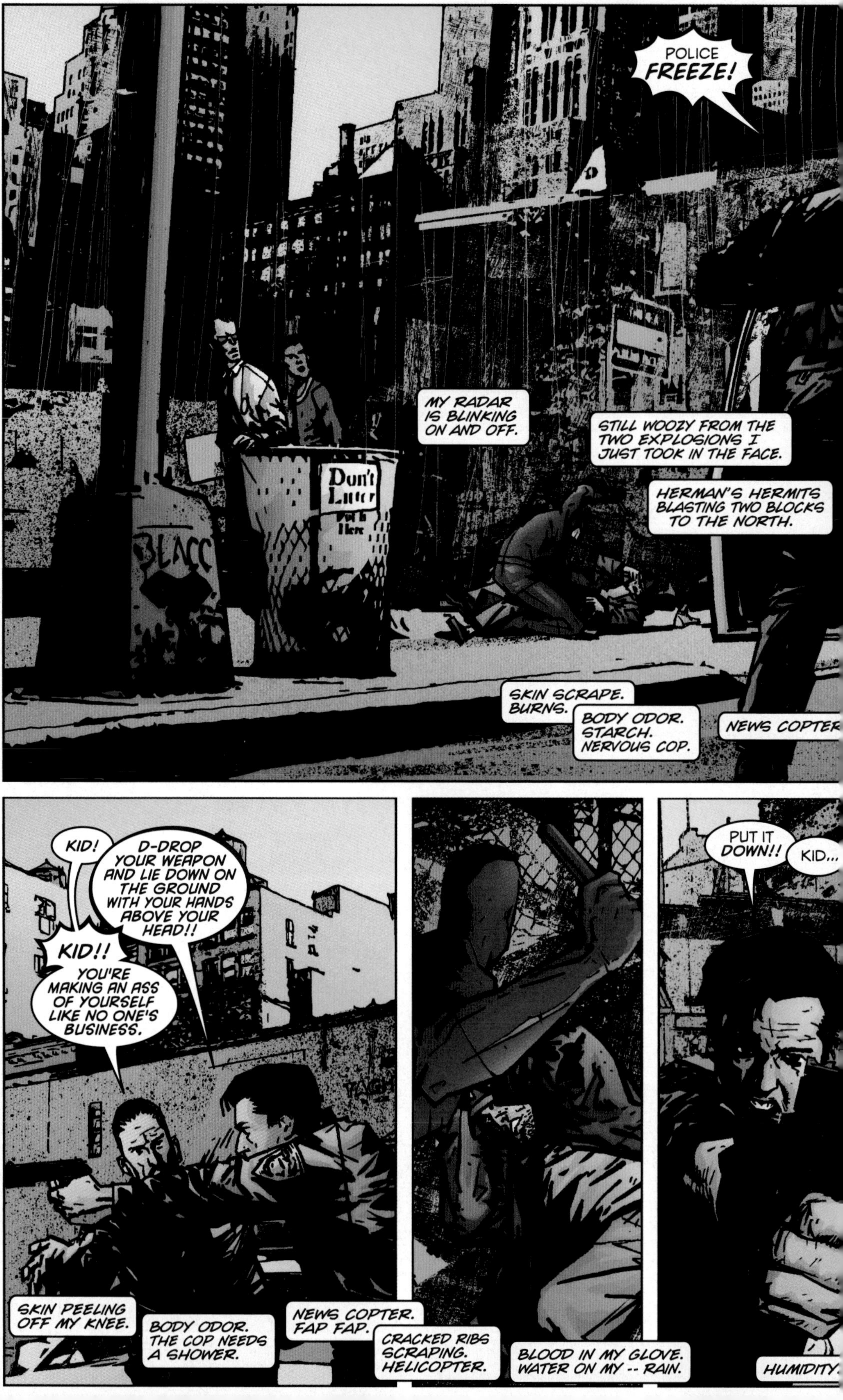
POLICE
FREEZE!
MY RADAR IS BLINKING ON AND OFF.
STILL WOOZY FROM THE TWO EXPLOSIONS I JUST TOOK IN THE FACE.
HERMAN'S HERMITS BLASTING TWO BLOCKS TO THE NORTH.
Don't Litter
SKIN SCRAPE. BURNS.
BODY ODOR. STARCH. NERVOUS COP.
NEWS COPTER
KID!
D-DROP YOUR WEAPON AND LIE DOWN ON THE GROUND WITH YOUR HANDS ABOVE YOUR HEAD!!
KID!!
YOU'RE MAKING AN ASS OF YOURSELF LIKE NO ONE'S BUSINESS.
SKIN PEELING OFF MY KNEE.
BODY ODOR. THE COP NEEDS A SHOWER.
NEWS COPTER. FAP FAP.
CRACKED RIBS SCRAPING. HELICOPTER.
BLOOD IN MY GLOVE. WATER ON MY -- RAIN.
PUT IT DOWN!!
KID...
HUMIDITY.

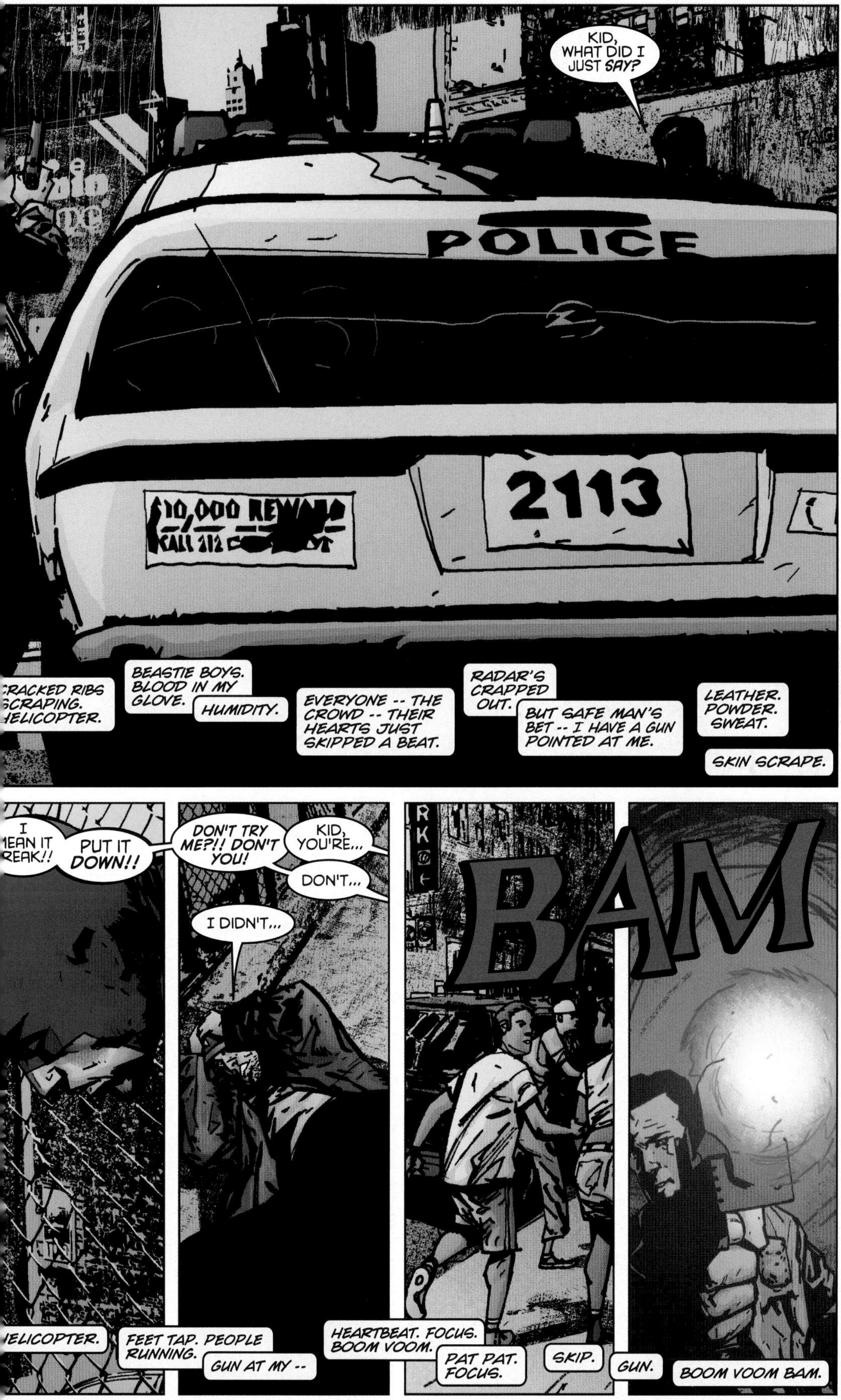
KID, WHAT DID I JUST SAY?
POLICE
2113
RACKED RIBS SCRAPING. ELICOPTER.
BEASTIE BOYS. BLOOD IN MY GLOVE.
HUMIDITY.
EVERYONE -- THE CROWD -- THEIR HEARTS JUST SKIPPED A BEAT.
RADAR'S CRAPPED OUT.
BUT SAFE MAN'S BET -- I HAVE A GUN POINTED AT ME.
LEATHER. POWDER. SWEAT.
SKIN SCRAPE.
I MEAN IT REAK!!
PUT IT DOWN!!
ELICOPTER.
DON'T TRY ME?!! DON'T YOU!
KID, YOU'RE...
DON'T...
I DIDN'T...
FEET TAP. PEOPLE RUNNING.
GUN AT MY --
BAM
HEARTBEAT. FOCUS. BOOM VOOM.
PAT PAT. FOCUS.
SKIP.
GUN.
BOOM VOOM BAM.

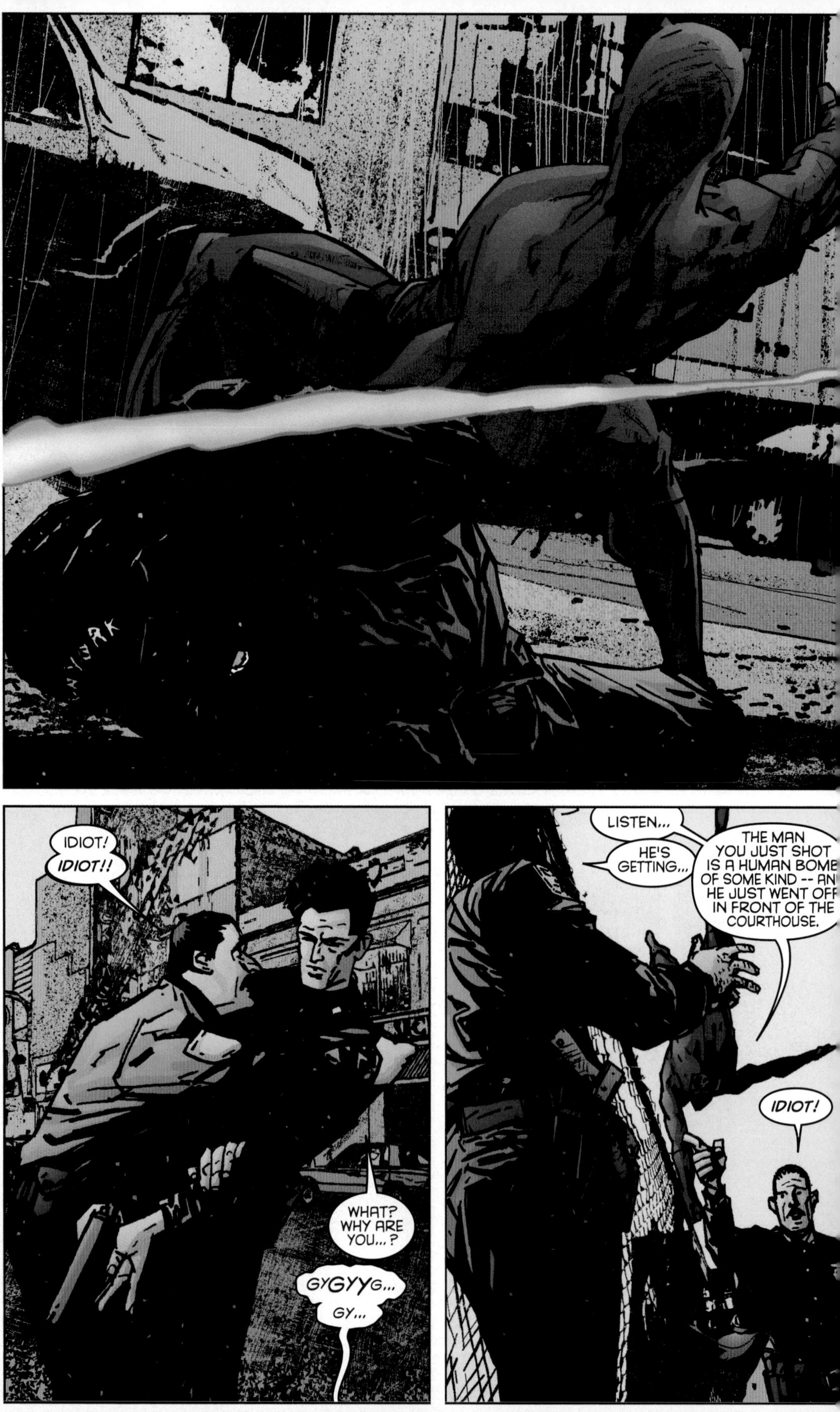
IDIOT! IDIOT!!
WHAT? WHY ARE YOU...?
GYGYYG... GY...
LISTEN...
HE'S GETTING...
THE MAN YOU JUST SHOT IS A HUMAN BOM OF SOME KIND -- AN HE JUST WENT OF IN FRONT OF THE COURTHOUSE.
IDIOT!

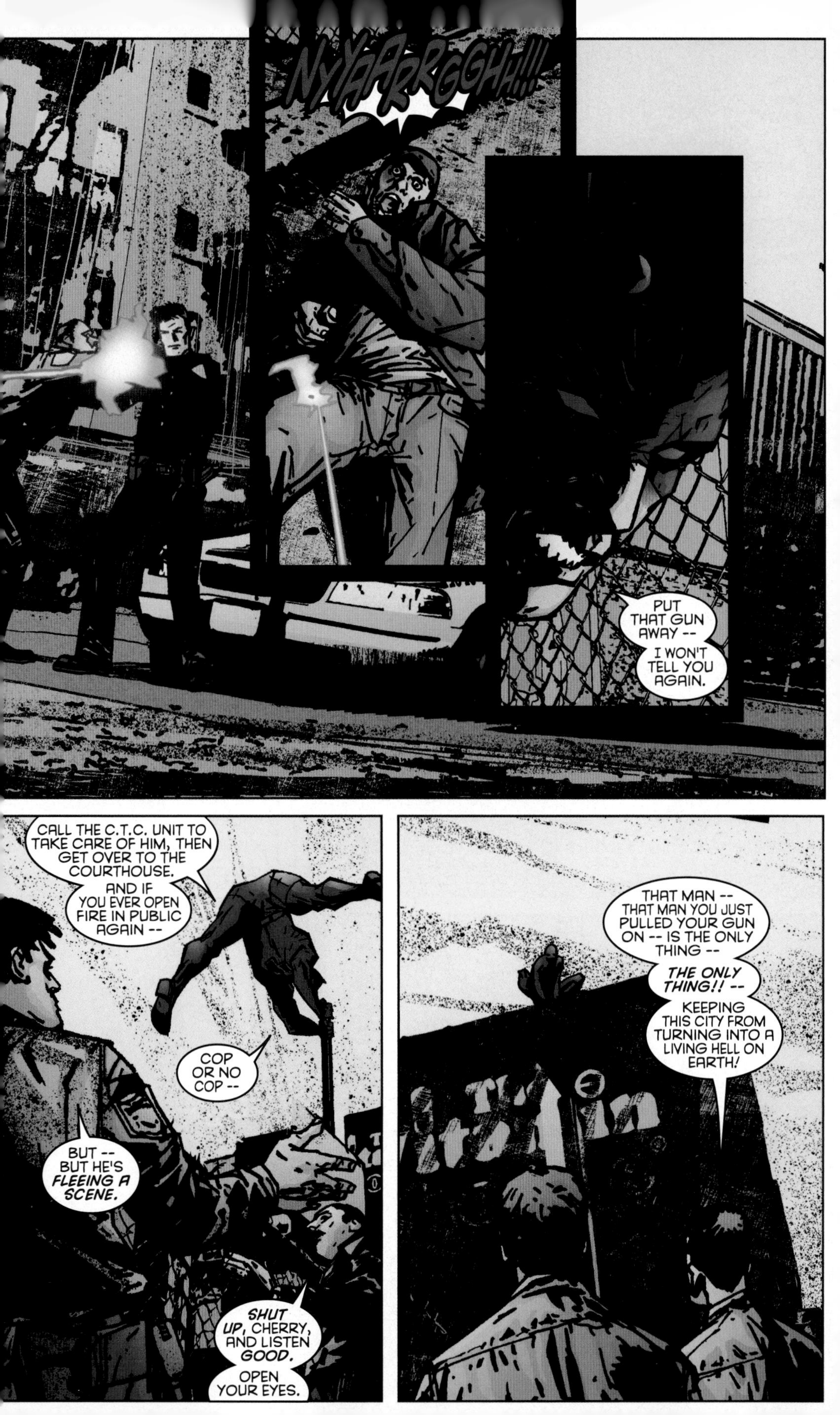
NYYAARRGGHH!!!
PUT THAT GUN AWAY -- I WON'T TELL YOU AGAIN.
CALL THE C.T.C. UNIT TO TAKE CARE OF HIM, THEN GET OVER TO THE COURTHOUSE.
AND IF YOU EVER OPEN FIRE IN PUBLIC AGAIN --
COP OR NO COP --
BUT -- BUT HE'S *FLEEING A SCENE.*
SHUT UP, CHERRY, AND LISTEN *GOOD.*
OPEN YOUR EYES.
THAT MAN -- THAT MAN YOU JUST PULLED YOUR GUN ON -- IS THE ONLY THING --
THE ONLY THING!! --
KEEPING THIS CITY FROM TURNING INTO A LIVING HELL ON EARTH!

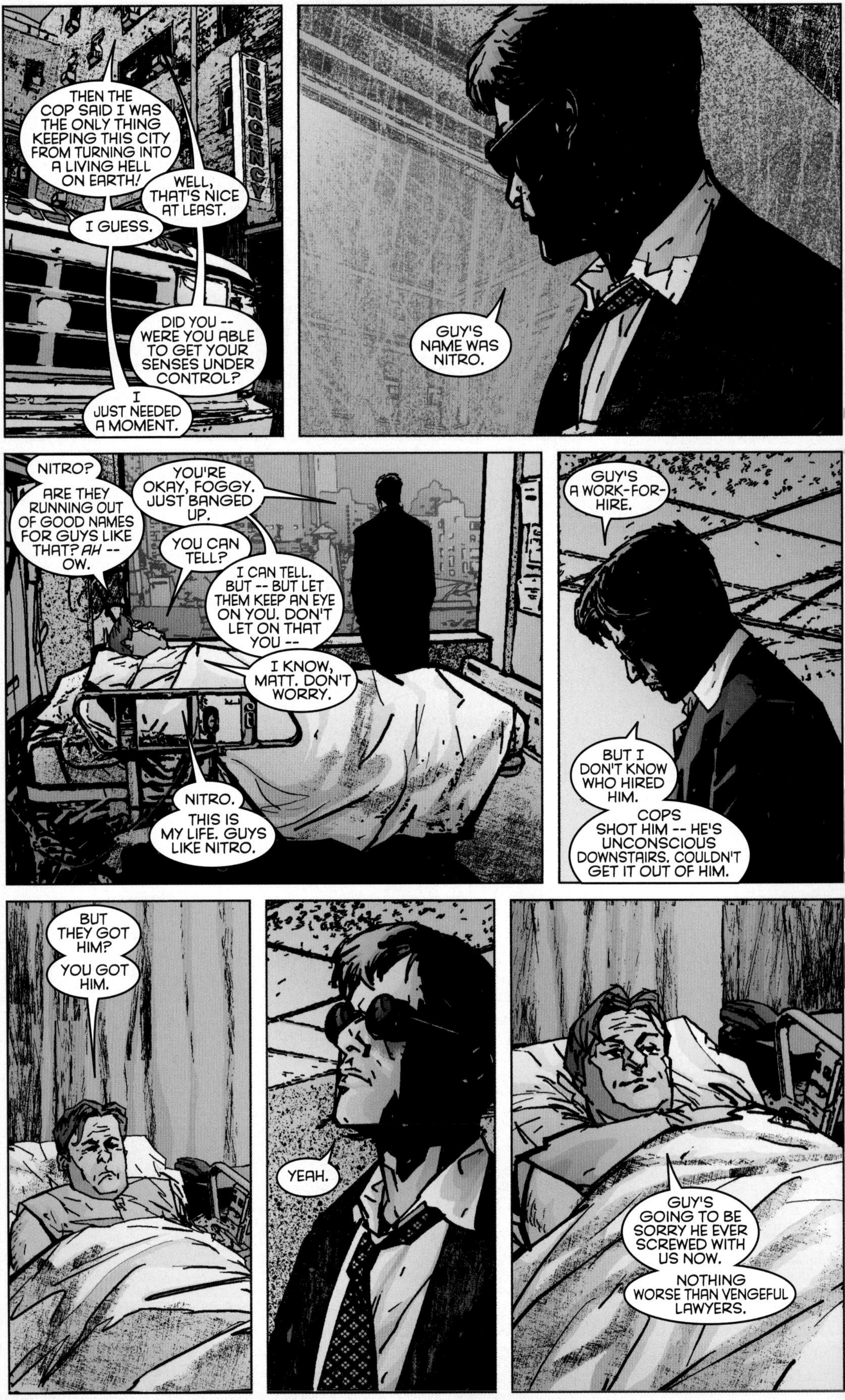
THEN THE COP SAID I WAS THE ONLY THING KEEPING THIS CITY FROM TURNING INTO A LIVING HELL ON EARTH!
I GUESS.
WELL, THAT'S NICE AT LEAST.
DID YOU -- WERE YOU ABLE TO GET YOUR SENSES UNDER CONTROL?
I JUST NEEDED A MOMENT.
GUY'S NAME WAS NITRO.
NITRO?
ARE THEY RUNNING OUT OF GOOD NAMES FOR GUYS LIKE THAT? AH -- OW.
YOU'RE OKAY, FOGGY. JUST BANGED UP.
YOU CAN TELL?
I CAN TELL. BUT -- BUT LET THEM KEEP AN EYE ON YOU. DON'T LET ON THAT YOU --
I KNOW, MATT. DON'T WORRY.
NITRO.
THIS IS MY LIFE. GUYS LIKE NITRO.
GUY'S A WORK-FOR-HIRE.
BUT I DON'T KNOW WHO HIRED HIM.
COPS SHOT HIM -- HE'S UNCONSCIOUS DOWNSTAIRS. COULDN'T GET IT OUT OF HIM.
BUT THEY GOT HIM?
YOU GOT HIM.
YEAH.
GUY'S GOING TO BE SORRY HE EVER SCREWED WITH US NOW.
NOTHING WORSE THAN VENGEFUL LAWYERS.

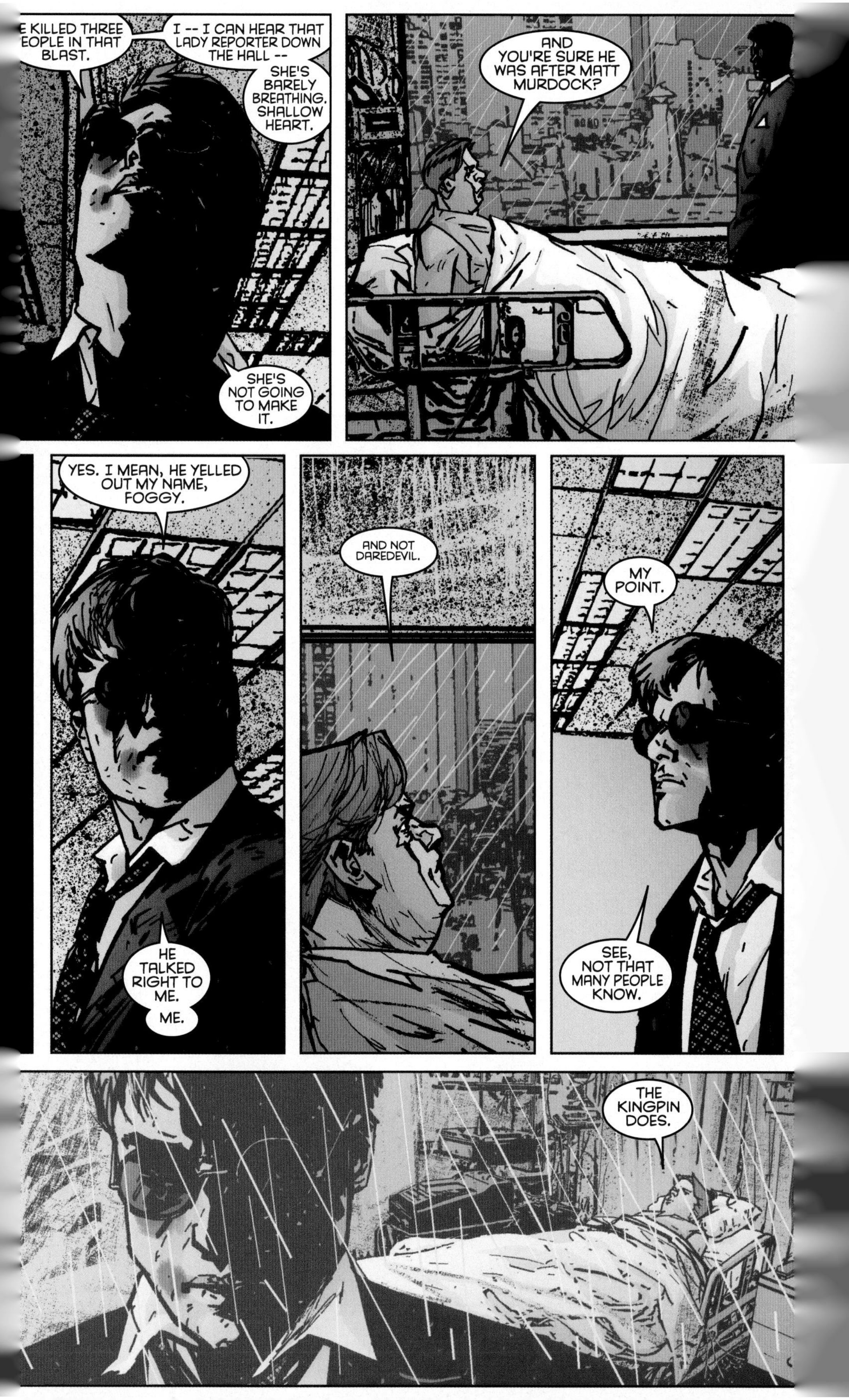
E KILLED THREE EOPLE IN THAT BLAST.
I -- I CAN HEAR THAT LADY REPORTER DOWN THE HALL --
SHE'S BARELY BREATHING. SHALLOW HEART.
SHE'S NOT GOING TO MAKE IT.
AND YOU'RE SURE HE WAS AFTER MATT MURDOCK?
YES. I MEAN, HE YELLED OUT MY NAME, FOGGY.
HE TALKED RIGHT TO ME.
ME.
AND NOT DAREDEVIL.
MY POINT.
SEE, NOT THAT MANY PEOPLE KNOW.
THE KINGPIN DOES.

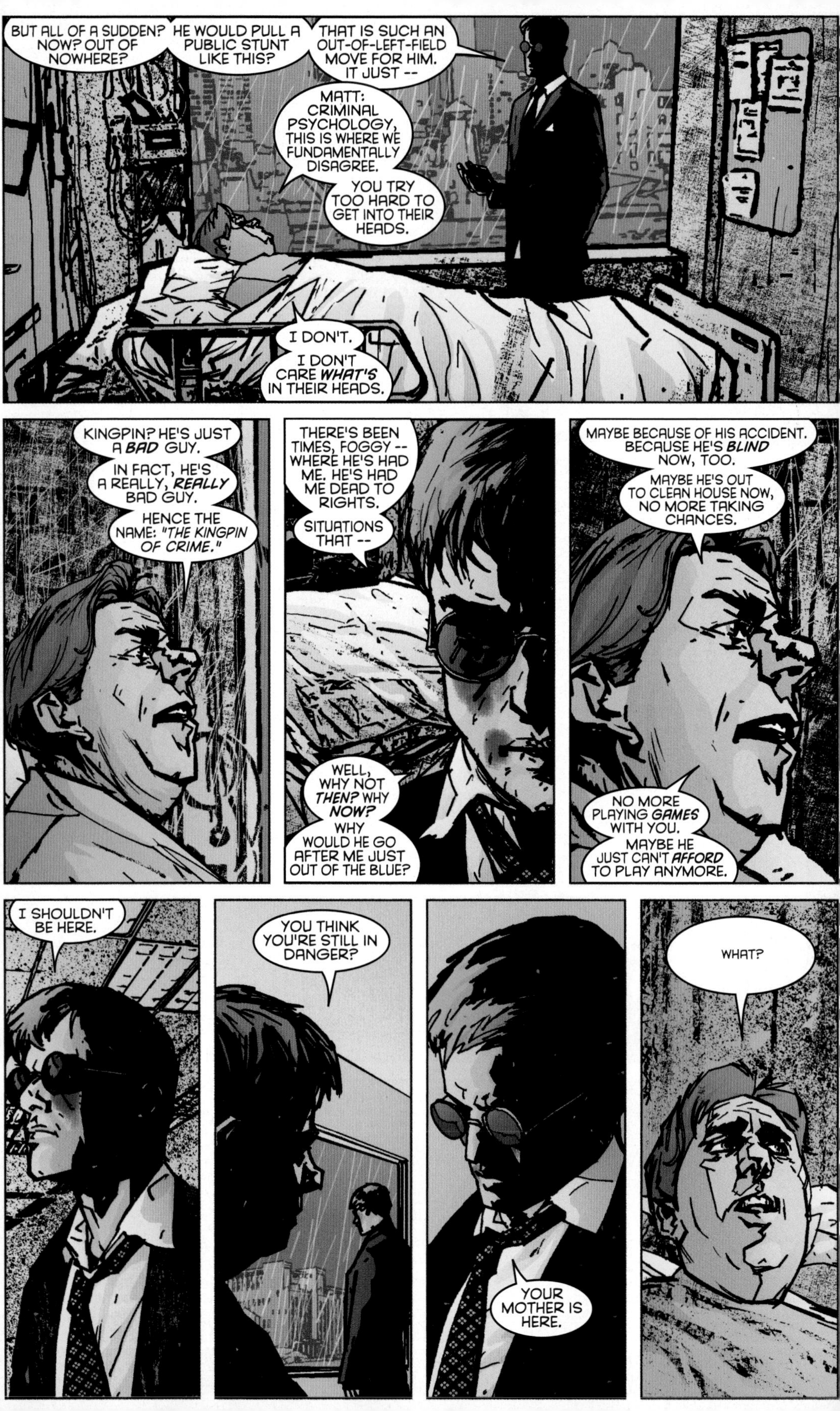

BUT ALL OF A SUDDEN? NOW? OUT OF NOWHERE?
HE WOULD PULL A PUBLIC STUNT LIKE THIS?
THAT IS SUCH AN OUT-OF-LEFT-FIELD MOVE FOR HIM. IT JUST --
MATT: CRIMINAL PSYCHOLOGY, THIS IS WHERE WE FUNDAMENTALLY DISAGREE.
YOU TRY TOO HARD TO GET INTO THEIR HEADS.
I DON'T.
I DON'T CARE WHAT'S IN THEIR HEADS.
KINGPIN? HE'S JUST A BAD GUY.
IN FACT, HE'S A REALLY, REALLY BAD GUY.
HENCE THE NAME: "THE KINGPIN OF CRIME."
THERE'S BEEN TIMES, FOGGY -- WHERE HE'S HAD ME. HE'S HAD ME DEAD TO RIGHTS.
SITUATIONS THAT --
WELL, WHY NOT THEN? WHY NOW?
WHY WOULD HE GO AFTER ME JUST OUT OF THE BLUE?
MAYBE BECAUSE OF HIS ACCIDENT. BECAUSE HE'S BLIND NOW, TOO.
MAYBE HE'S OUT TO CLEAN HOUSE NOW, NO MORE TAKING CHANCES.
NO MORE PLAYING GAMES WITH YOU.
MAYBE HE JUST CAN'T AFFORD TO PLAY ANYMORE.
I SHOULDN'T BE HERE.
YOU THINK YOU'RE STILL IN DANGER?
YOUR MOTHER IS HERE.
WHAT?

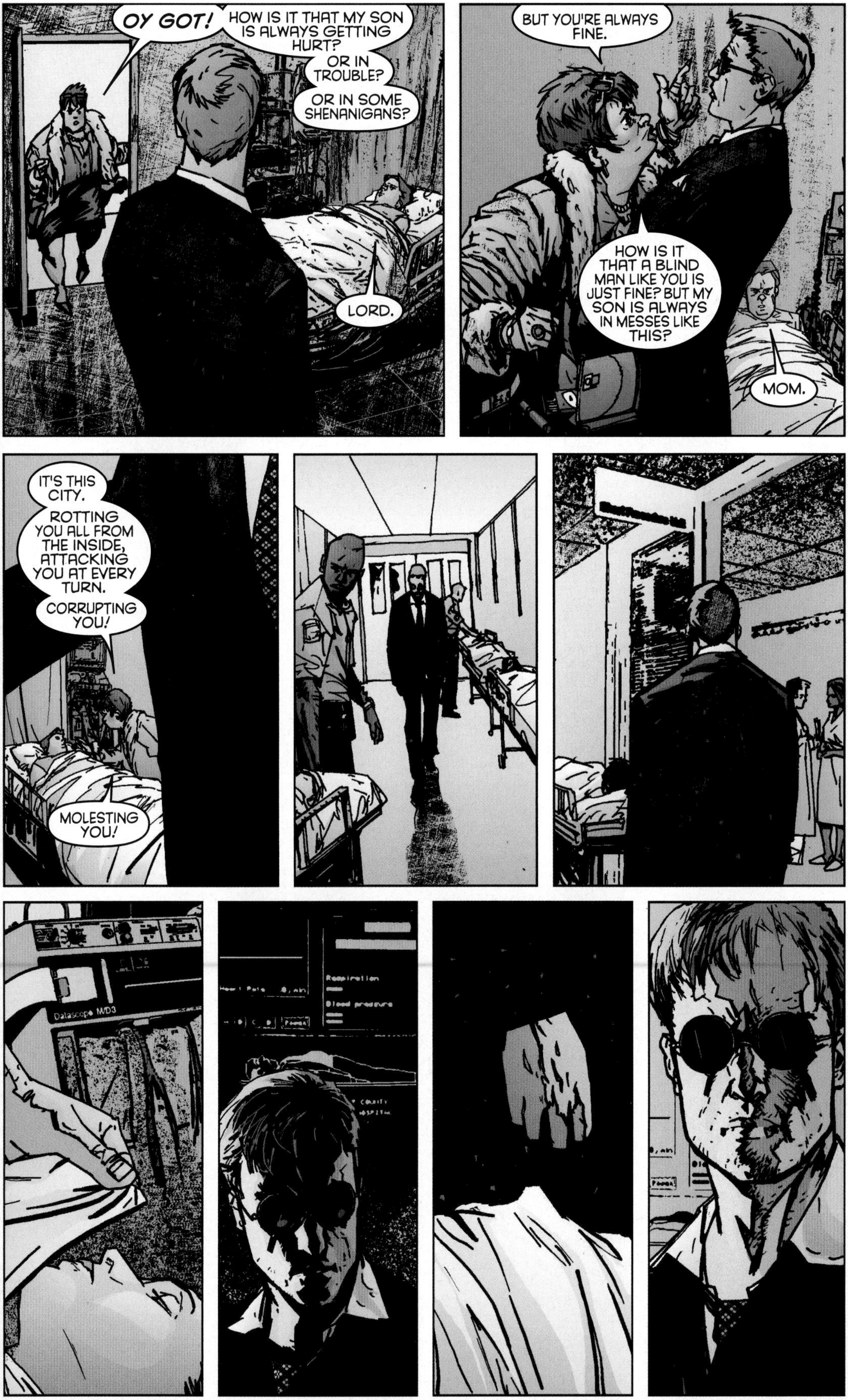
OY GOT!
HOW IS IT THAT MY SON IS ALWAYS GETTING HURT?
OR IN TROUBLE?
OR IN SOME SHENANIGANS?
LORD.
BUT YOU'RE ALWAYS FINE.
HOW IS IT THAT A BLIND MAN LIKE YOU IS JUST FINE? BUT MY SON IS ALWAYS IN MESSES LIKE THIS?
MOM.
IT'S THIS CITY.
ROTTING YOU ALL FROM THE INSIDE, ATTACKING YOU AT EVERY TURN.
CORRUPTING YOU!
MOLESTING YOU!
Datascope M/D3
Respiration
Blood pressure

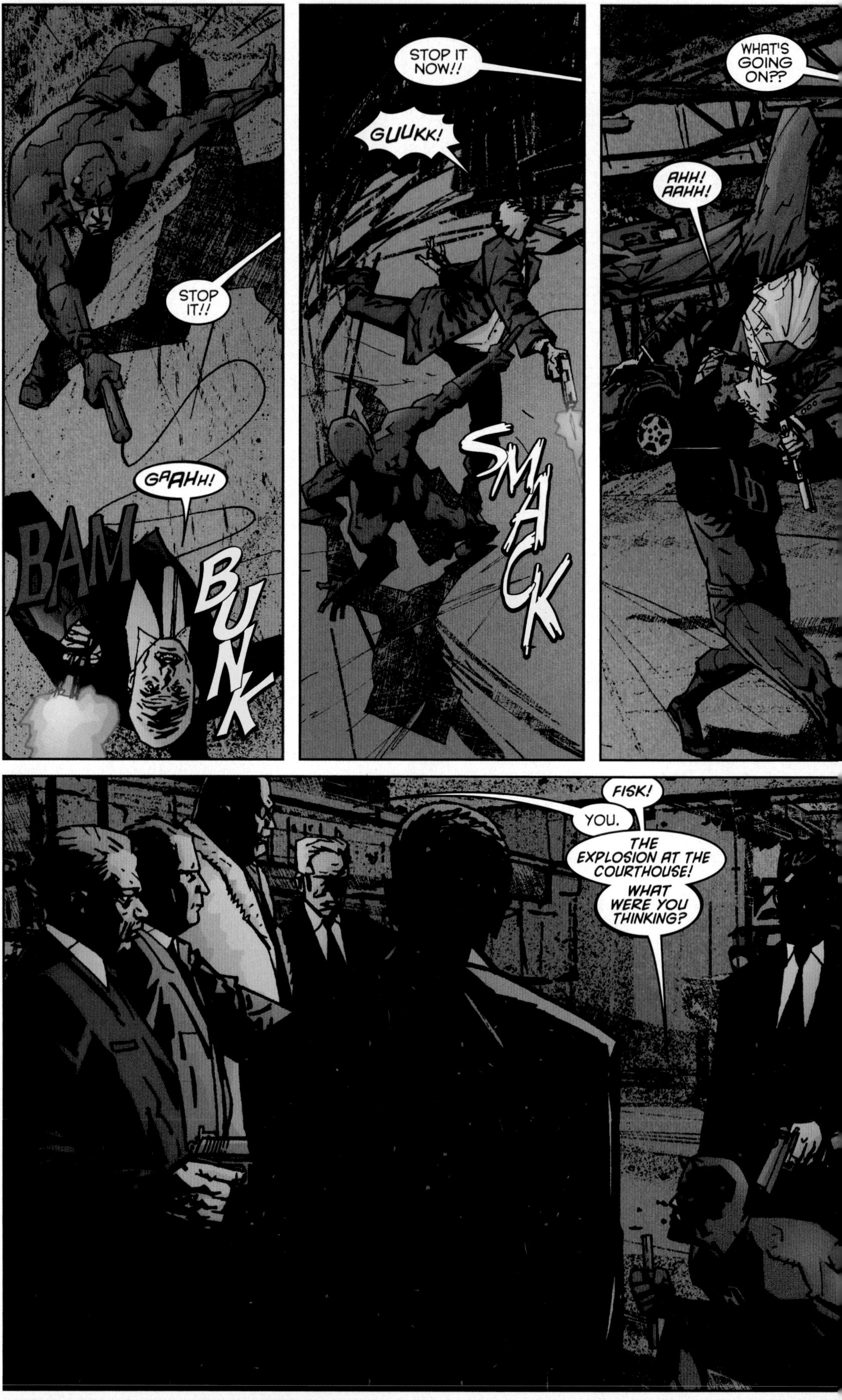
STOP IT!!
GAAHH!
BAM
BUNK
STOP IT NOW!!
GUUKK!
SMACK
WHAT'S GOING ON??
AHH! AAHH!
FISK!
YOU.
THE EXPLOSION AT THE COURTHOUSE!
WHAT WERE YOU THINKING?

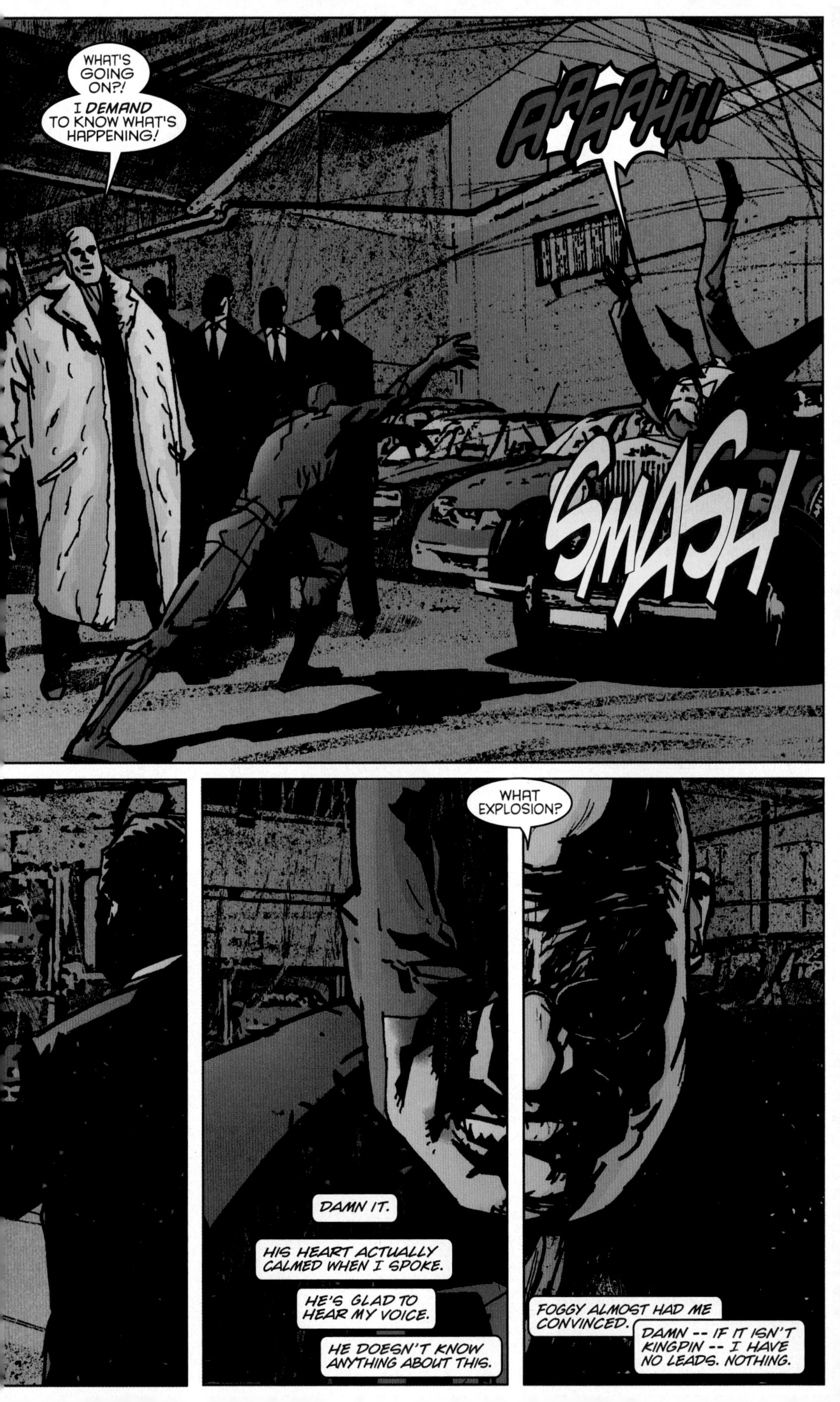
WHAT'S GOING ON?!
I DEMAND TO KNOW WHAT'S HAPPENING!
AAAAHH!
SMASH
WHAT EXPLOSION?
DAMN IT.
HIS HEART ACTUALLY CALMED WHEN I SPOKE.
HE'S GLAD TO HEAR MY VOICE.
HE DOESN'T KNOW ANYTHING ABOUT THIS.
FOGGY ALMOST HAD ME CONVINCED.
DAMN -- IF IT ISN'T KINGPIN -- I HAVE NO LEADS. NOTHING.

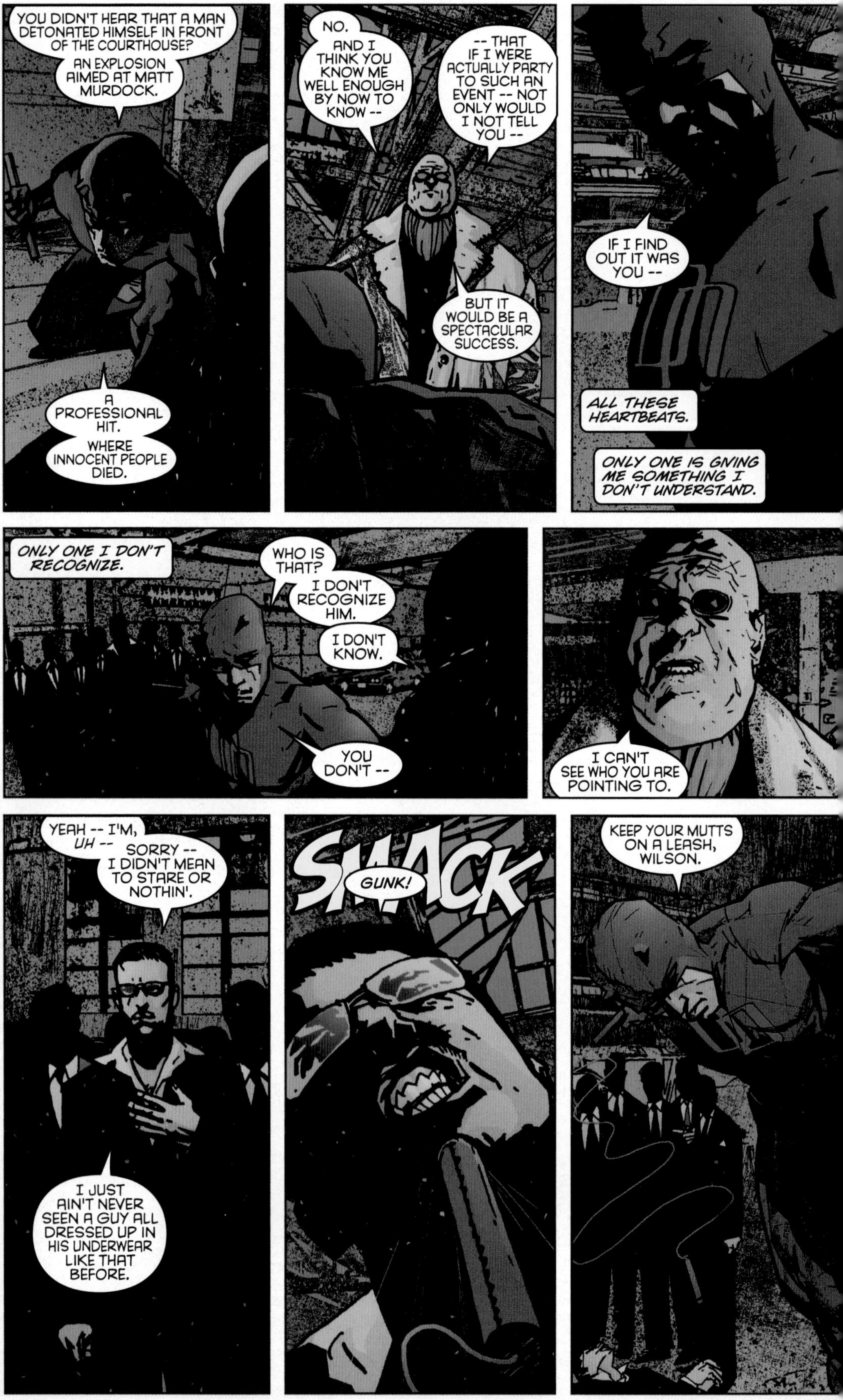
YOU DIDN'T HEAR THAT A MAN DETONATED HIMSELF IN FRONT OF THE COURTHOUSE?
AN EXPLOSION AIMED AT MATT MURDOCK.
A PROFESSIONAL HIT.
WHERE INNOCENT PEOPLE DIED.
NO.
AND I THINK YOU KNOW ME WELL ENOUGH BY NOW TO KNOW --
-- THAT IF I WERE ACTUALLY PARTY TO SUCH AN EVENT -- NOT ONLY WOULD I NOT TELL YOU --
BUT IT WOULD BE A SPECTACULAR SUCCESS.
IF I FIND OUT IT WAS YOU --
ALL THESE HEARTBEATS.
ONLY ONE IS GIVING ME SOMETHING I DON'T UNDERSTAND.
ONLY ONE I DON'T RECOGNIZE.
WHO IS THAT?
I DON'T RECOGNIZE HIM.
I DON'T KNOW.
YOU DON'T --
I CAN'T SEE WHO YOU ARE POINTING TO.
YEAH -- I'M, UH --
SORRY -- I DIDN'T MEAN TO STARE OR NOTHIN'.
I JUST AIN'T NEVER SEEN A GUY ALL DRESSED UP IN HIS UNDERWEAR LIKE THAT BEFORE.
SMACK
GUNK!
KEEP YOUR MUTTS ON A LEASH, WILSON.

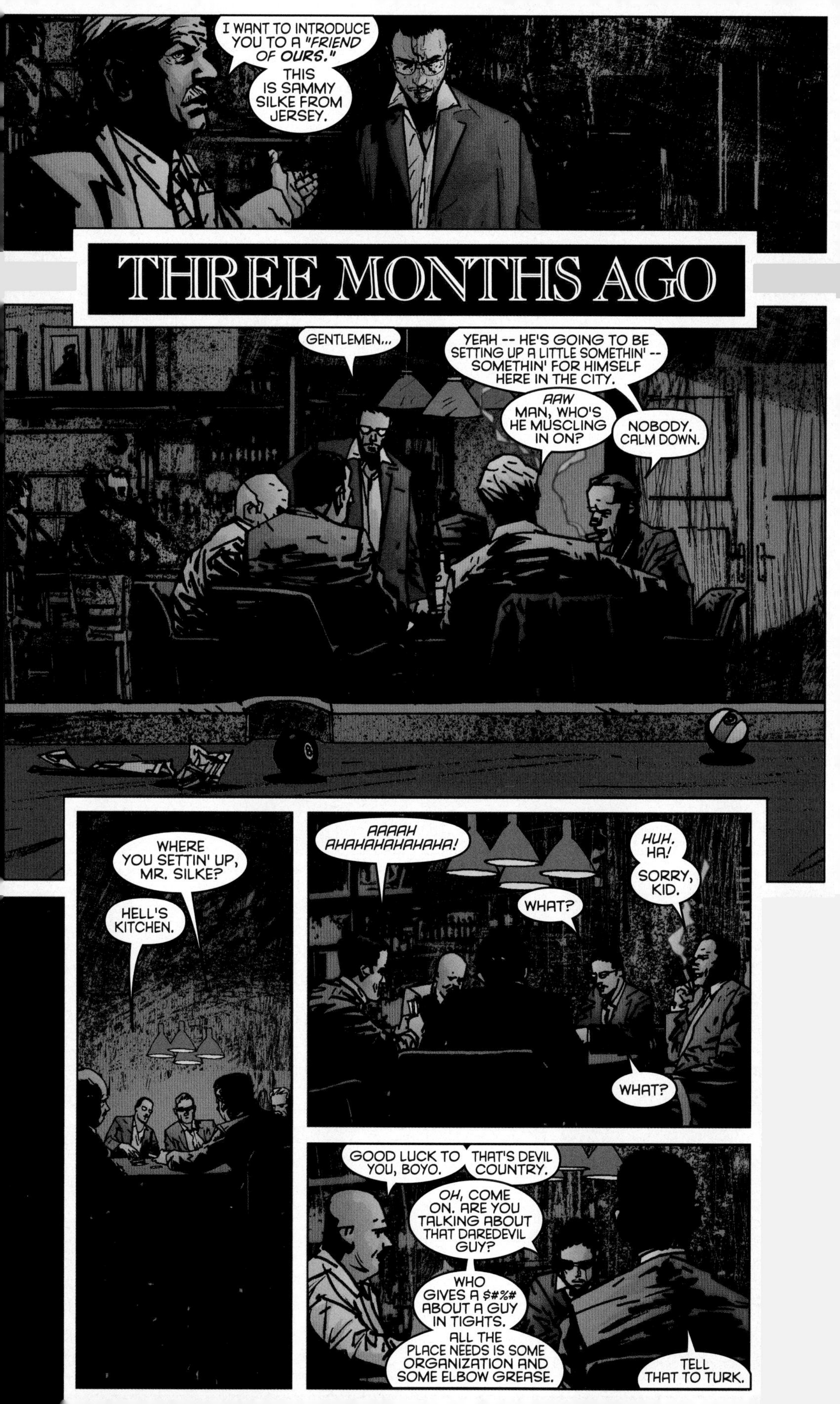

I WANT TO INTRODUCE YOU TO A "FRIEND OF OURS."
THIS IS SAMMY SILKE FROM JERSEY.
THREE MONTHS AGO
GENTLEMEN...
YEAH -- HE'S GOING TO BE SETTING UP A LITTLE SOMETHIN' -- SOMETHIN' FOR HIMSELF HERE IN THE CITY.
AAW MAN, WHO'S HE MUSCLING IN ON?
NOBODY. CALM DOWN.
WHERE YOU SETTIN' UP, MR. SILKE?
HELL'S KITCHEN.
AAAAH AHAHAHAHAHAHA!
HUH. HA!
SORRY, KID.
WHAT?
WHAT?
GOOD LUCK TO YOU, BOYO.
THAT'S DEVIL COUNTRY.
OH, COME ON. ARE YOU TALKING ABOUT THAT DAREDEVIL GUY?
WHO GIVES A $#%# ABOUT A GUY IN TIGHTS.
ALL THE PLACE NEEDS IS SOME ORGANIZATION AND SOME ELBOW GREASE.
TELL THAT TO TURK.

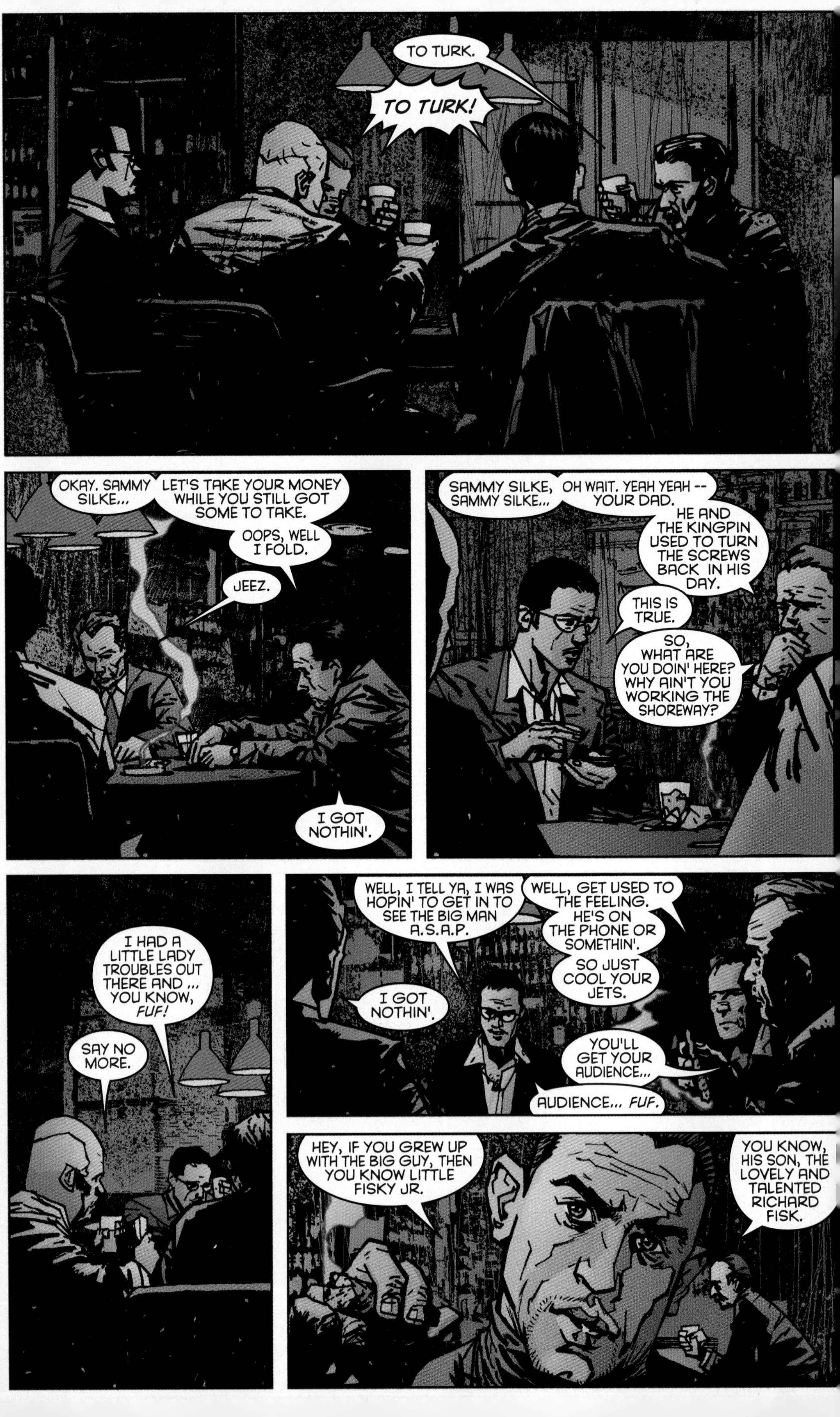

TO TURK.
TO TURK!
OKAY. SAMMY SILKE...
LET'S TAKE YOUR MONEY WHILE YOU STILL GOT SOME TO TAKE.
OOPS, WELL I FOLD.
JEEZ.
I GOT NOTHIN'.
SAMMY SILKE, SAMMY SILKE...
OH WAIT. YEAH YEAH -- YOUR DAD.
HE AND THE KINGPIN USED TO TURN THE SCREWS BACK IN HIS DAY.
THIS IS TRUE.
SO, WHAT ARE YOU DOIN' HERE? WHY AIN'T YOU WORKING THE SHOREWAY?
I HAD A LITTLE LADY TROUBLES OUT THERE AND ... YOU KNOW, *FUF!*
SAY NO MORE.
WELL, I TELL YA, I WAS HOPIN' TO GET IN TO SEE THE BIG MAN A.S.A.P.
WELL, GET USED TO THE FEELING.
HE'S ON THE PHONE OR SOMETHIN'.
SO JUST COOL YOUR JETS.
I GOT NOTHIN'.
YOU'LL GET YOUR AUDIENCE...
AUDIENCE... *FUF*.
HEY, IF YOU GREW UP WITH THE BIG GUY, THEN YOU KNOW LITTLE FISKY JR.
YOU KNOW, HIS SON, THE LOVELY AND TALENTED RICHARD FISK.

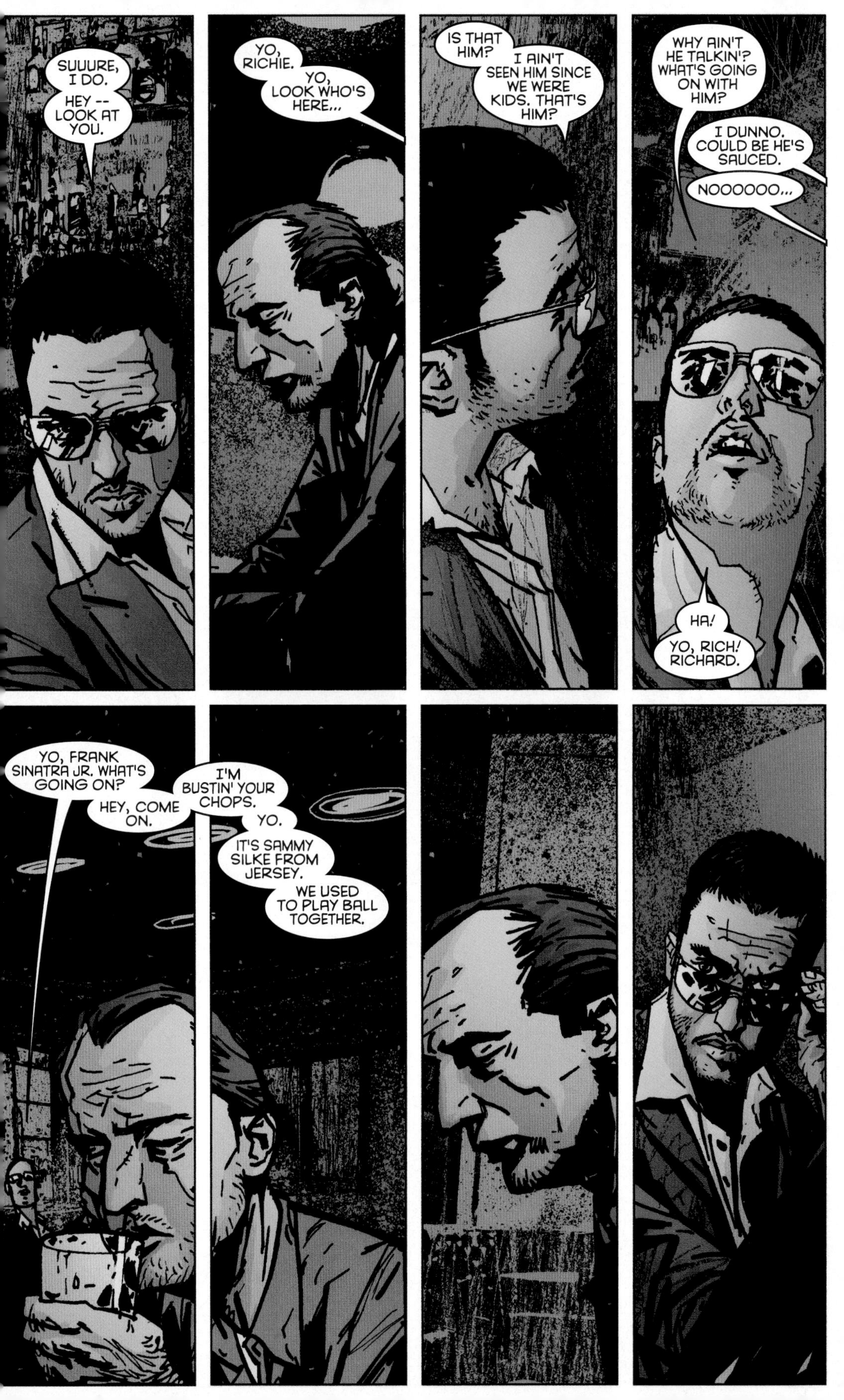
SUUURE, I DO.
HEY -- LOOK AT YOU.
YO, RICHIE.
YO, LOOK WHO'S HERE...
IS THAT HIM?
I AIN'T SEEN HIM SINCE WE WERE KIDS. THAT'S HIM?
WHY AIN'T HE TALKIN'? WHAT'S GOING ON WITH HIM?
I DUNNO. COULD BE HE'S SAUCED.
NOOOOOO...
HA!
YO, RICH! RICHARD.
YO, FRANK SINATRA JR. WHAT'S GOING ON?
HEY, COME ON.
I'M BUSTIN' YOUR CHOPS.
YO.
IT'S SAMMY SILKE FROM JERSEY.
WE USED TO PLAY BALL TOGETHER.

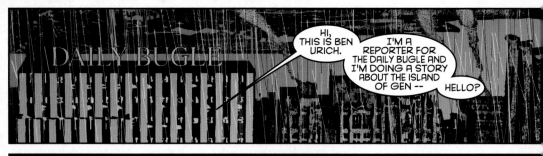

DAILY BUGLE

HI, THIS IS BEN URICH.

I'M A REPORTER FOR THE DAILY BUGLE AND I'M DOING A STORY ABOUT THE ISLAND OF GEN --

HELLO?

TODAY

LORD -- WHATEVER HAPPENED TO "NO COMMENT"?

CALL ON LINE SEVENTEEN, BEN.

THIS IS BEN URICH.

WHAT?

HEY BEN, DID YOU SEE THE INSANE THING THE MAYOR SAID ABOUT THE AVENGERS MAN --

WHAT'S GOING ON, BEN?

KINGPIN'S DEAD.

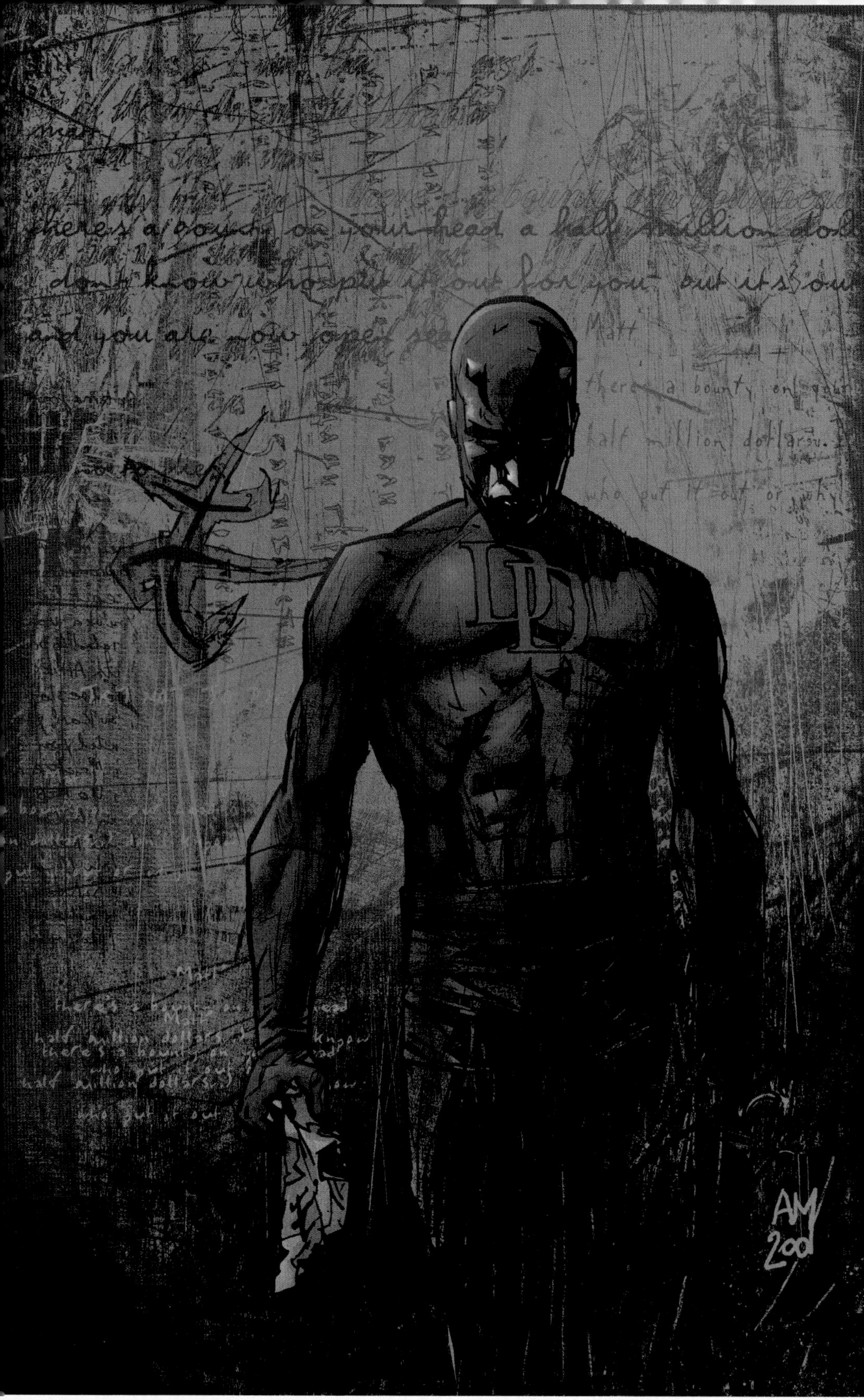

there's a bounty on your head a half million doll
Matt
there's a bounty on your
half million dollars
who put it out or why

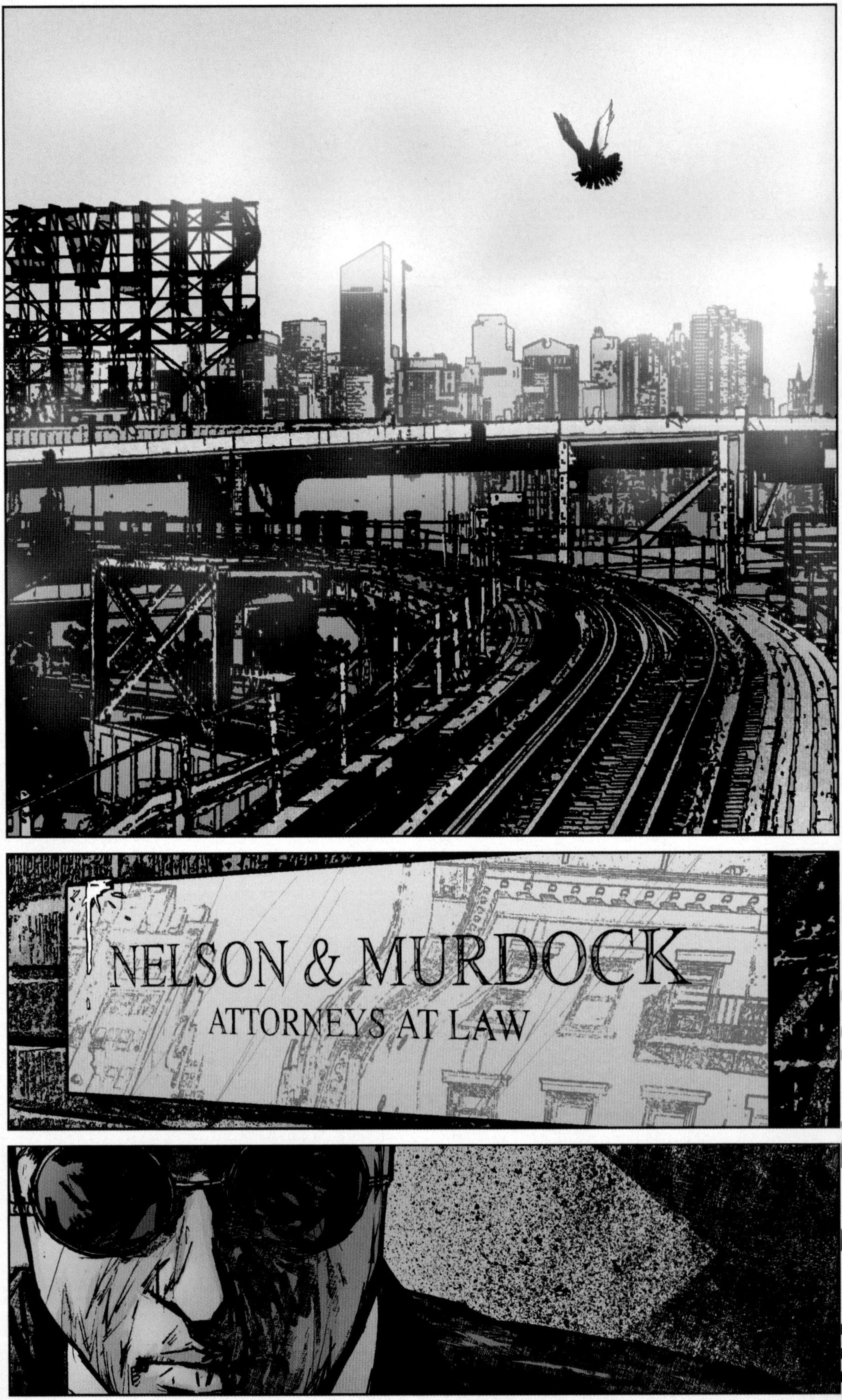
NELSON & MURDOCK
ATTORNEYS AT LAW

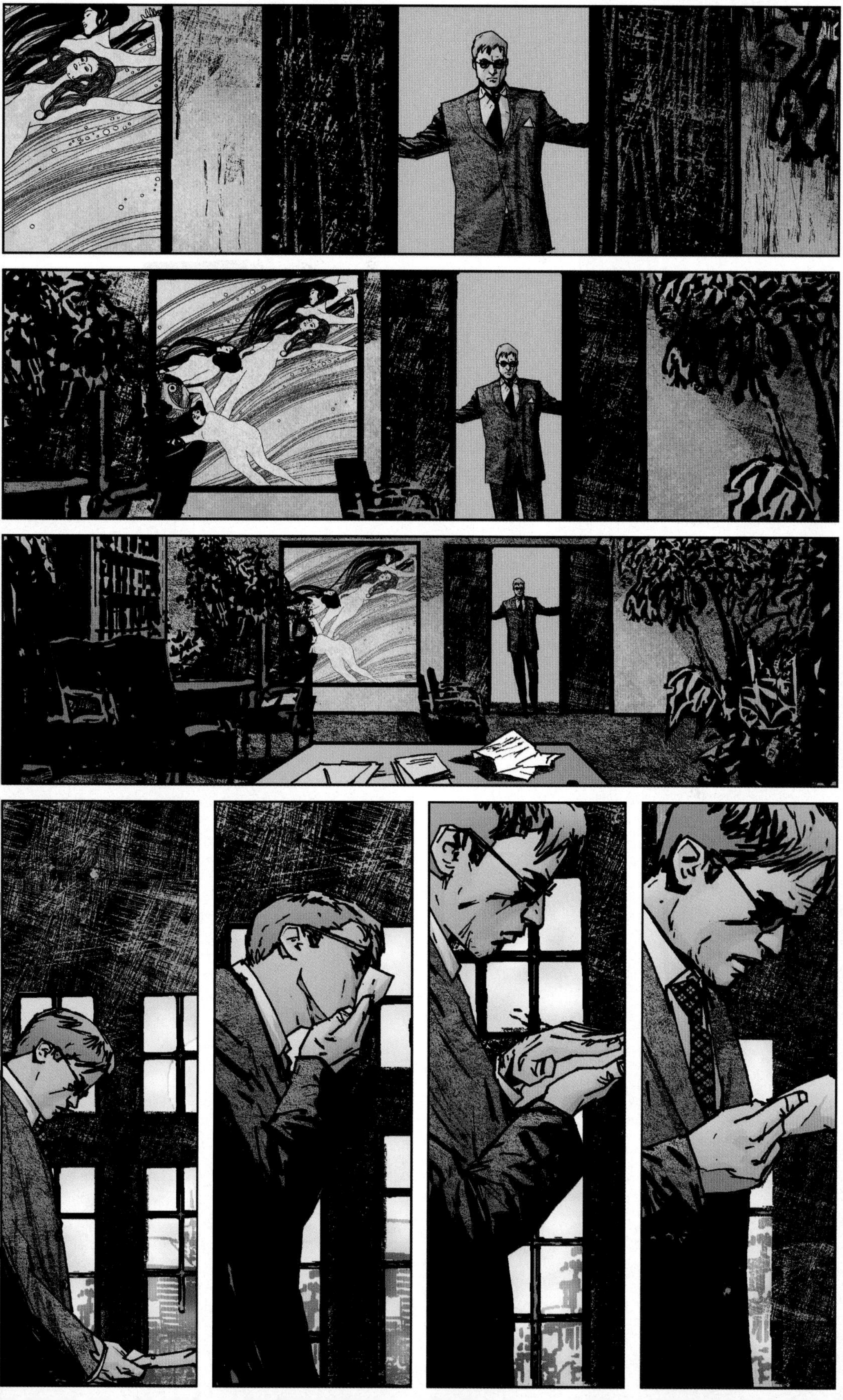

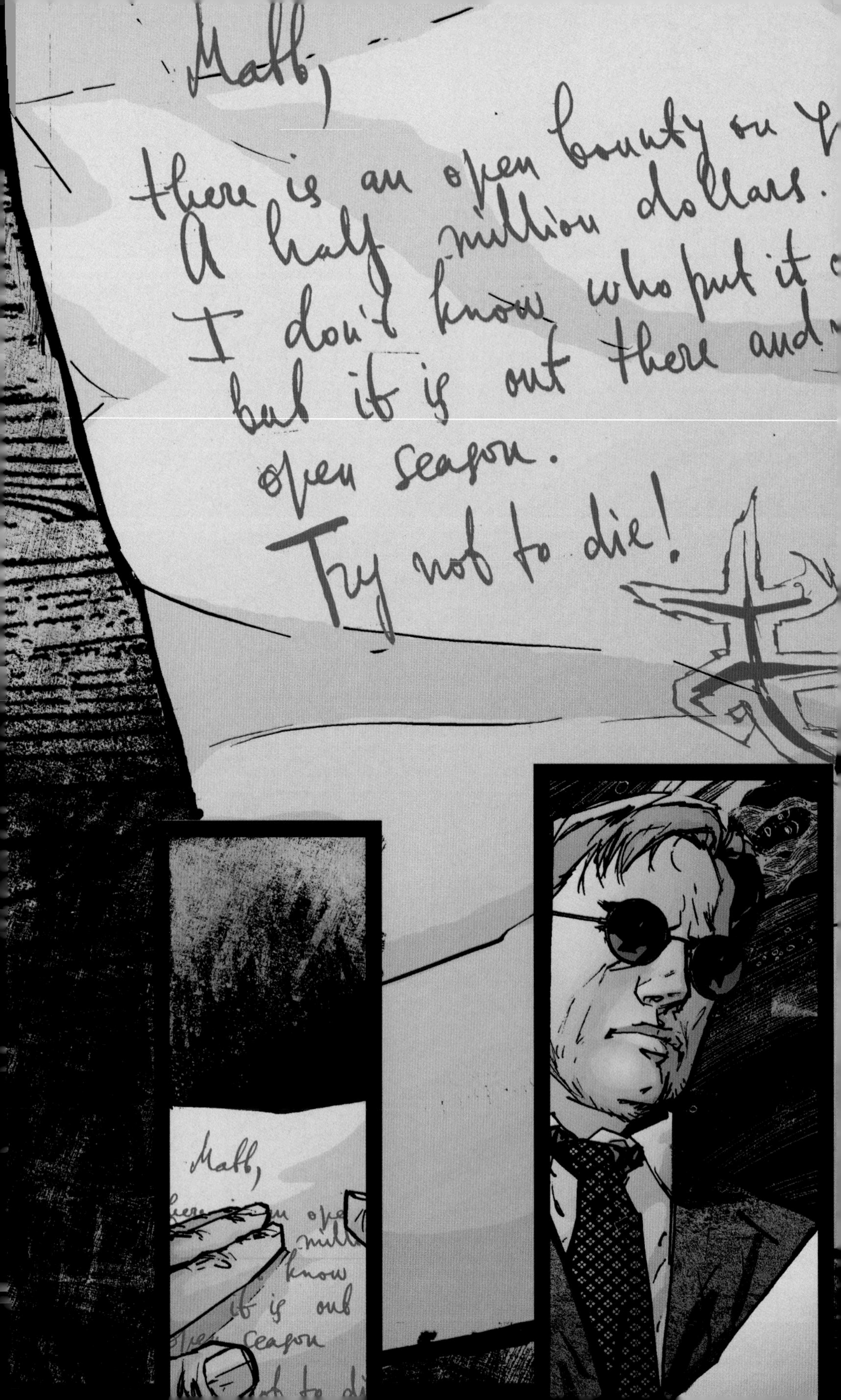
Matt,
There is an open bounty on
A half million dollars.
I don't know who put it
but it is out there and
open season.
Try not to die!

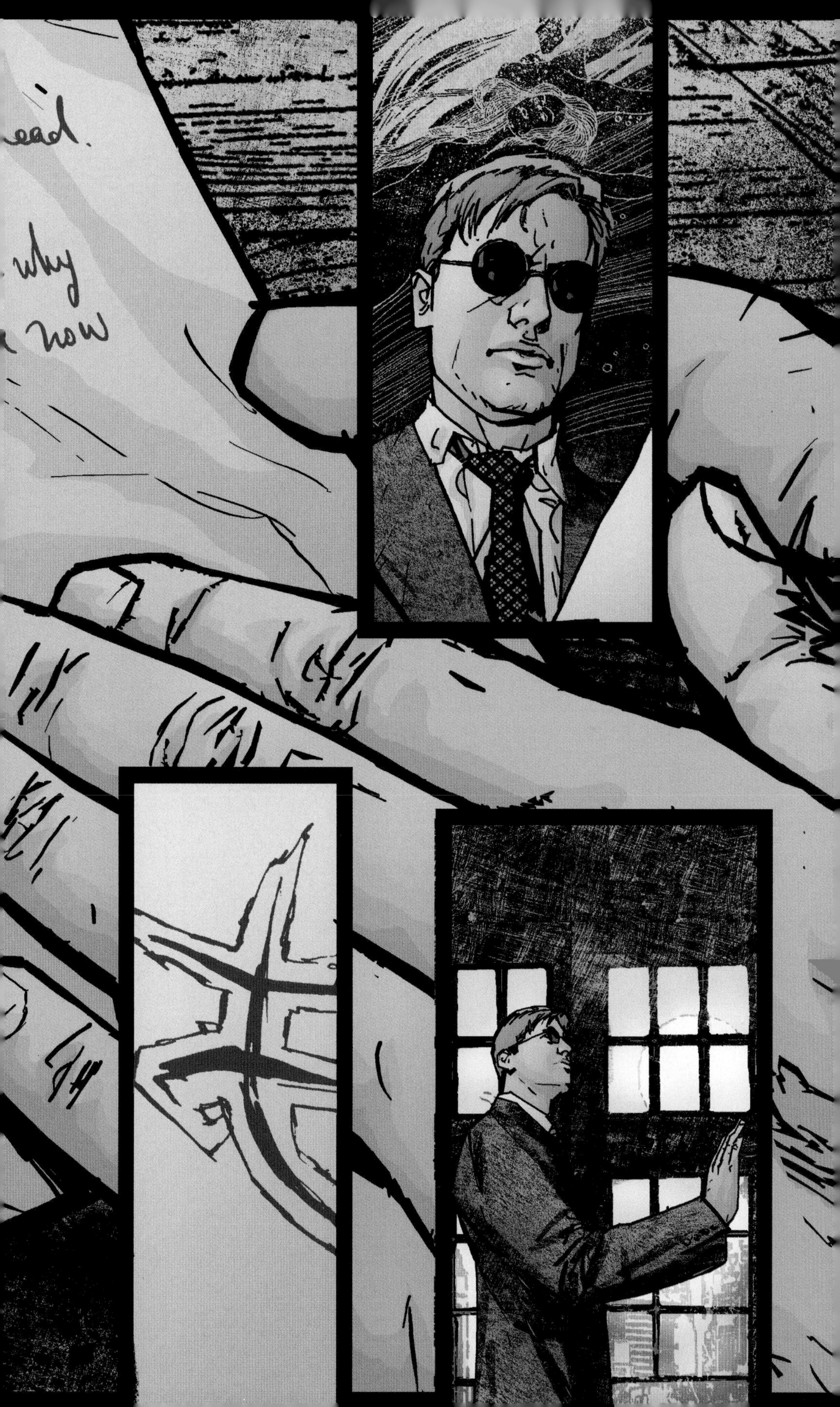
ead.
why
now

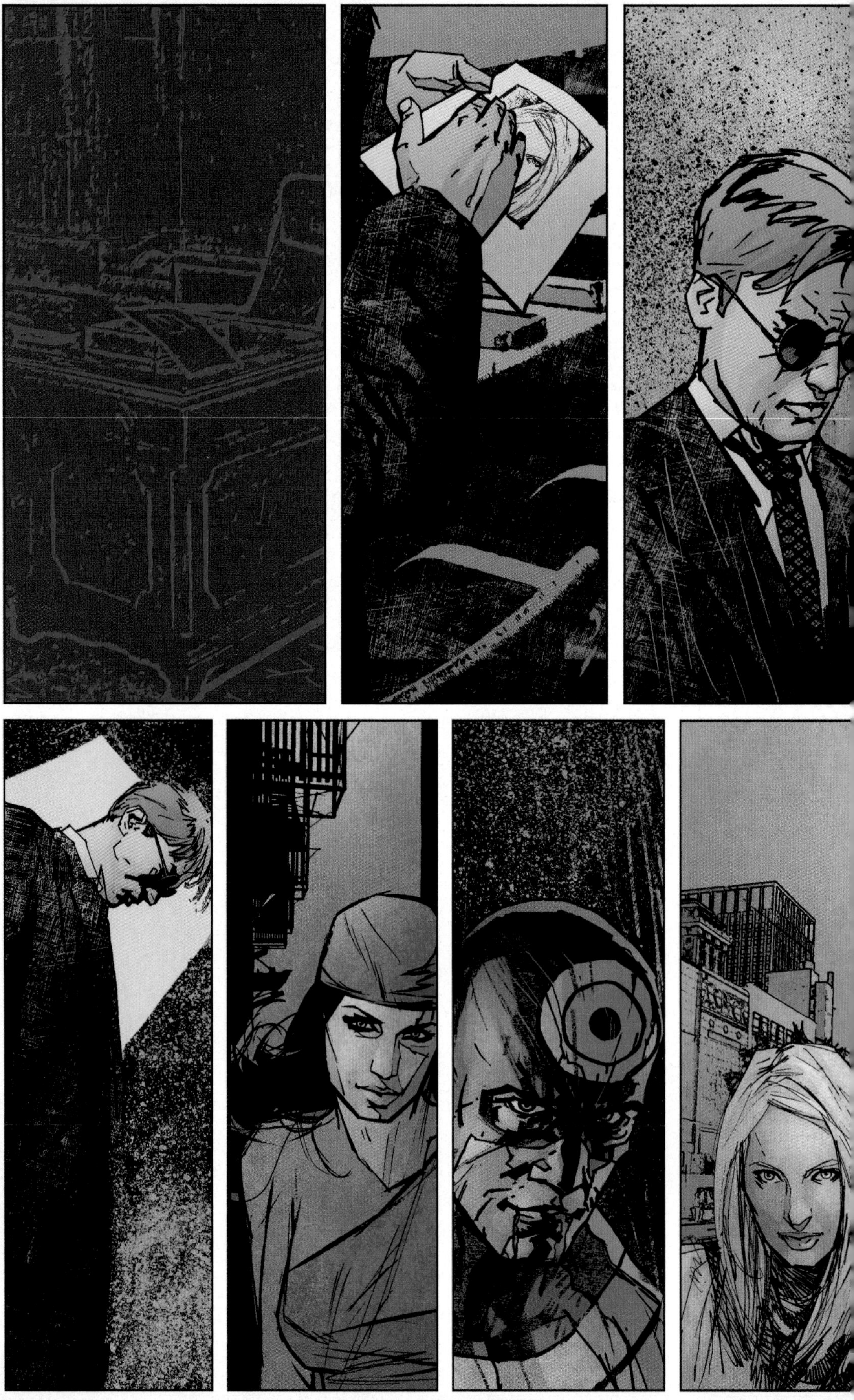

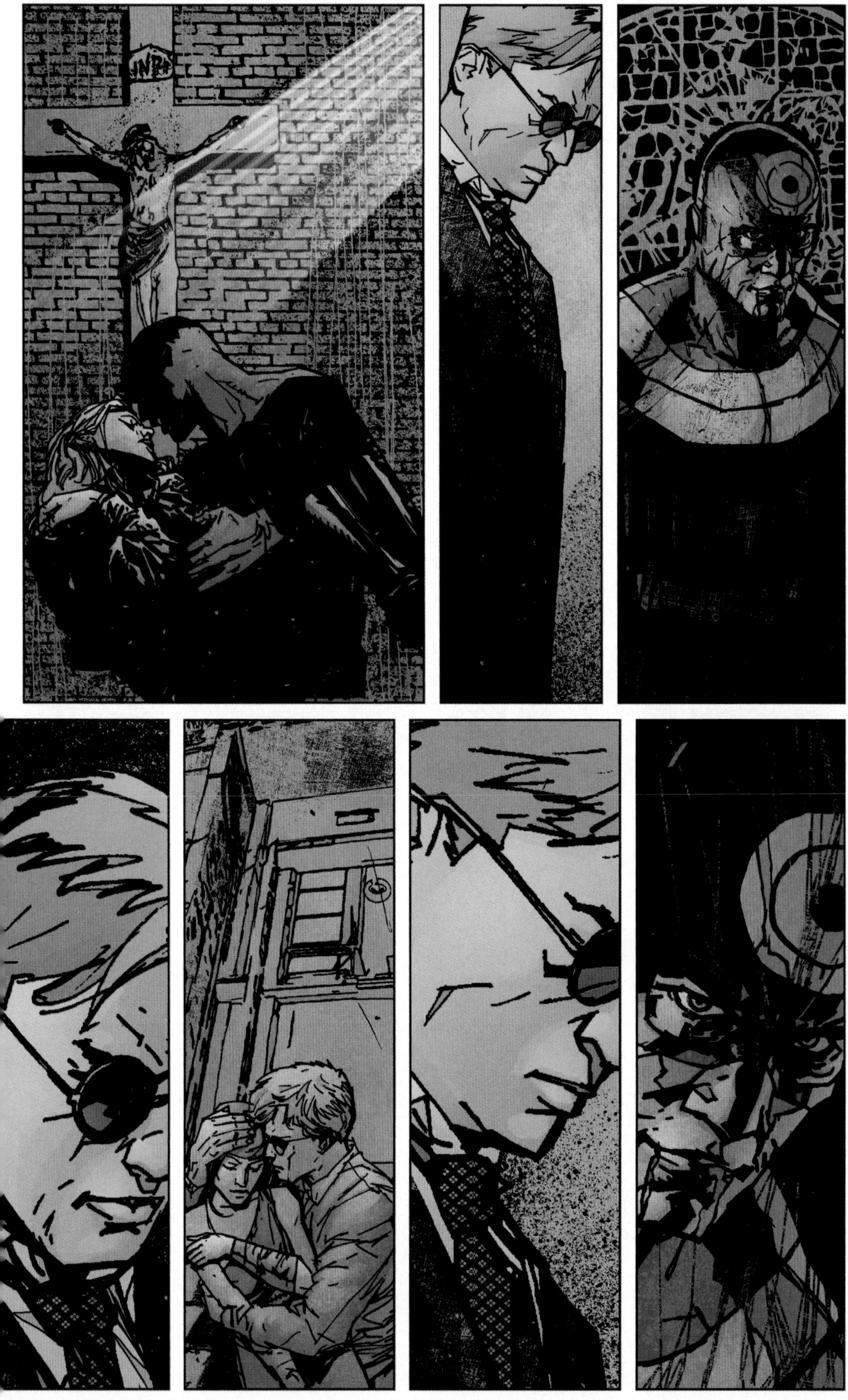

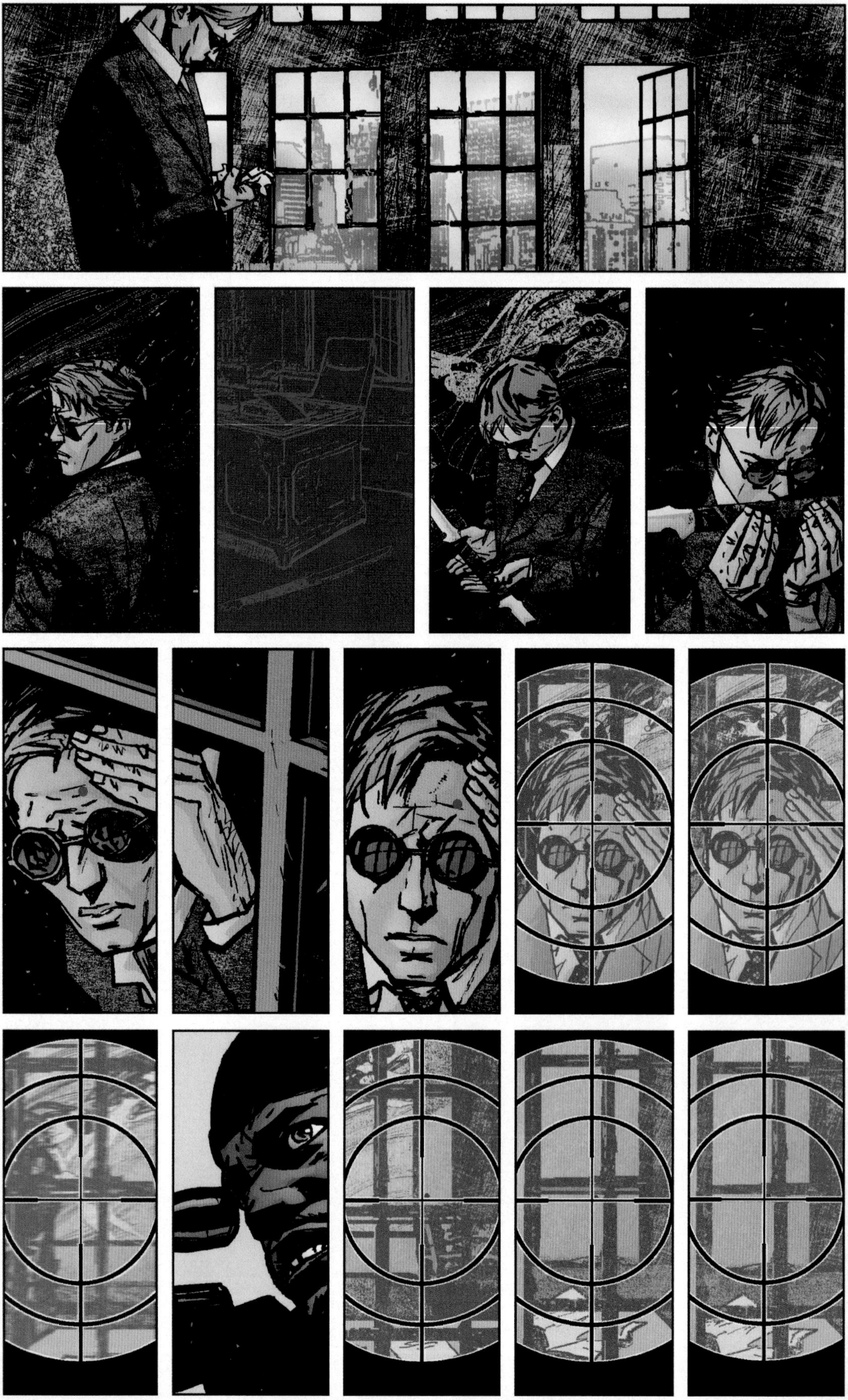

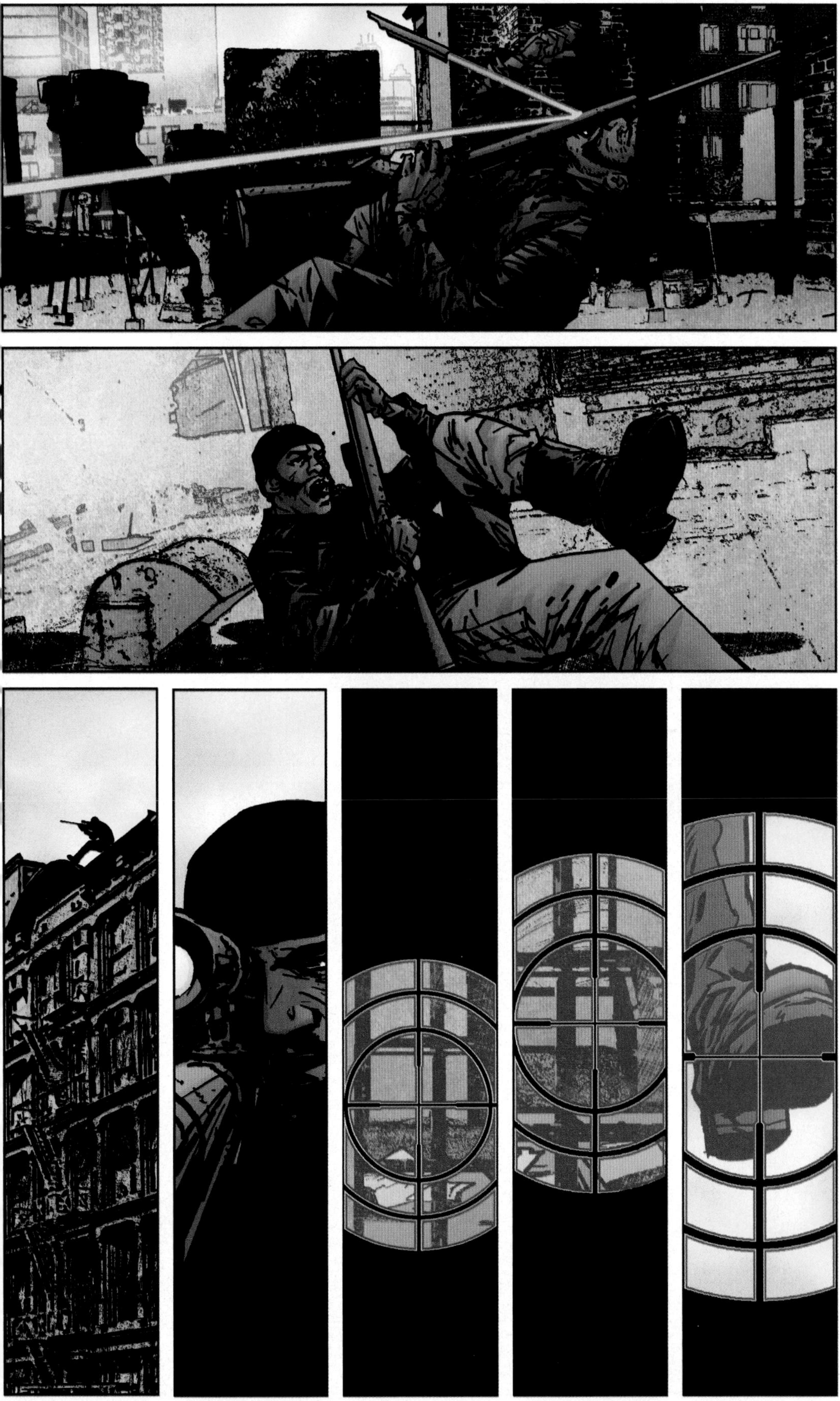

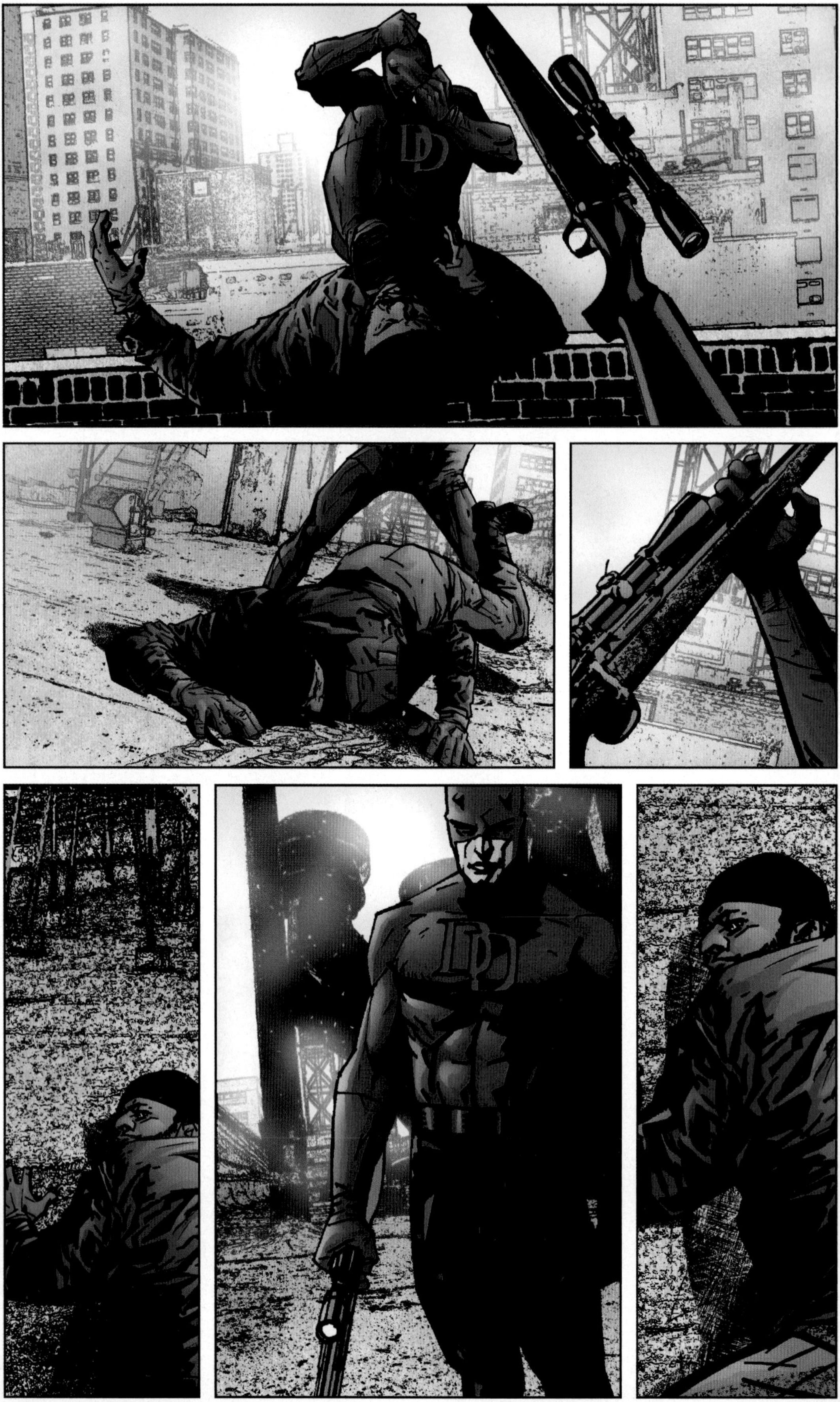

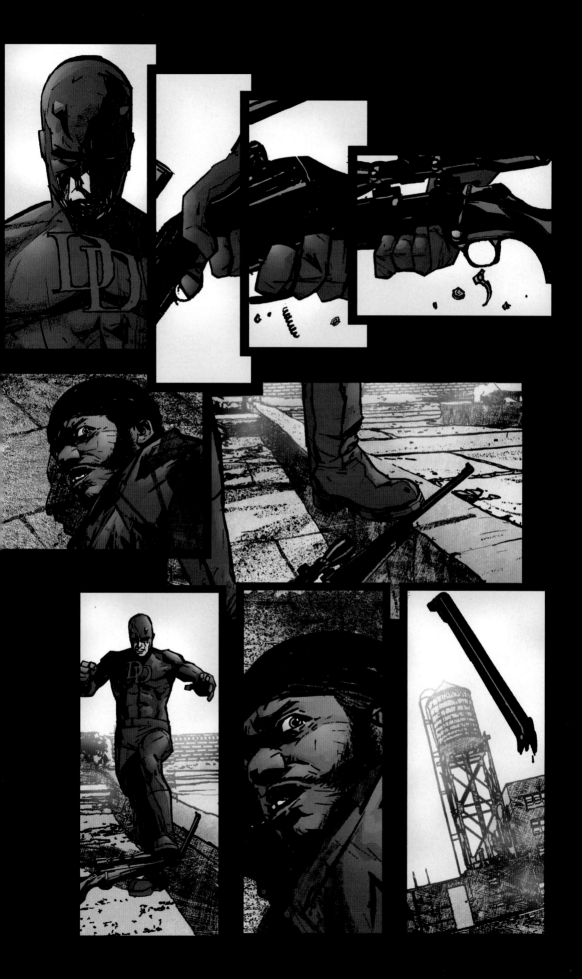

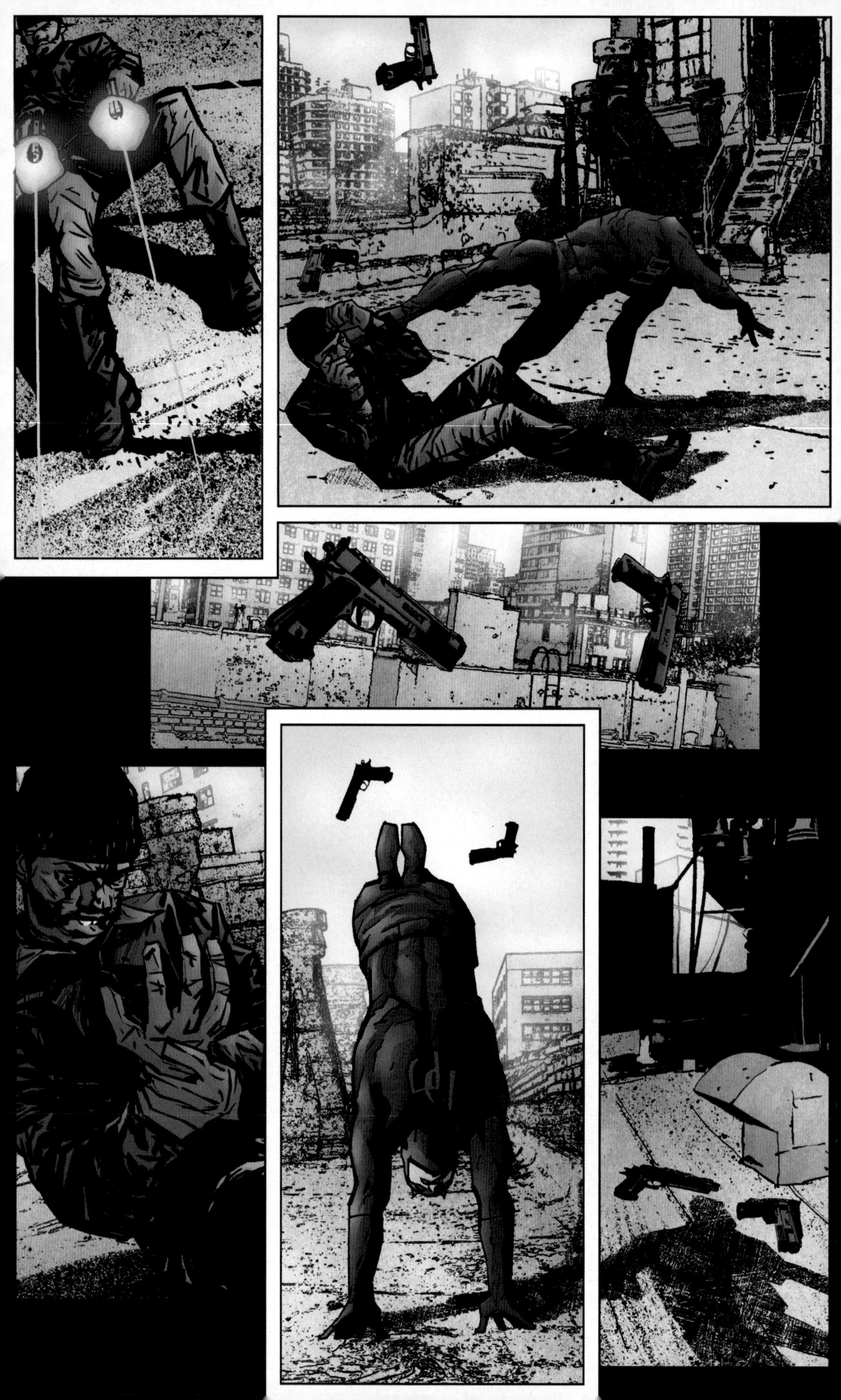

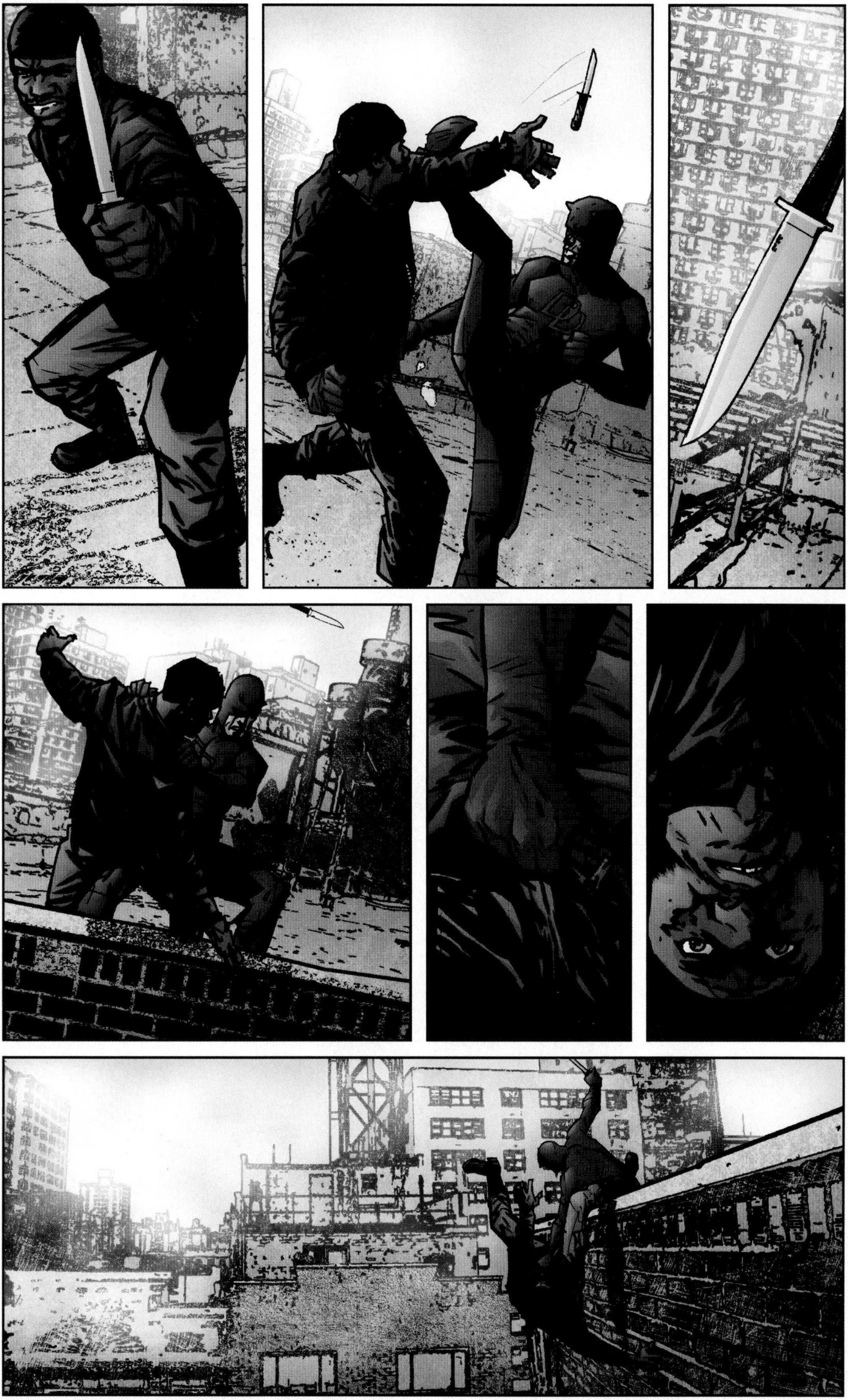

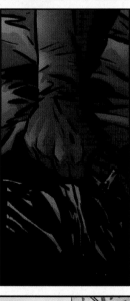

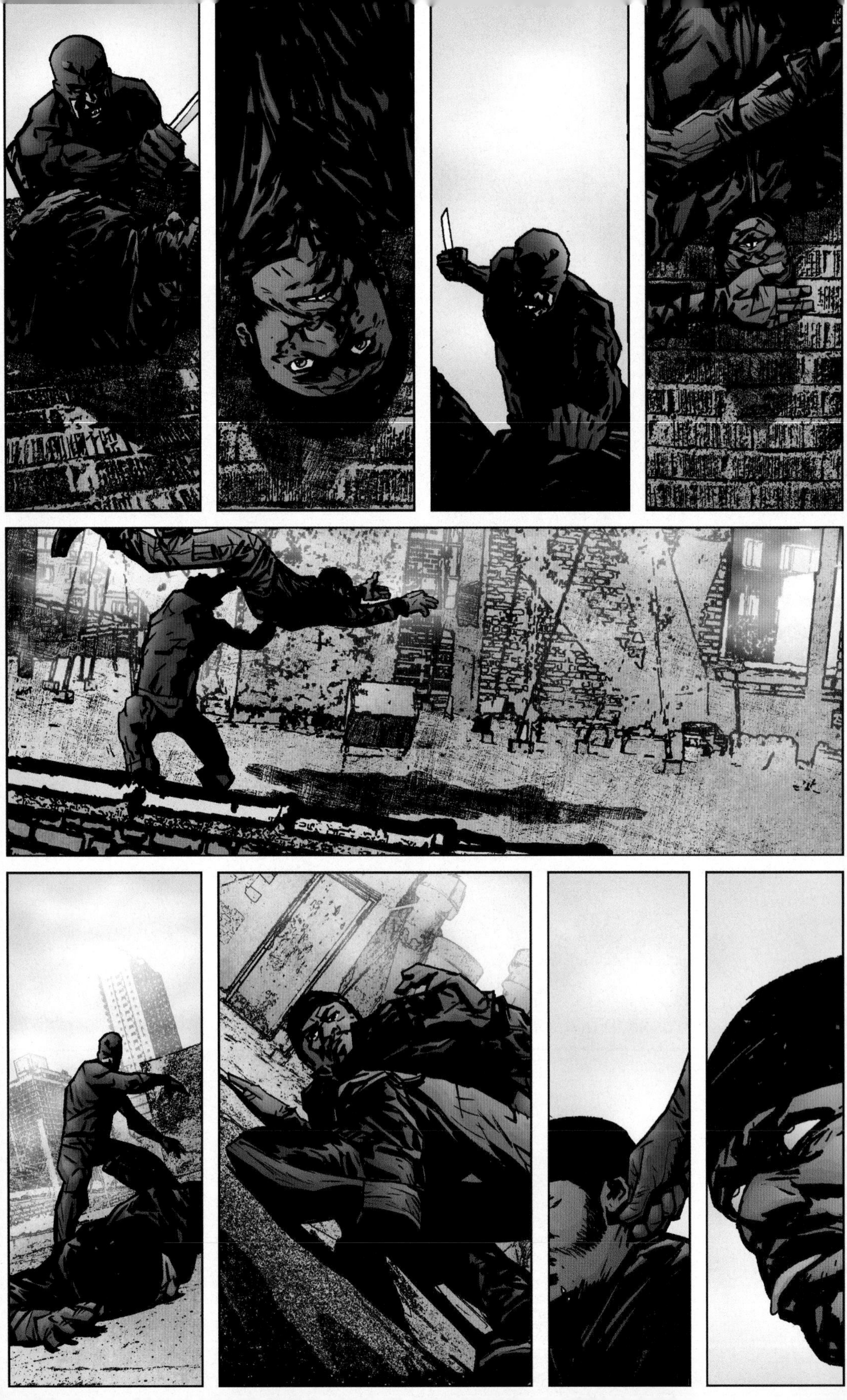

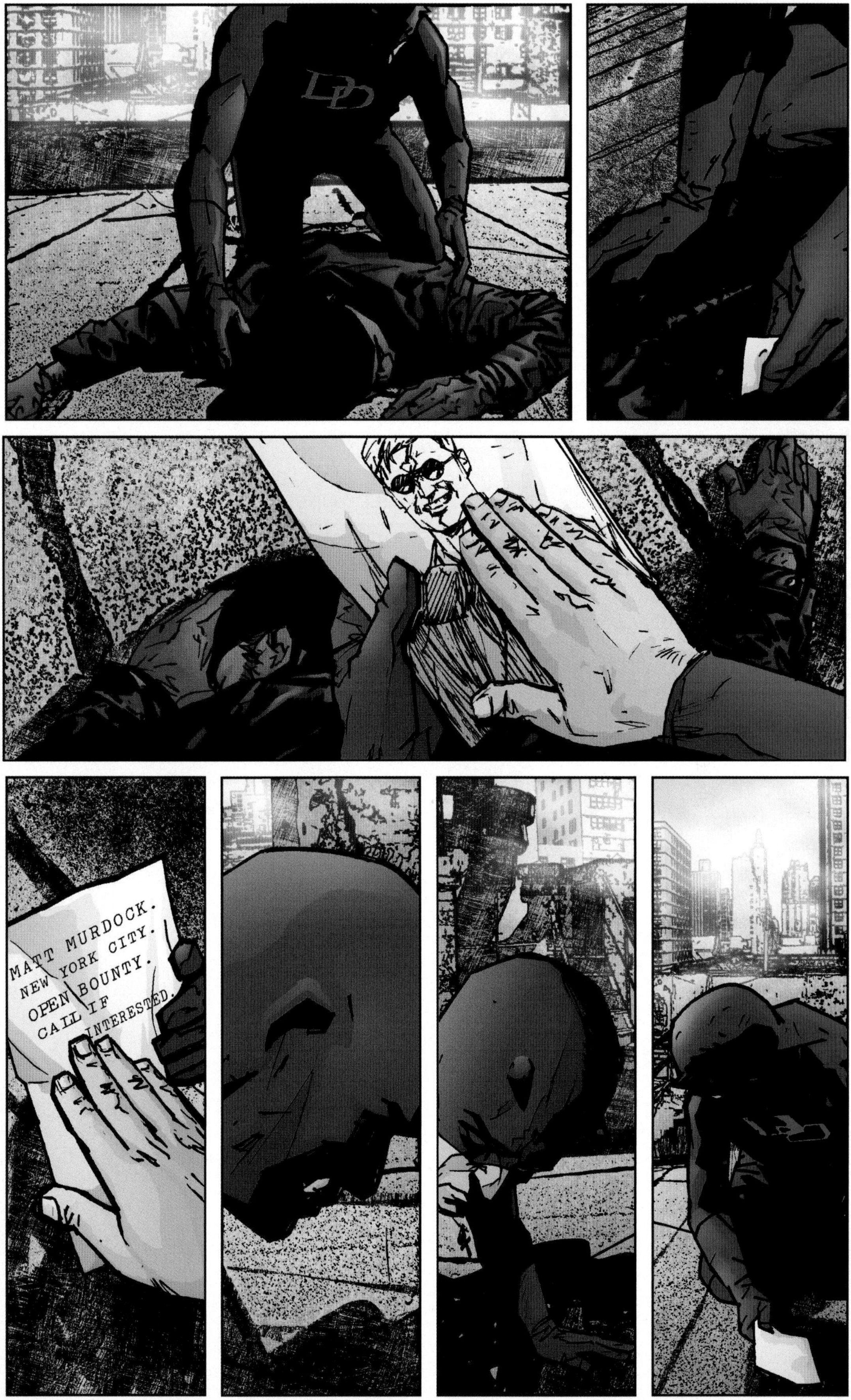
MATT MURDOCK.
NEW YORK CITY.
OPEN BOUNTY.
CALL IF
INTERESTED.

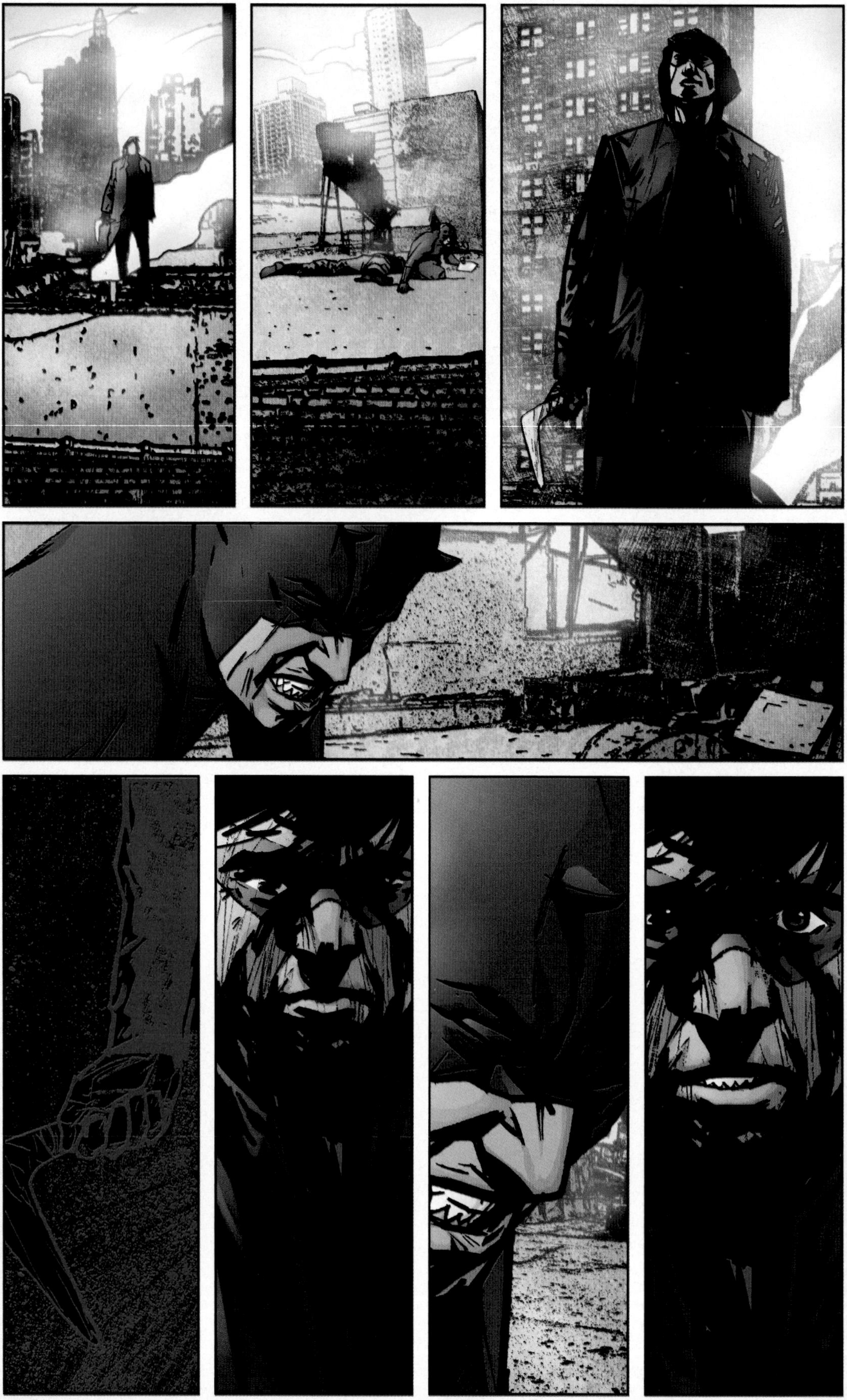

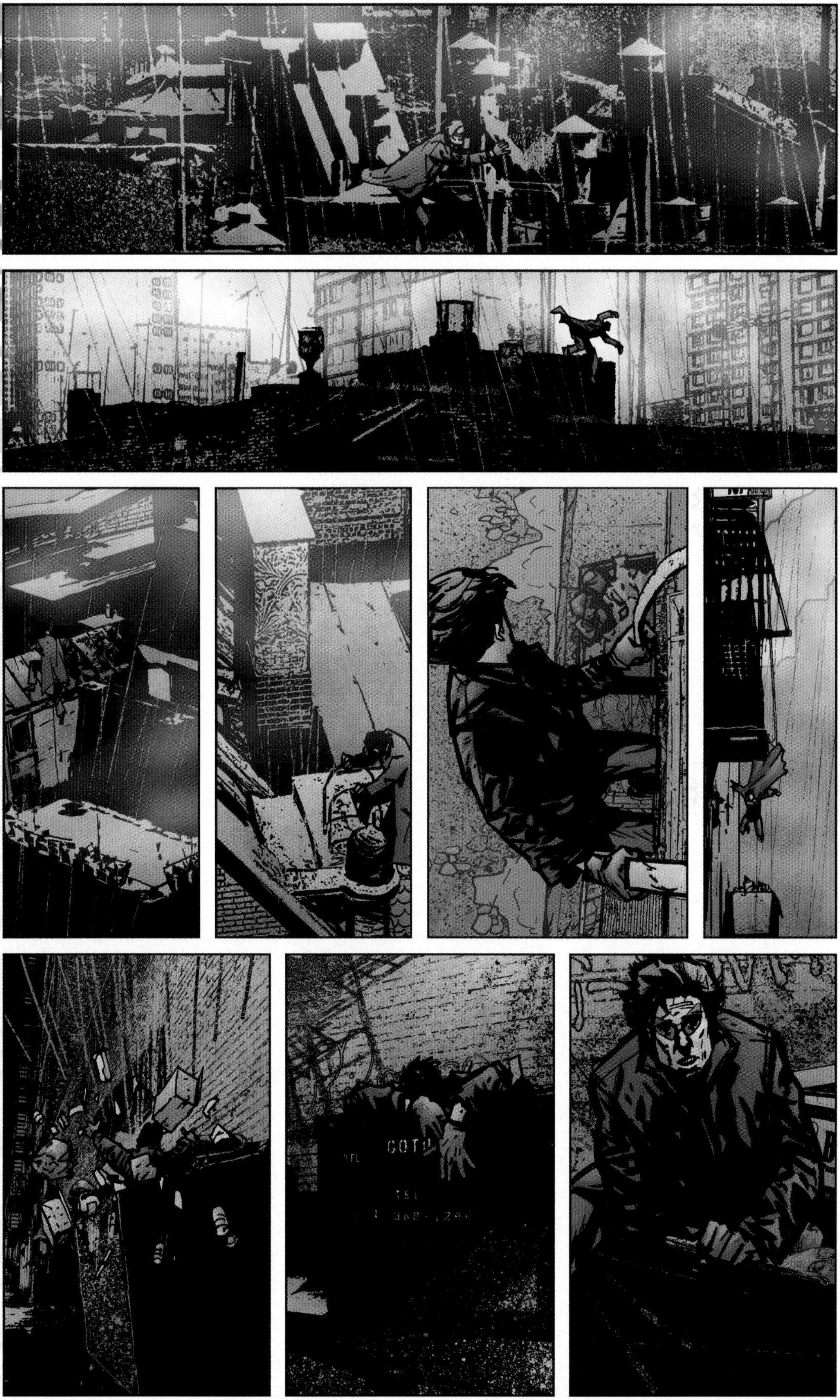
TEL

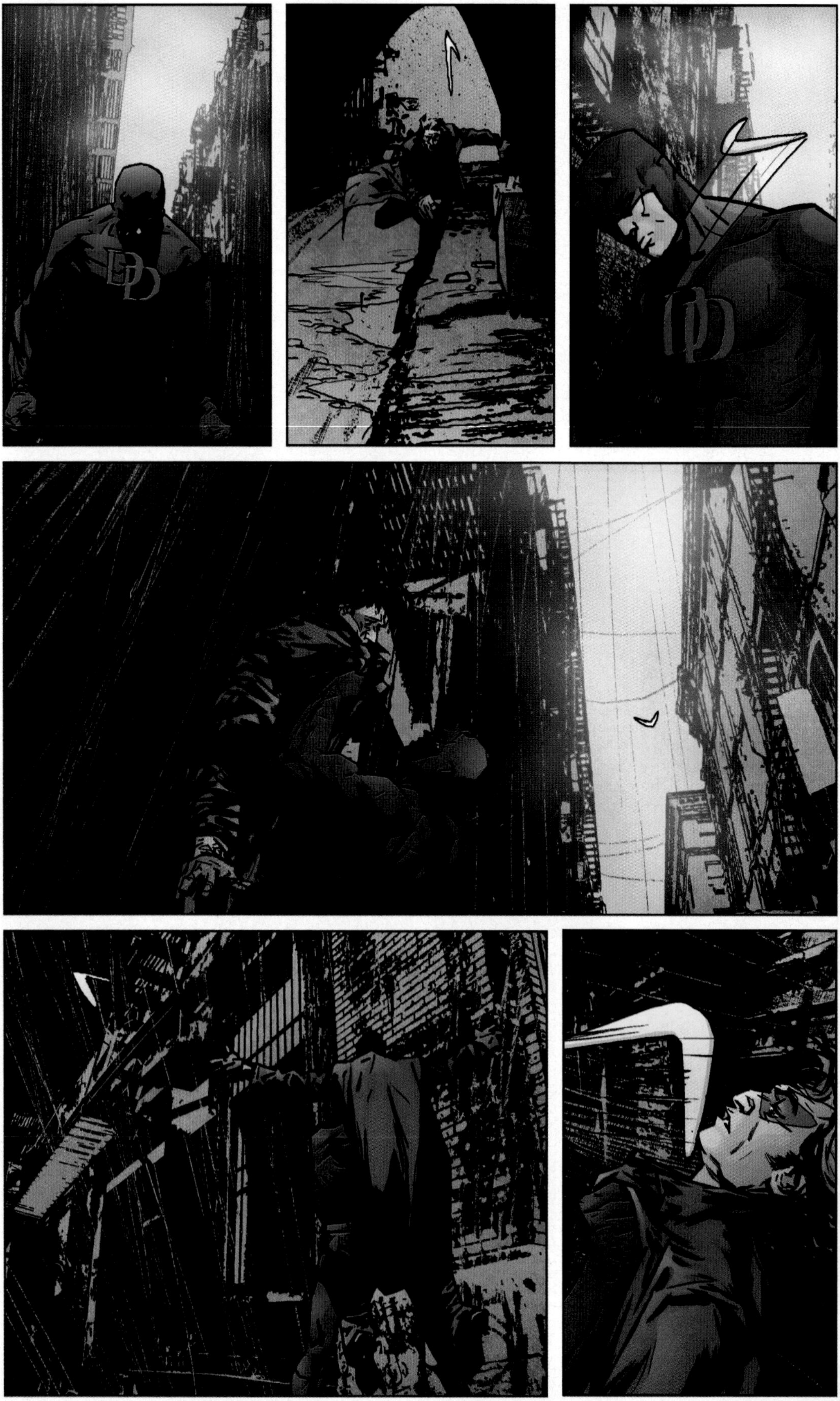

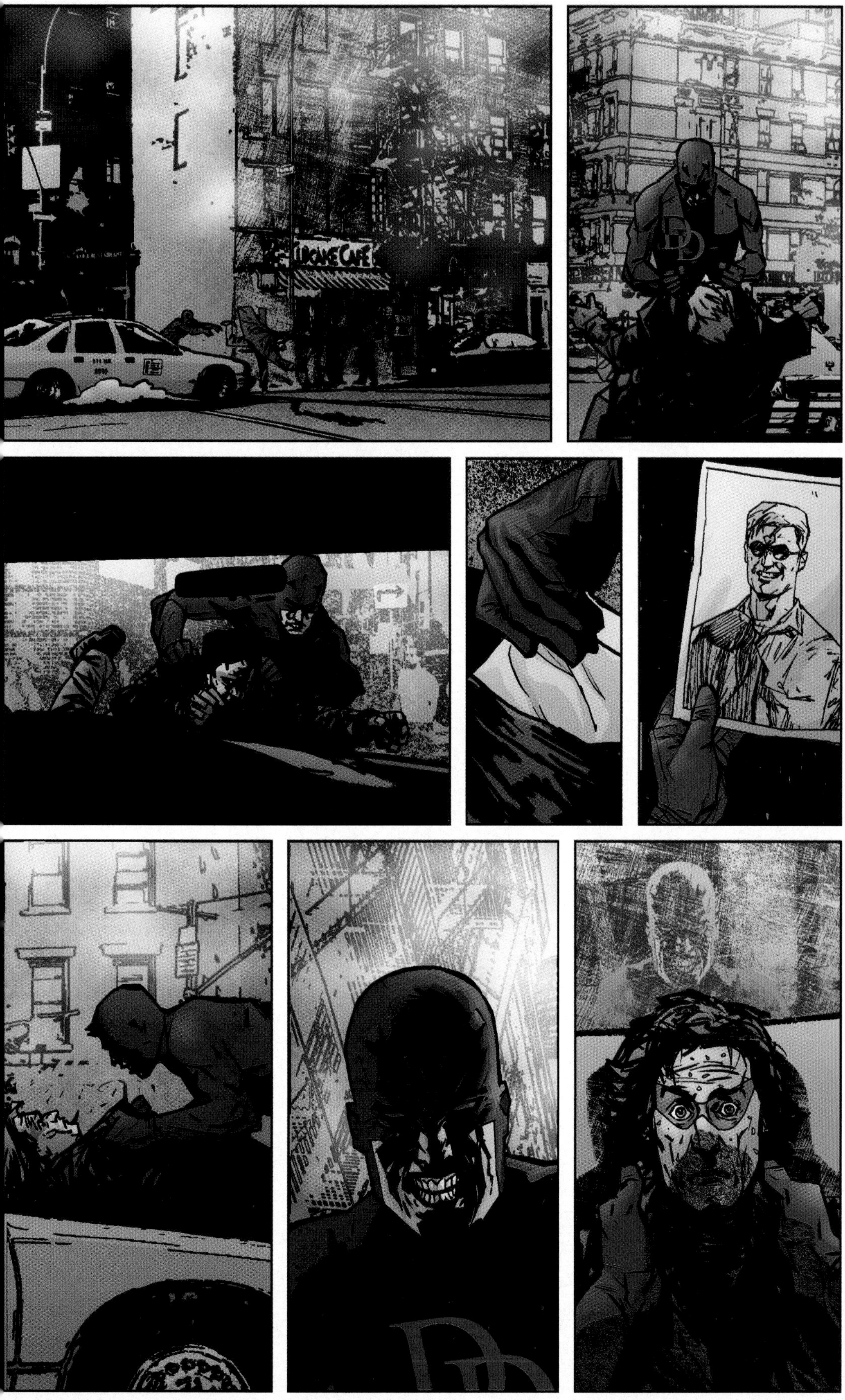
CAFE

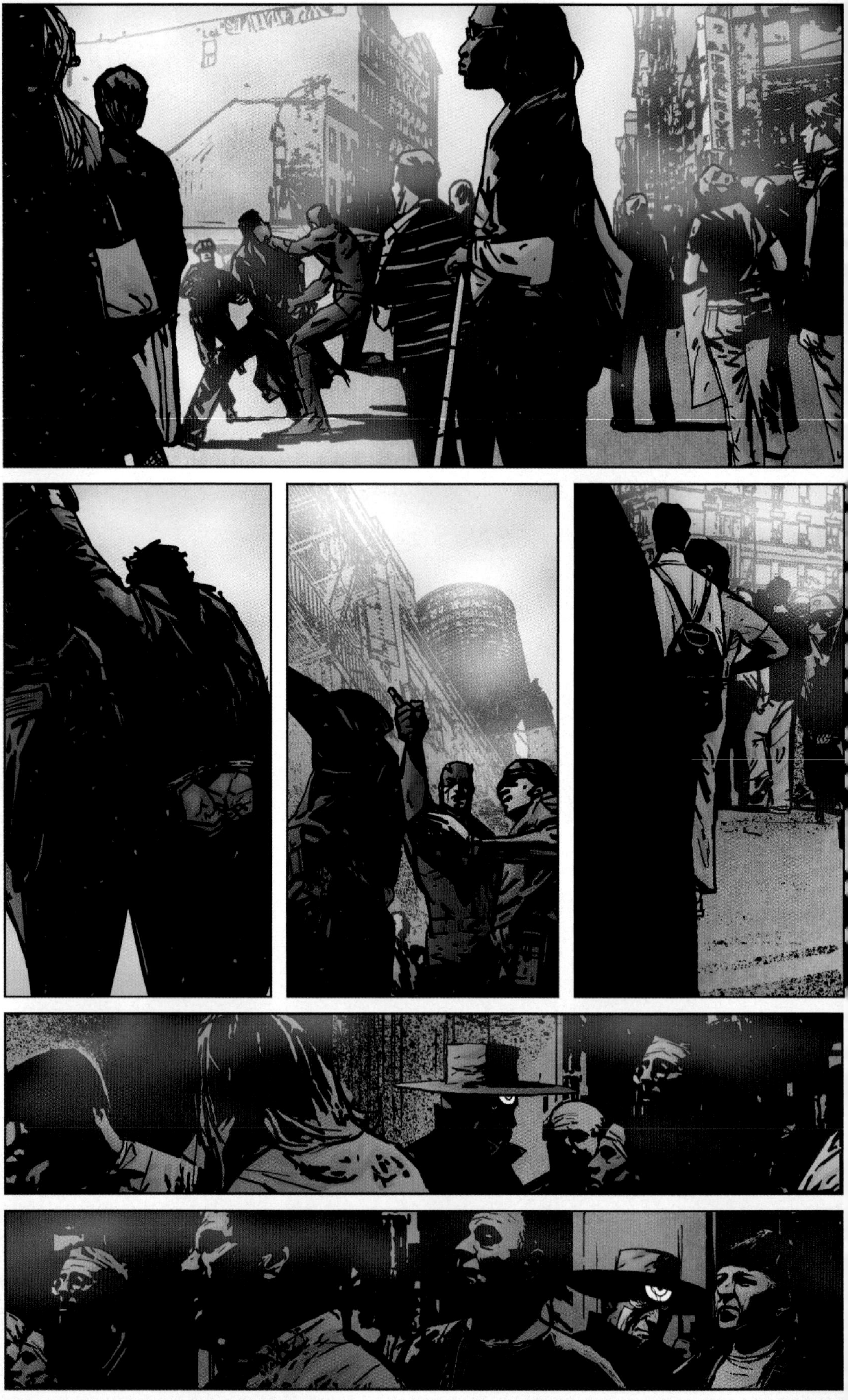

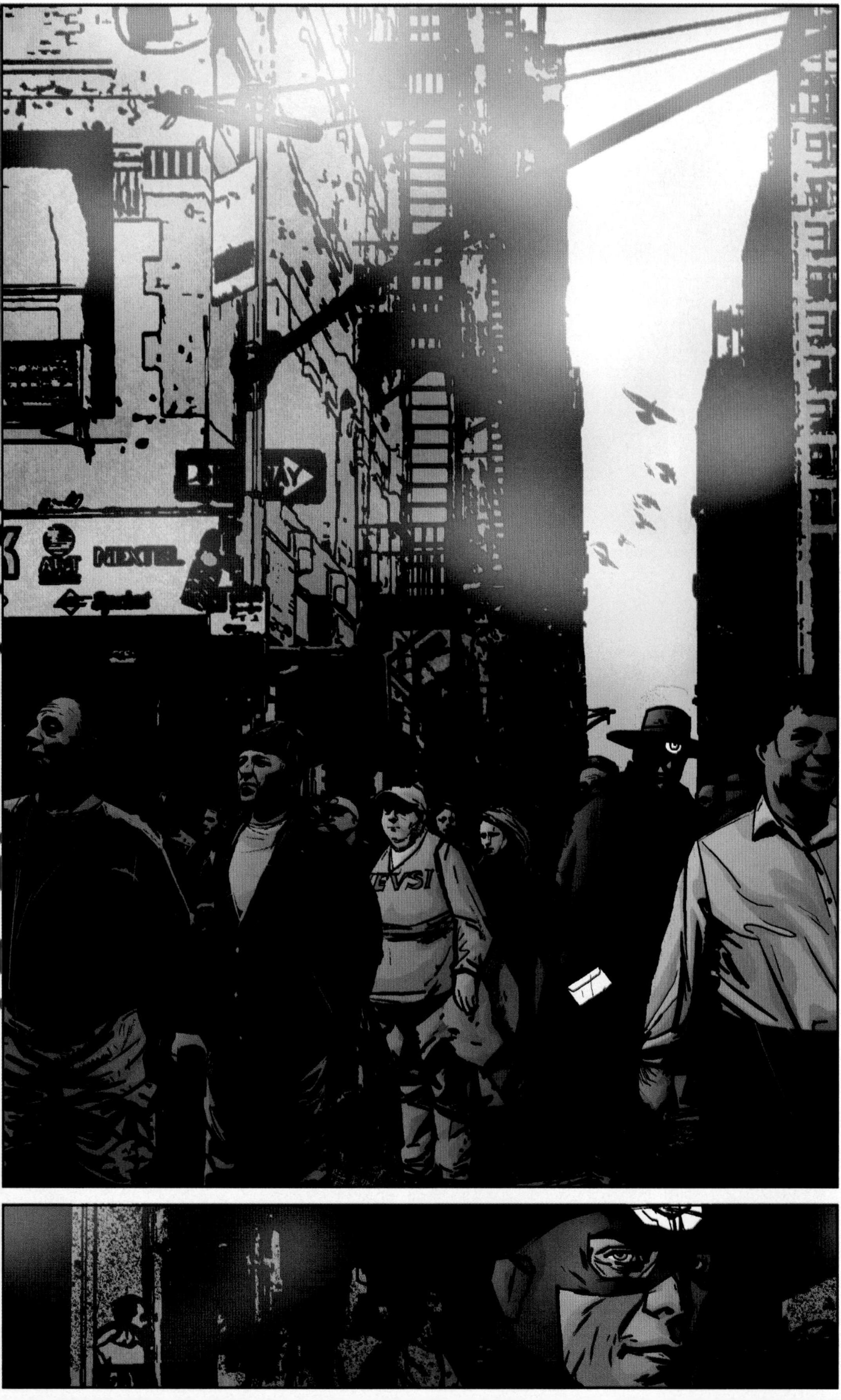
NEXTEL

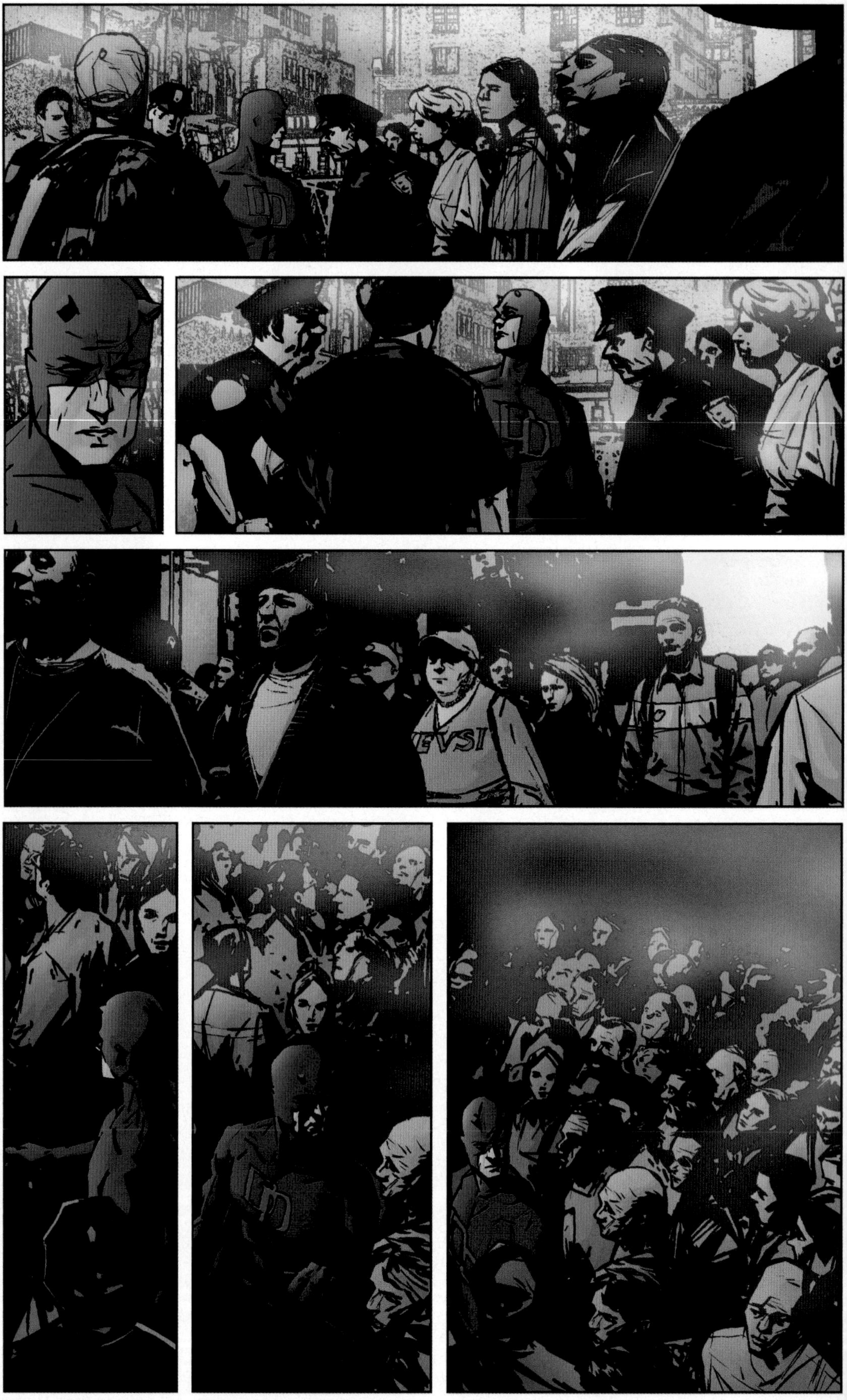

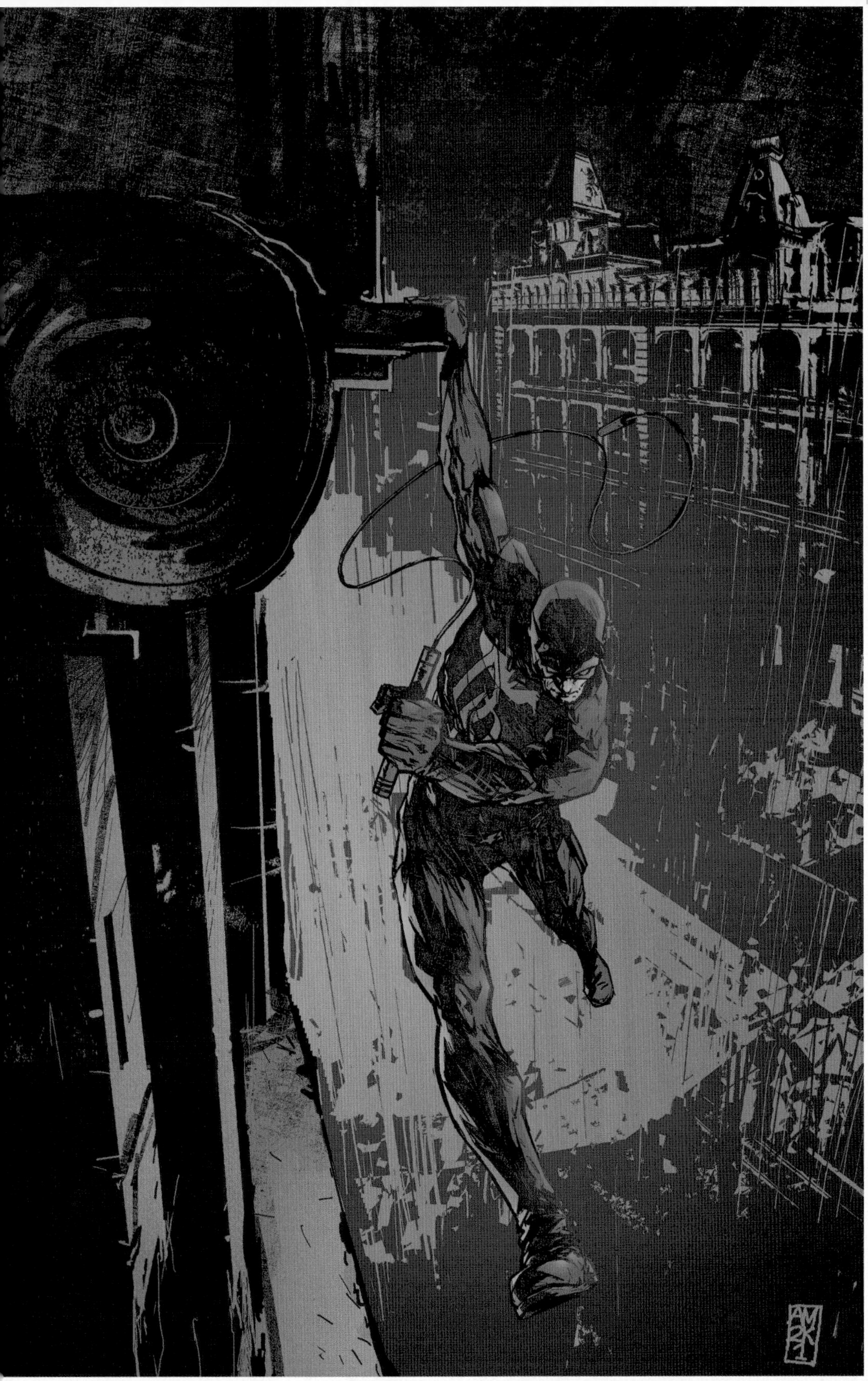

29

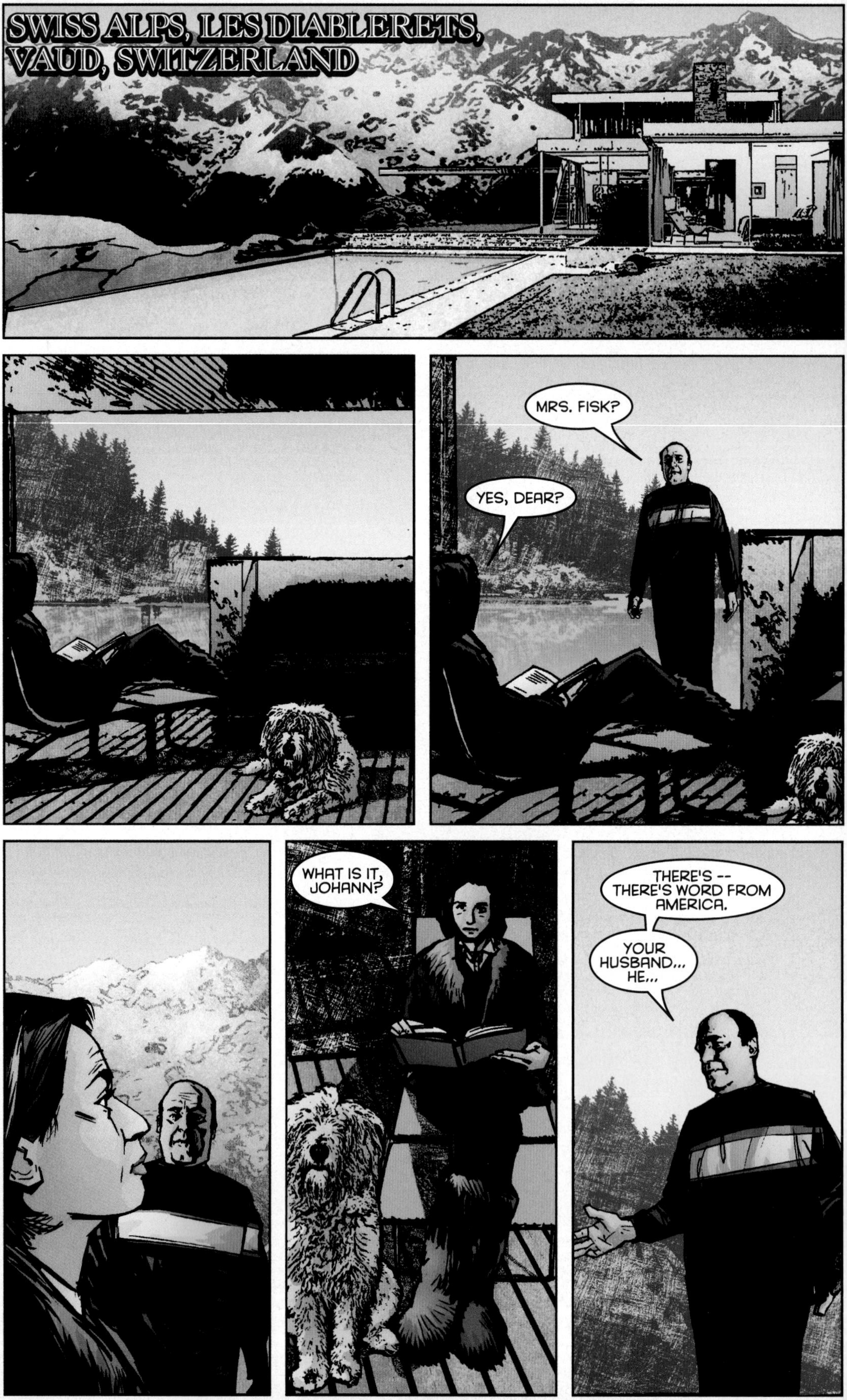
SWISS ALPS, LES DIABLERETS, VAUD, SWITZERLAND
MRS. FISK?
YES, DEAR?
WHAT IS IT, JOHANN?
THERE'S -- THERE'S WORD FROM AMERICA.
YOUR HUSBAND... HE...

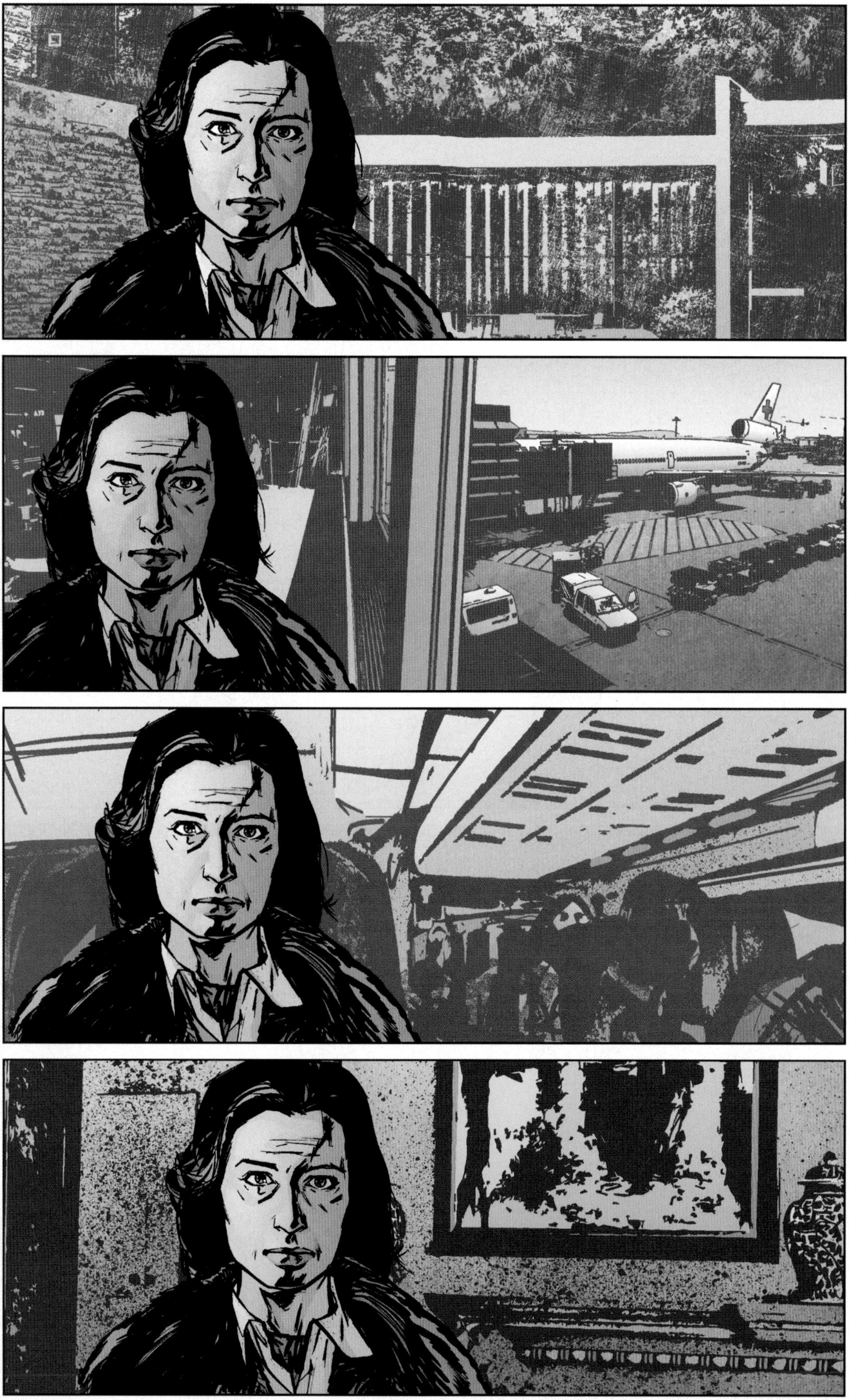

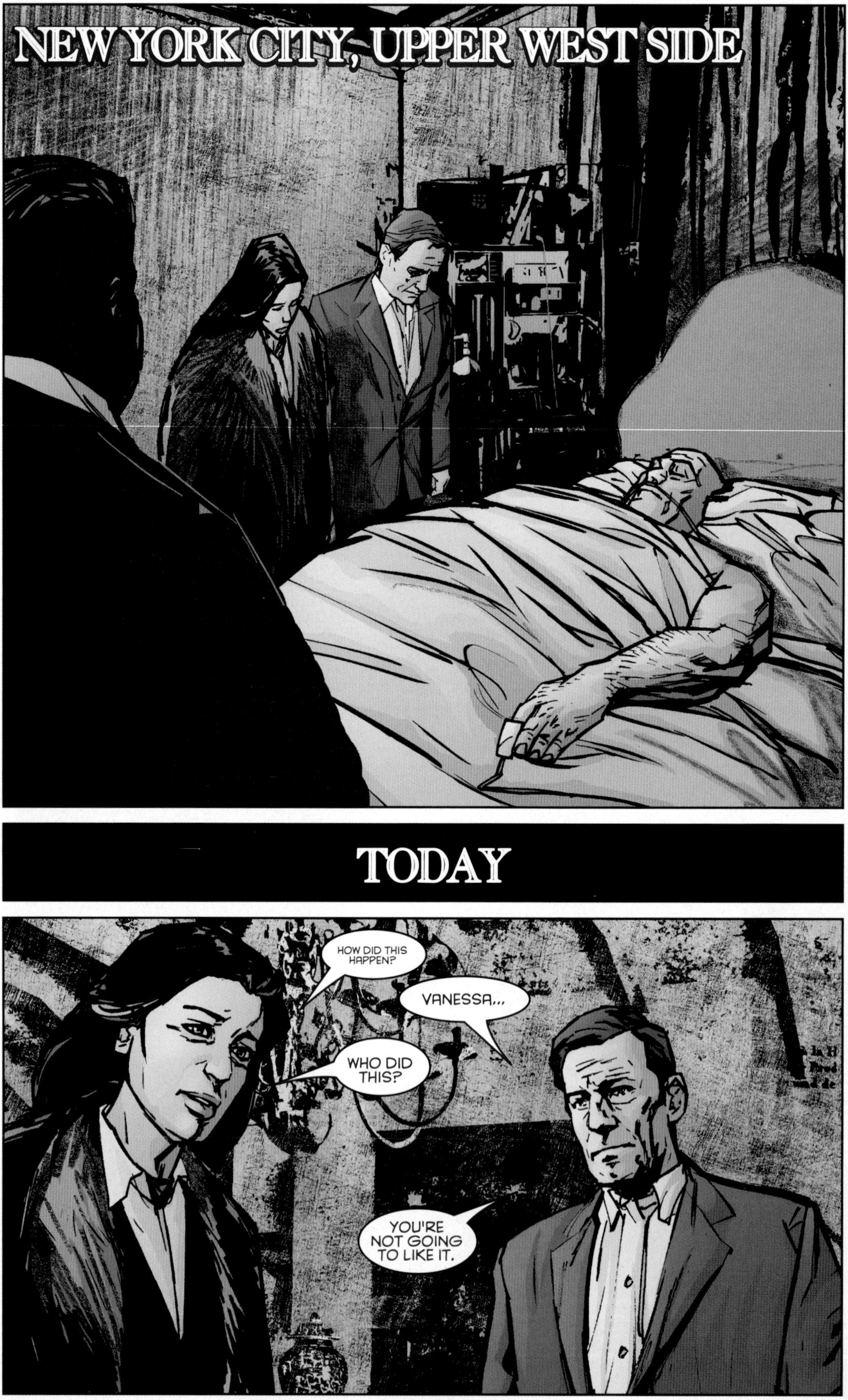
NEW YORK CITY, UPPER WEST SIDE
TODAY
HOW DID THIS HAPPEN?
VANESSA...
WHO DID THIS?
YOU'RE NOT GOING TO LIKE IT.

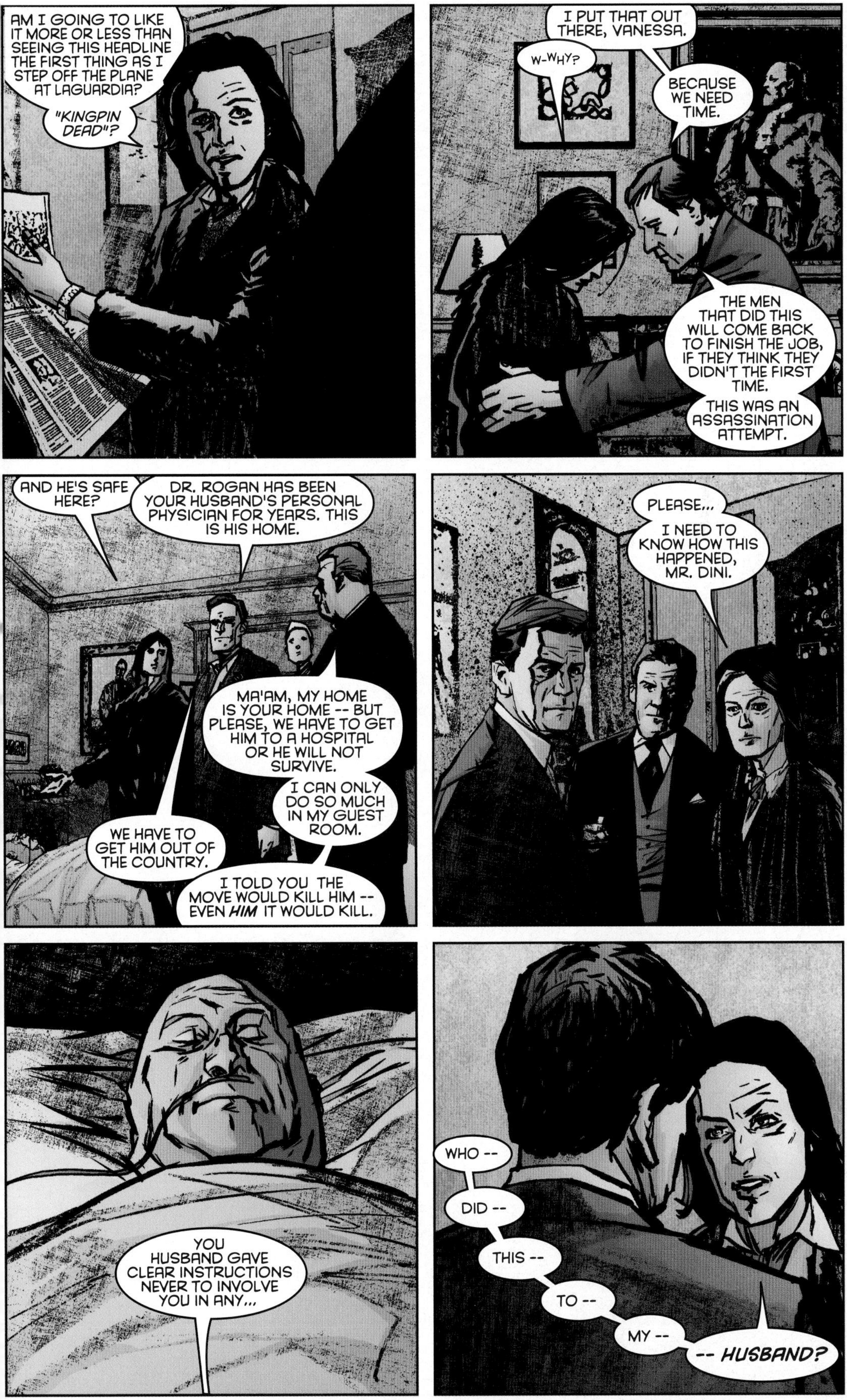
AM I GOING TO LIKE IT MORE OR LESS THAN SEEING THIS HEADLINE THE FIRST THING AS I STEP OFF THE PLANE AT LAGUARDIA?
"KINGPIN DEAD"?
I PUT THAT OUT THERE, VANESSA.
W-WHY?
BECAUSE WE NEED TIME.
THE MEN THAT DID THIS WILL COME BACK TO FINISH THE JOB, IF THEY THINK THEY DIDN'T THE FIRST TIME.
THIS WAS AN ASSASSINATION ATTEMPT.
AND HE'S SAFE HERE?
DR. ROGAN HAS BEEN YOUR HUSBAND'S PERSONAL PHYSICIAN FOR YEARS. THIS IS HIS HOME.
MA'AM, MY HOME IS YOUR HOME -- BUT PLEASE, WE HAVE TO GET HIM TO A HOSPITAL OR HE WILL NOT SURVIVE.
I CAN ONLY DO SO MUCH IN MY GUEST ROOM.
WE HAVE TO GET HIM OUT OF THE COUNTRY.
I TOLD YOU THE MOVE WOULD KILL HIM -- EVEN HIM IT WOULD KILL.
PLEASE...
I NEED TO KNOW HOW THIS HAPPENED, MR. DINI.
YOU HUSBAND GAVE CLEAR INSTRUCTIONS NEVER TO INVOLVE YOU IN ANY...
WHO --
DID --
THIS --
TO --
MY --
-- HUSBAND?

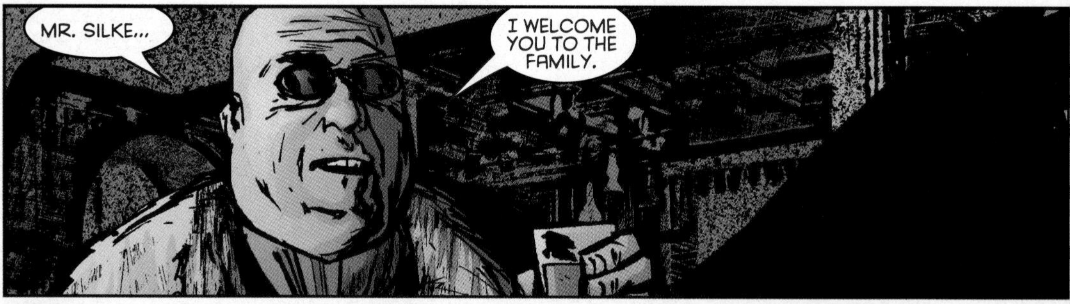
MR. SILKE...
I WELCOME YOU TO THE FAMILY.

THREE MONTHS AGO

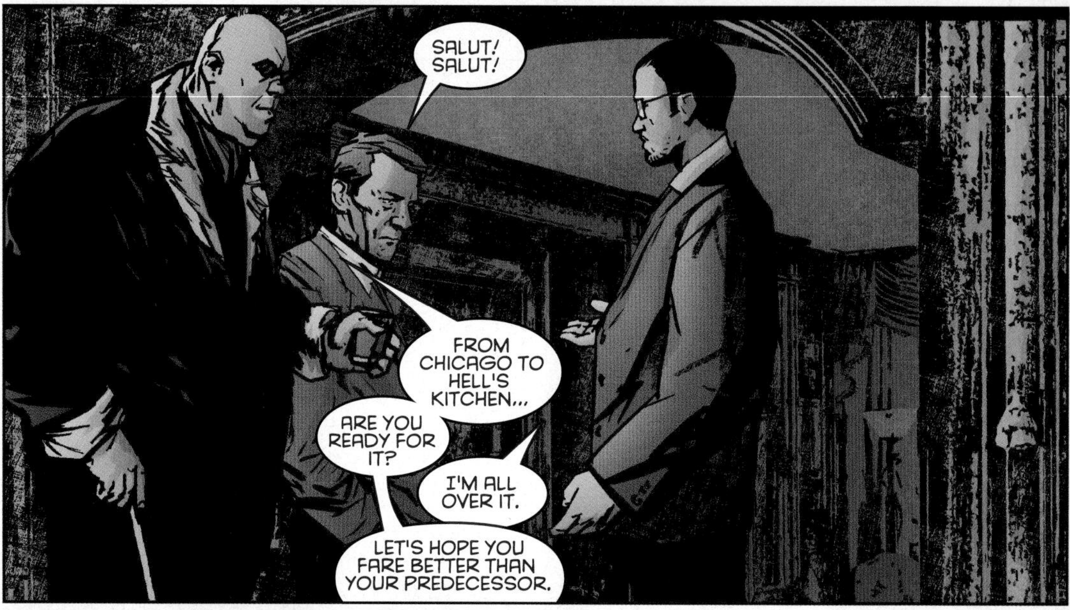
SALUT! SALUT!
FROM CHICAGO TO HELL'S KITCHEN...
ARE YOU READY FOR IT?
I'M ALL OVER IT.
LET'S HOPE YOU FARE BETTER THAN YOUR PREDECESSOR.

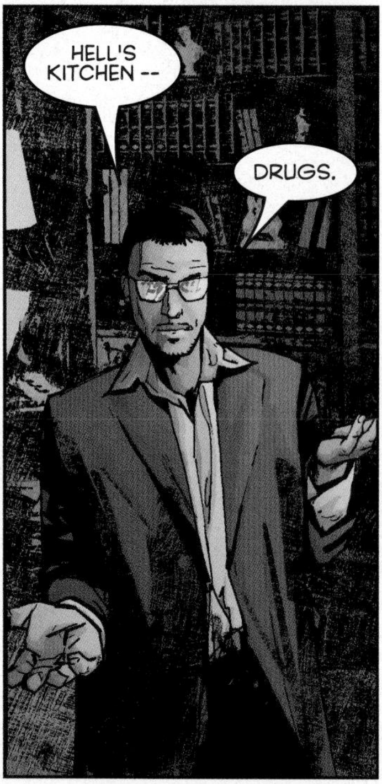
HELL'S KITCHEN --
DRUGS.

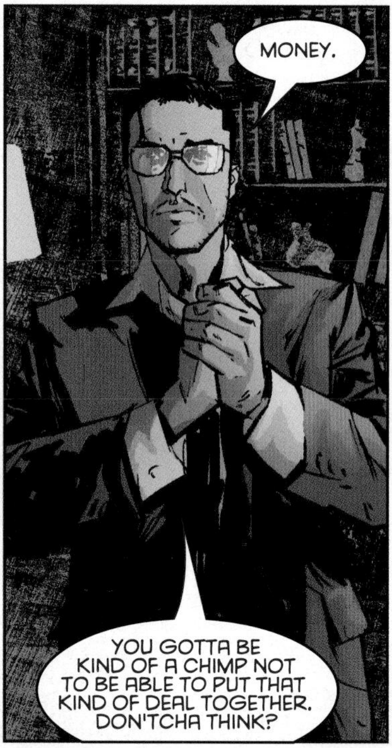
MONEY.
YOU GOTTA BE KIND OF A CHIMP NOT TO BE ABLE TO PUT THAT KIND OF DEAL TOGETHER. DON'TCHA THINK?

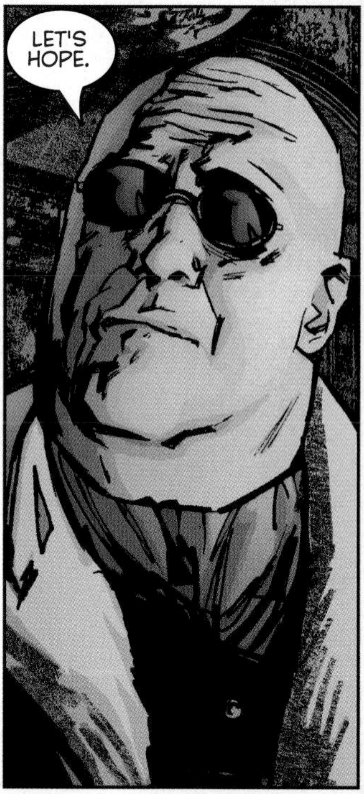
LET'S HOPE.

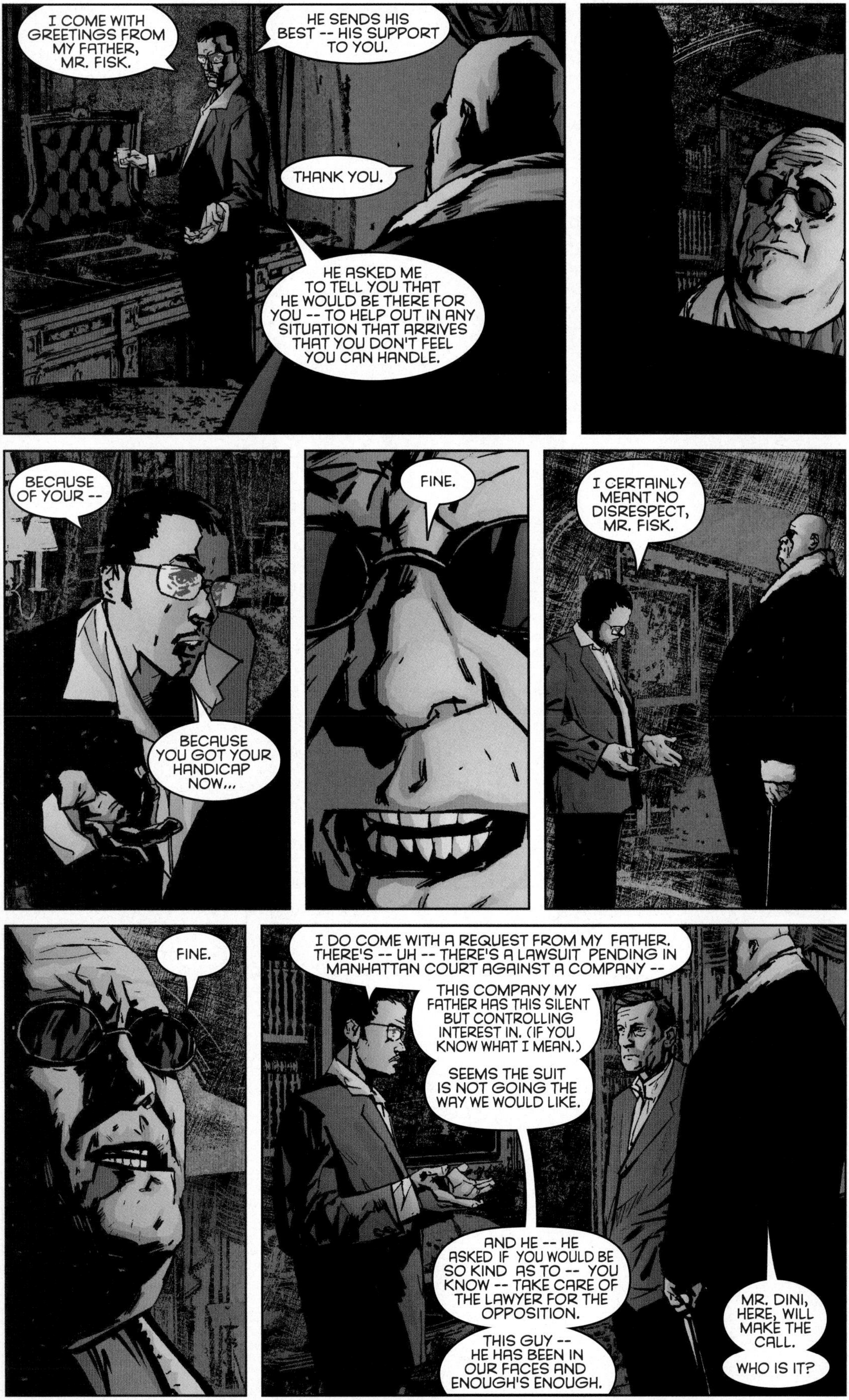

I COME WITH GREETINGS FROM MY FATHER, MR. FISK.
HE SENDS HIS BEST -- HIS SUPPORT TO YOU.
THANK YOU.
HE ASKED ME TO TELL YOU THAT HE WOULD BE THERE FOR YOU -- TO HELP OUT IN ANY SITUATION THAT ARRIVES THAT YOU DON'T FEEL YOU CAN HANDLE.
BECAUSE OF YOUR --
BECAUSE YOU GOT YOUR HANDICAP NOW...
FINE.
I CERTAINLY MEANT NO DISRESPECT, MR. FISK.
FINE.
I DO COME WITH A REQUEST FROM MY FATHER. THERE'S -- UH -- THERE'S A LAWSUIT PENDING IN MANHATTAN COURT AGAINST A COMPANY --
THIS COMPANY MY FATHER HAS THIS SILENT BUT CONTROLLING INTEREST IN. (IF YOU KNOW WHAT I MEAN.)
SEEMS THE SUIT IS NOT GOING THE WAY WE WOULD LIKE.
AND HE -- HE ASKED IF YOU WOULD BE SO KIND AS TO -- YOU KNOW -- TAKE CARE OF THE LAWYER FOR THE OPPOSITION.
THIS GUY -- HE HAS BEEN IN OUR FACES AND ENOUGH'S ENOUGH.
MR. DINI, HERE, WILL MAKE THE CALL.
WHO IS IT?

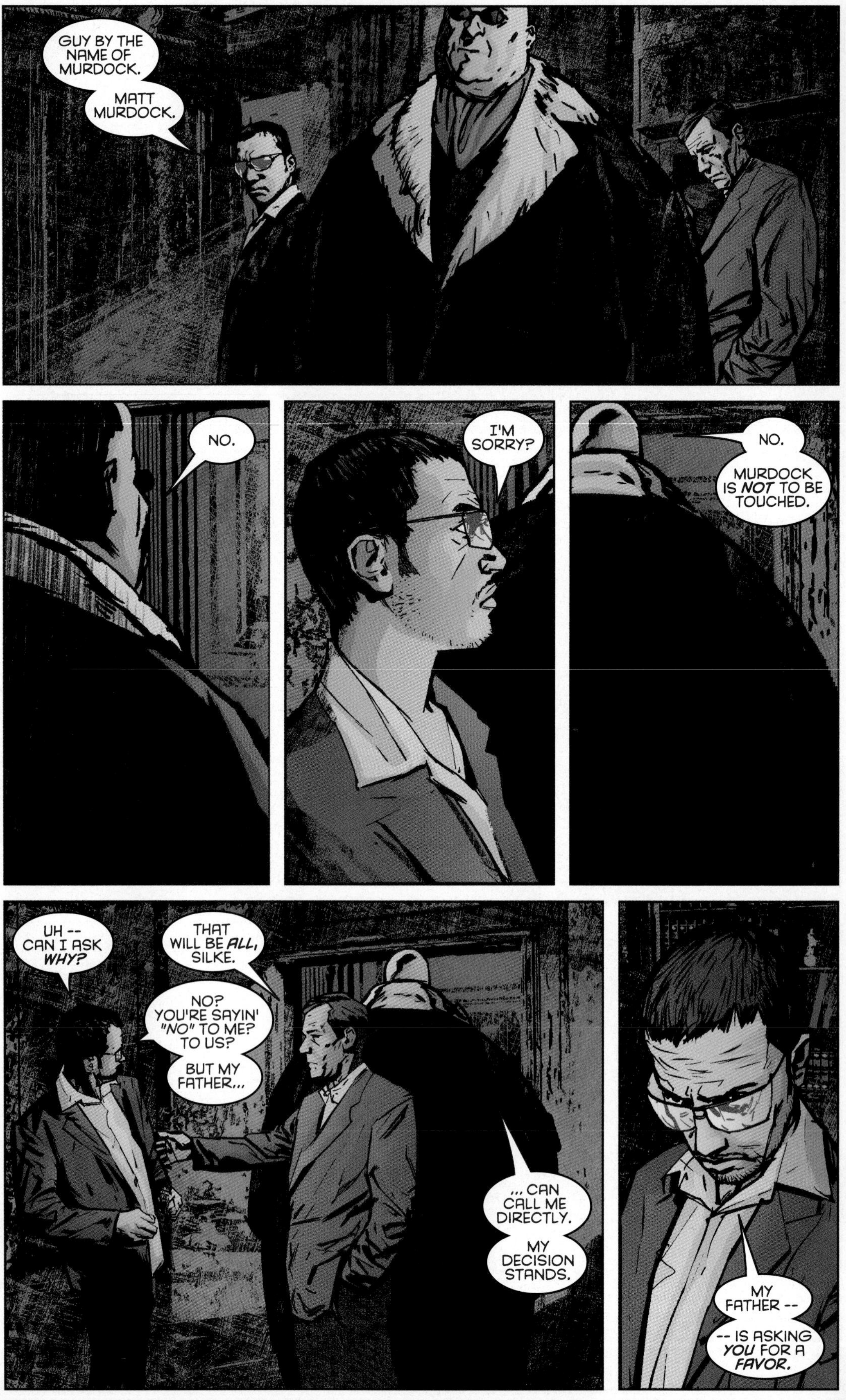
GUY BY THE NAME OF MURDOCK.
MATT MURDOCK.
NO.
I'M SORRY?
NO.
MURDOCK IS *NOT* TO BE TOUCHED.
UH -- CAN I ASK *WHY?*
THAT WILL BE *ALL,* SILKE.
NO? YOU'RE SAYIN' "*NO*" TO ME? TO US?
BUT MY FATHER...
... CAN CALL ME DIRECTLY.
MY DECISION STANDS.
MY FATHER --
-- IS ASKING *YOU* FOR A *FAVOR.*

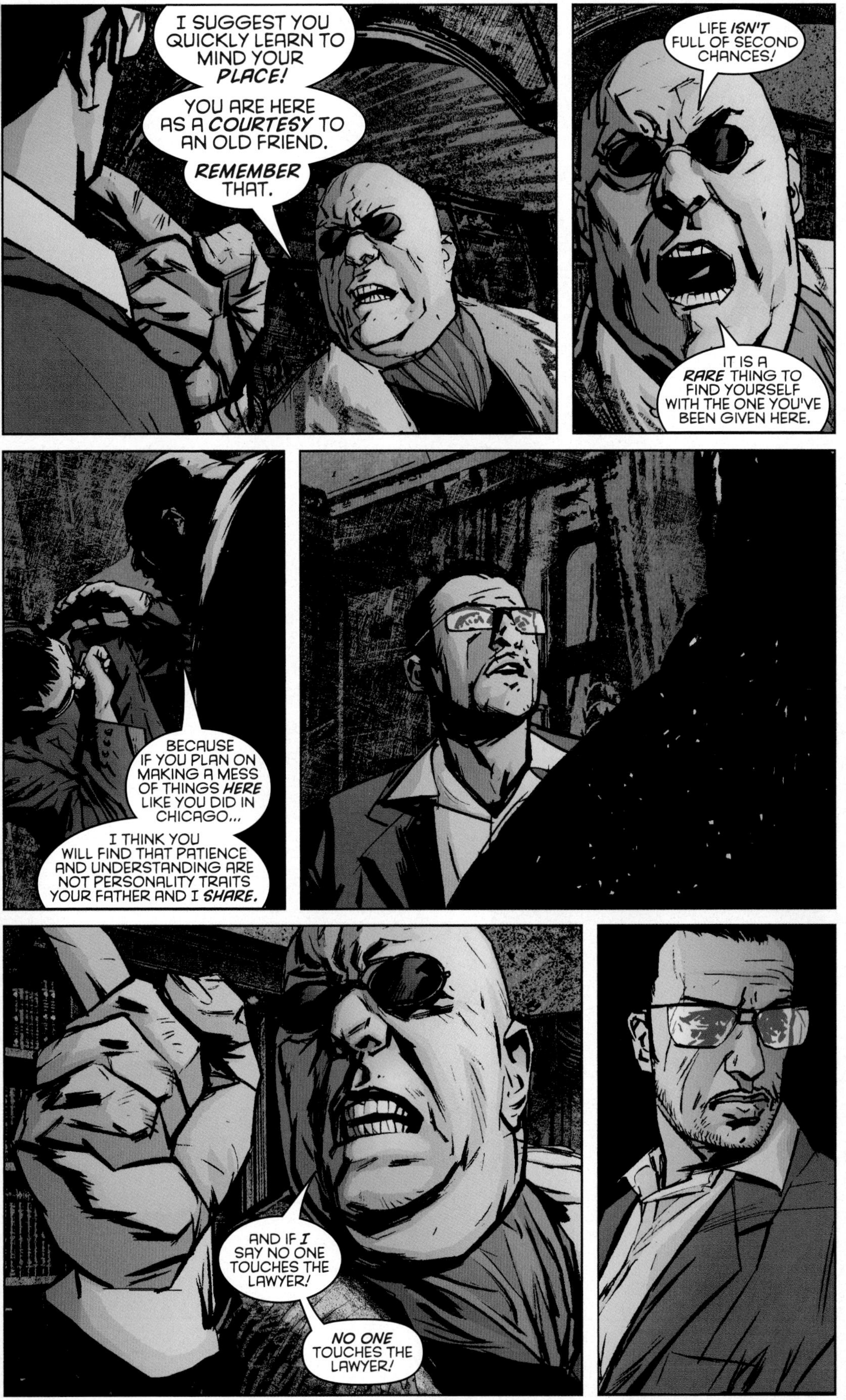
I SUGGEST YOU QUICKLY LEARN TO MIND YOUR PLACE!
YOU ARE HERE AS A COURTESY TO AN OLD FRIEND.
REMEMBER THAT.
LIFE ISN'T FULL OF SECOND CHANCES!
IT IS A RARE THING TO FIND YOURSELF WITH THE ONE YOU'VE BEEN GIVEN HERE.
BECAUSE IF YOU PLAN ON MAKING A MESS OF THINGS HERE LIKE YOU DID IN CHICAGO...
I THINK YOU WILL FIND THAT PATIENCE AND UNDERSTANDING ARE NOT PERSONALITY TRAITS YOUR FATHER AND I SHARE.
AND IF I SAY NO ONE TOUCHES THE LAWYER!
NO ONE TOUCHES THE LAWYER!

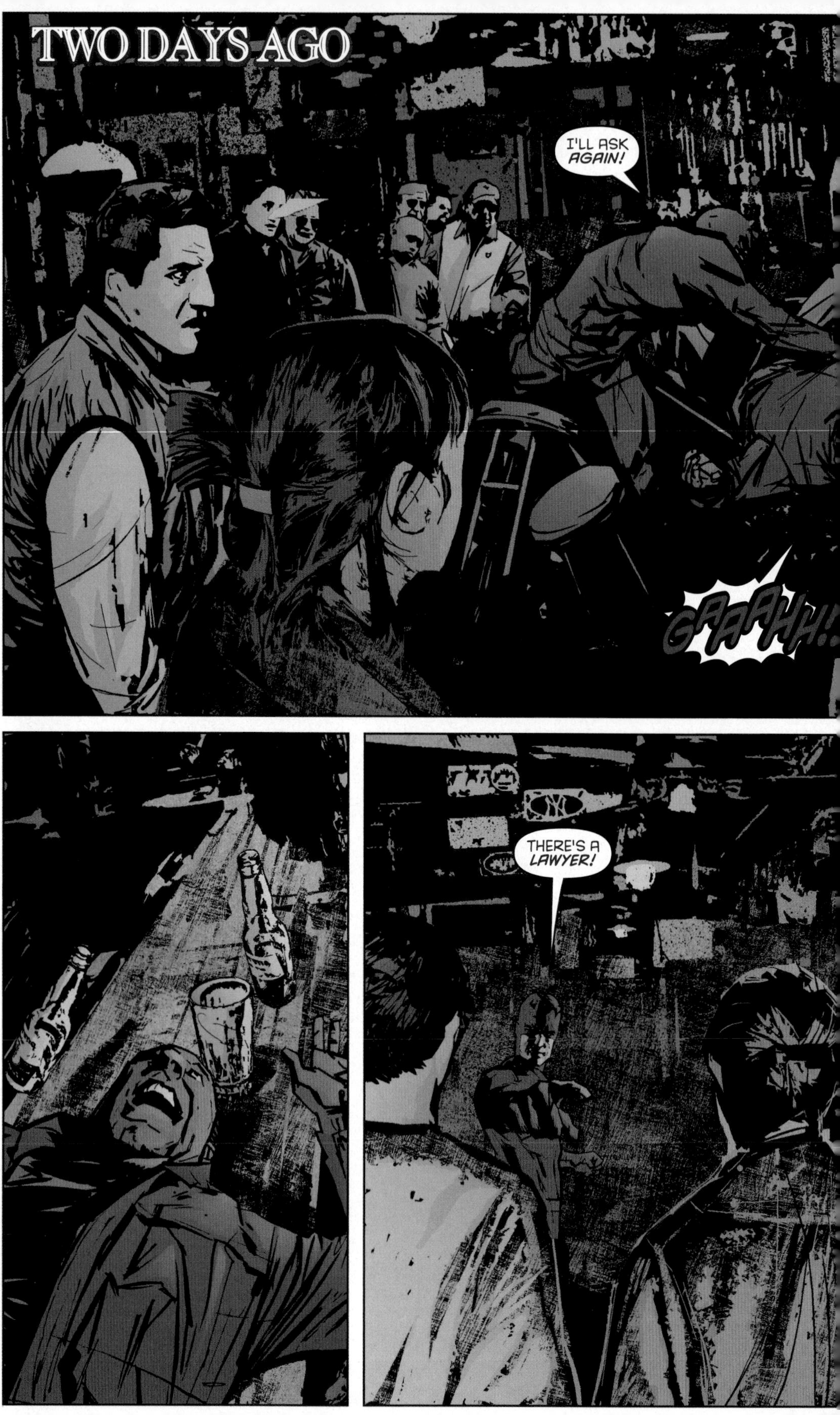
TWO DAYS AGO
I'LL ASK AGAIN!
GAAAHH!!
THERE'S A LAWYER!

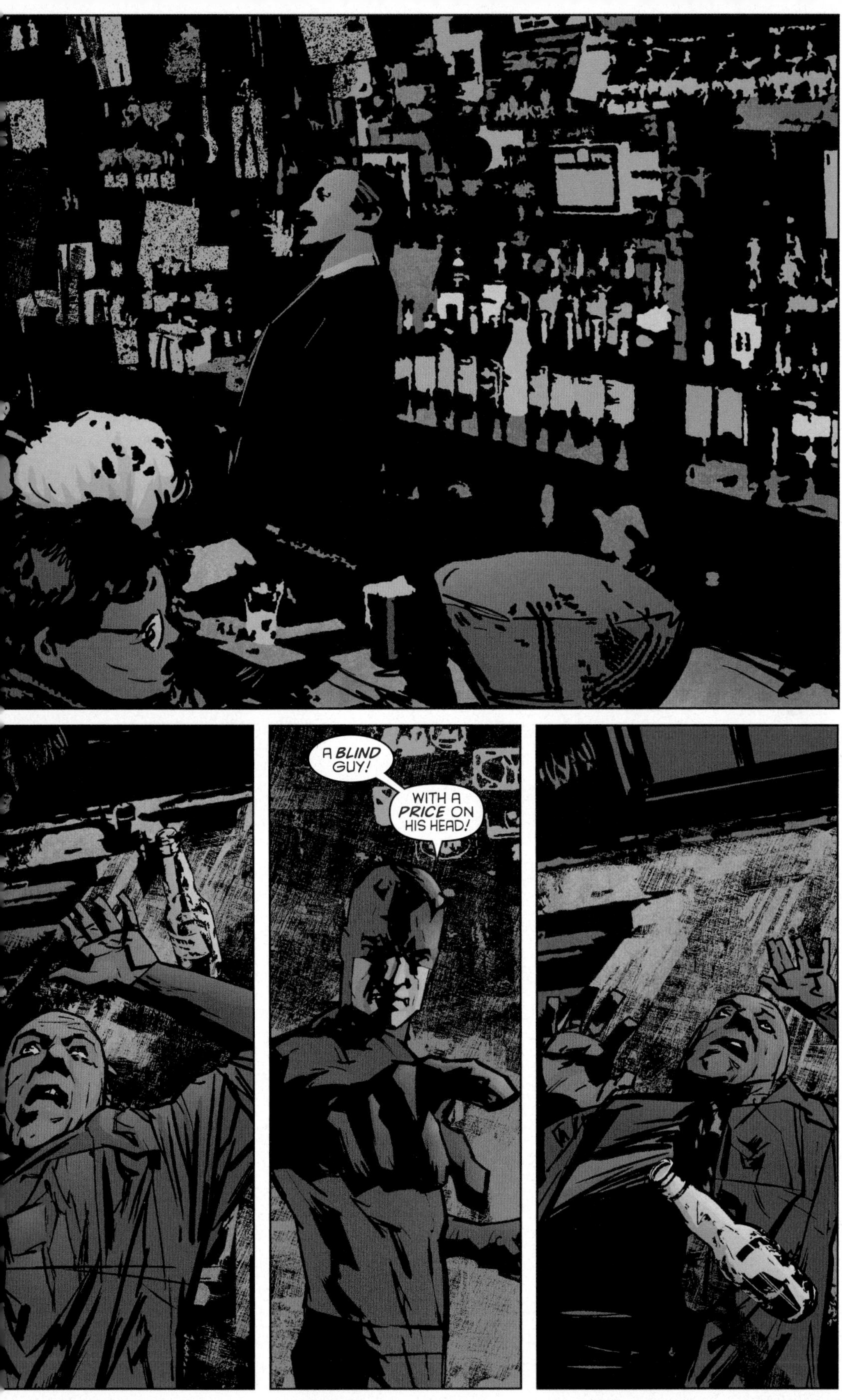
A BLIND GUY!
WITH A PRICE ON HIS HEAD!

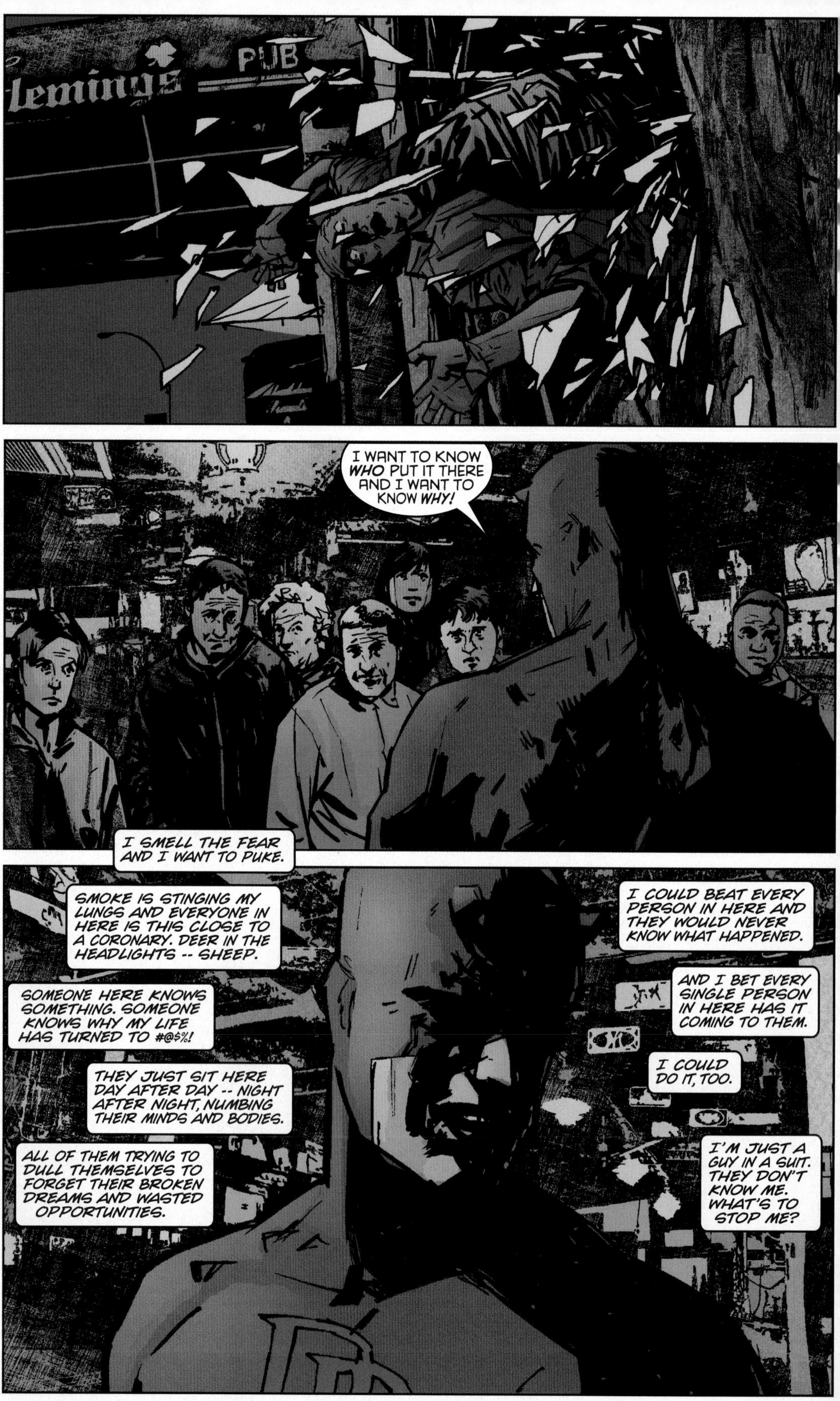
PUB
I WANT TO KNOW *WHO* PUT IT THERE AND I WANT TO KNOW *WHY!*
I SMELL THE FEAR AND I WANT TO PUKE.
SMOKE IS STINGING MY LUNGS AND EVERYONE IN HERE IS THIS CLOSE TO A CORONARY. DEER IN THE HEADLIGHTS -- SHEEP.
SOMEONE HERE KNOWS SOMETHING. SOMEONE KNOWS WHY MY LIFE HAS TURNED TO #@$%!
THEY JUST SIT HERE DAY AFTER DAY -- NIGHT AFTER NIGHT, NUMBING THEIR MINDS AND BODIES.
ALL OF THEM TRYING TO DULL THEMSELVES TO FORGET THEIR BROKEN DREAMS AND WASTED OPPORTUNITIES.
I COULD BEAT EVERY PERSON IN HERE AND THEY WOULD NEVER KNOW WHAT HAPPENED.
AND I BET EVERY SINGLE PERSON IN HERE HAS IT COMING TO THEM.
I COULD DO IT, TOO.
I'M JUST A GUY IN A SUIT. THEY DON'T KNOW ME. WHAT'S TO STOP ME?

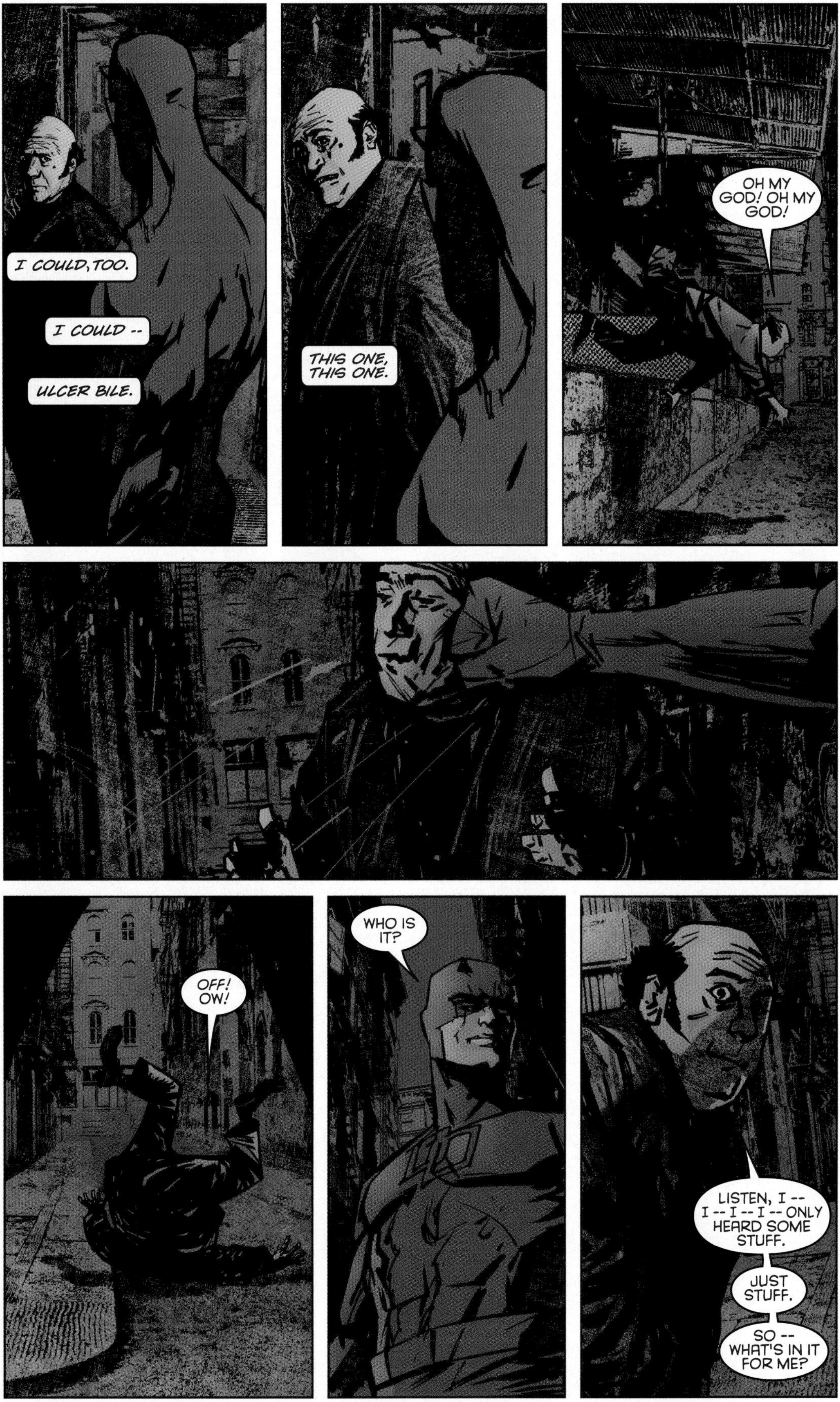
I COULD, TOO.
I COULD --
ULCER BILE.
THIS ONE, THIS ONE.
OH MY GOD! OH MY GOD!
OFF! OW!
WHO IS IT?
LISTEN, I -- I -- I -- I -- ONLY HEARD SOME STUFF.
JUST STUFF.
SO -- WHAT'S IN IT FOR ME?

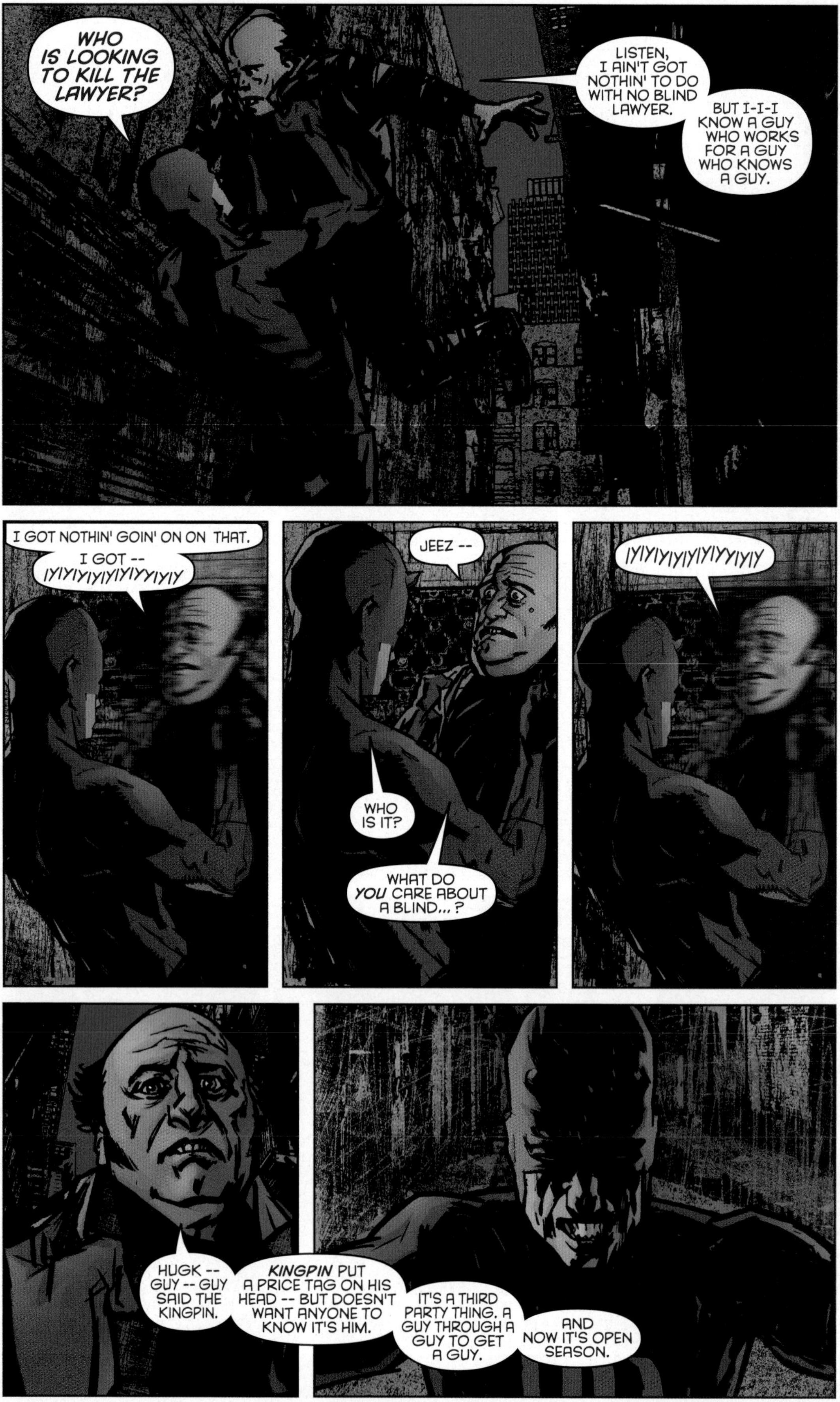
WHO IS LOOKING TO KILL THE LAWYER?
LISTEN, I AIN'T GOT NOTHIN' TO DO WITH NO BLIND LAWYER.
BUT I-I-I KNOW A GUY WHO WORKS FOR A GUY WHO KNOWS A GUY.
I GOT NOTHIN' GOIN' ON ON THAT.
I GOT -- IYIYIYIYIYIYIYYIYIY
JEEZ --
WHO IS IT?
WHAT DO *YOU* CARE ABOUT A BLIND... ?
IYIYIYIYIYIYIYYIYIY
HUGK -- GUY -- GUY SAID THE KINGPIN.
KINGPIN PUT A PRICE TAG ON HIS HEAD -- BUT DOESN'T WANT ANYONE TO KNOW IT'S HIM.
IT'S A THIRD PARTY THING. A GUY THROUGH A GUY TO GET A GUY.
AND NOW IT'S OPEN SEASON.

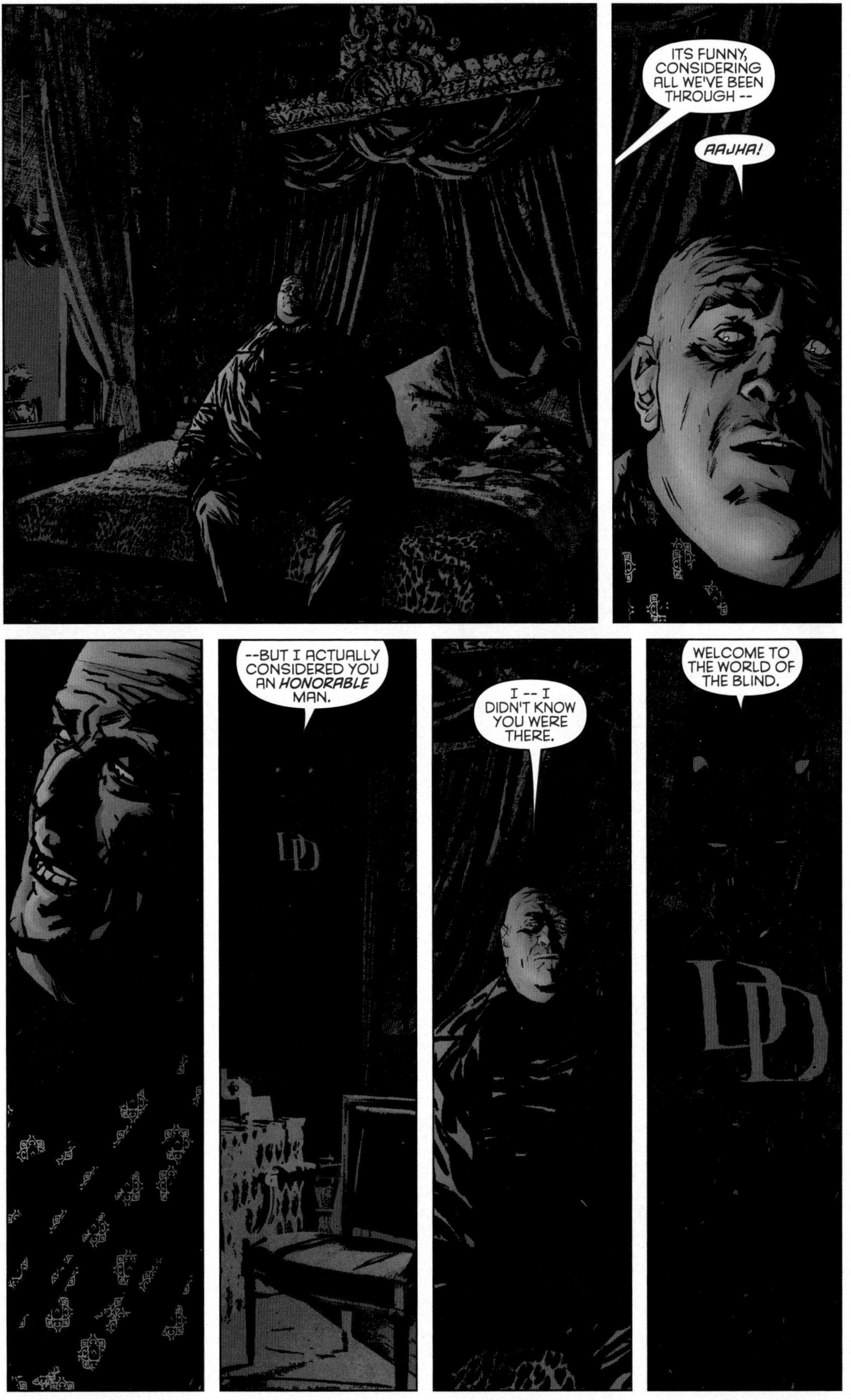
ITS FUNNY, CONSIDERING ALL WE'VE BEEN THROUGH --
AAJHA!
--BUT I ACTUALLY CONSIDERED YOU AN *HONORABLE* MAN.
I -- I DIDN'T KNOW YOU WERE THERE.
WELCOME TO THE WORLD OF THE BLIND.

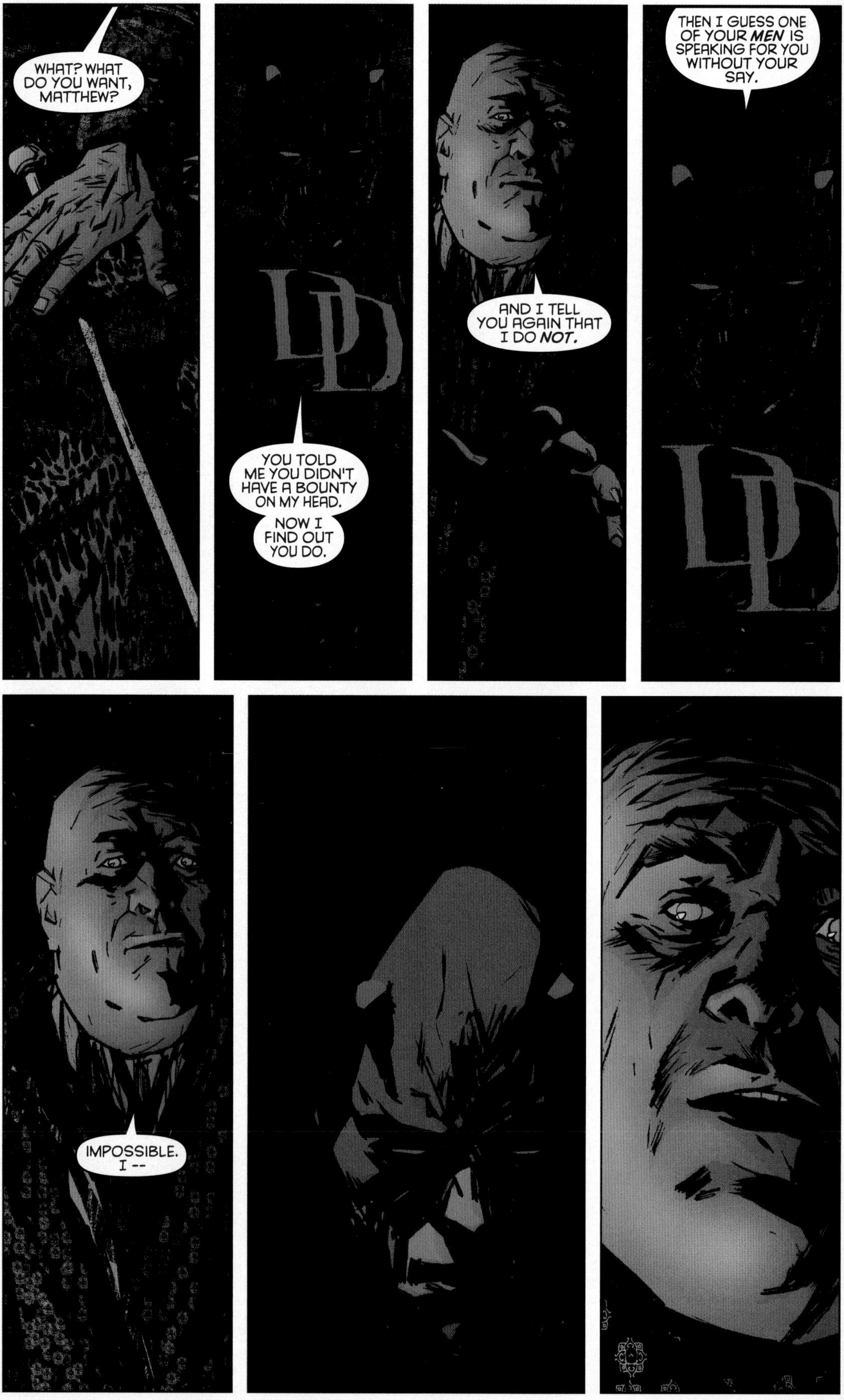
WHAT? WHAT DO YOU WANT, MATTHEW?
YOU TOLD ME YOU DIDN'T HAVE A BOUNTY ON MY HEAD.
NOW I FIND OUT YOU DO.
AND I TELL YOU AGAIN THAT I DO NOT.
THEN I GUESS ONE OF YOUR MEN IS SPEAKING FOR YOU WITHOUT YOUR SAY.
IMPOSSIBLE. I --

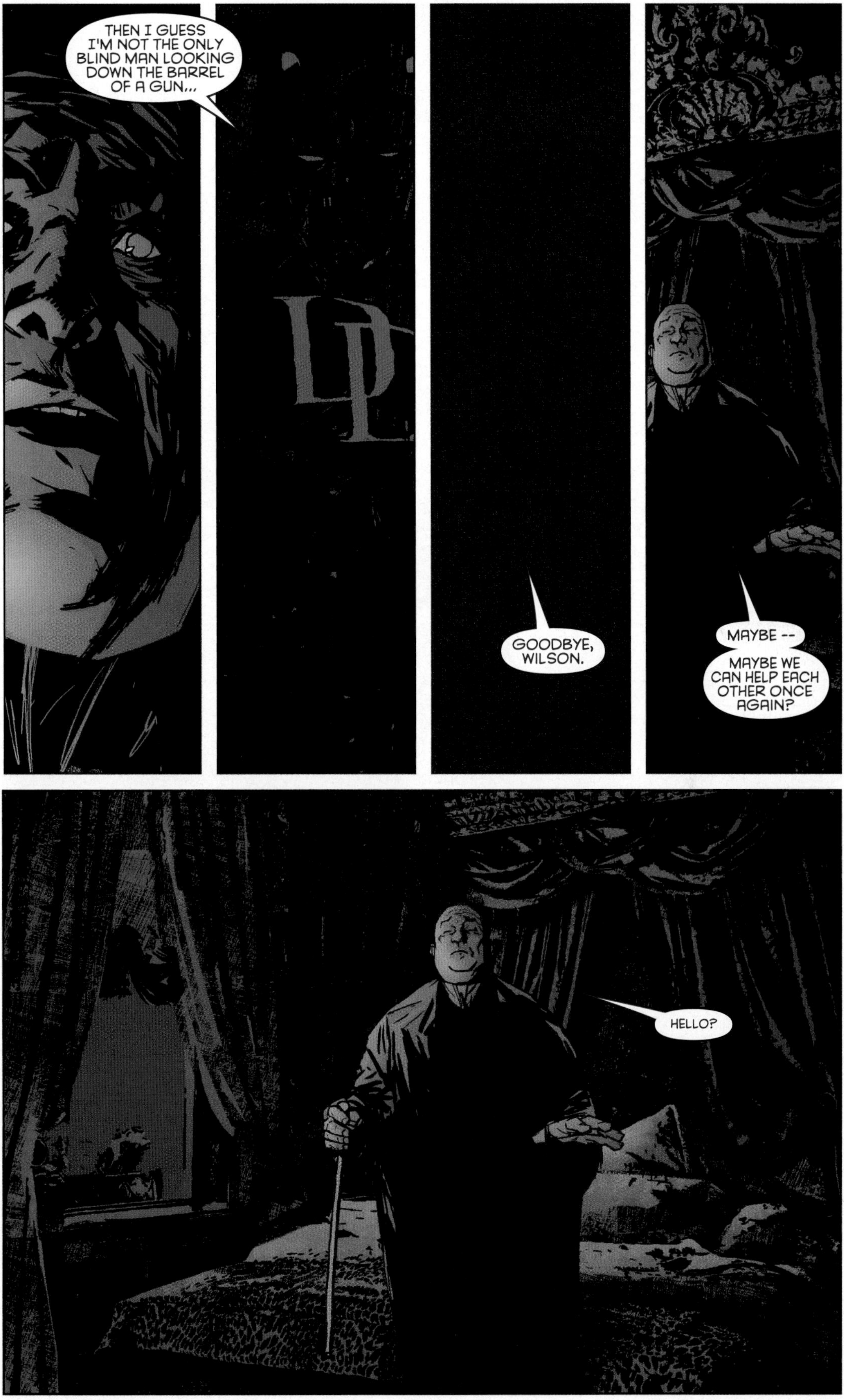
THEN I GUESS I'M NOT THE ONLY BLIND MAN LOOKING DOWN THE BARREL OF A GUN...
GOODBYE, WILSON.
MAYBE --
MAYBE WE CAN HELP EACH OTHER ONCE AGAIN?
HELLO?

TWO MONTHS AGO

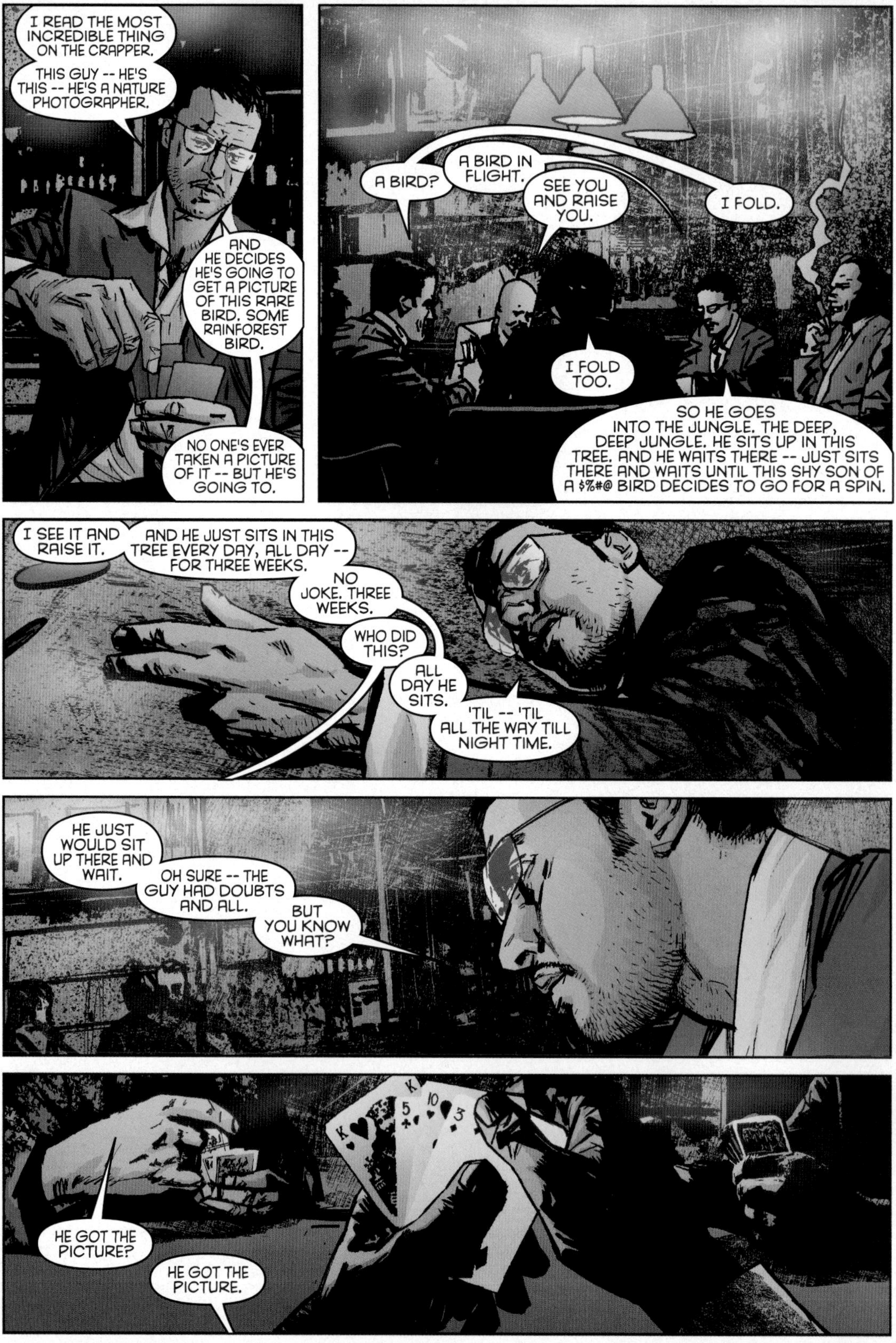

I READ THE MOST INCREDIBLE THING ON THE CRAPPER.
THIS GUY -- HE'S THIS -- HE'S A NATURE PHOTOGRAPHER.
AND HE DECIDES HE'S GOING TO GET A PICTURE OF THIS RARE BIRD. SOME RAINFOREST BIRD.
NO ONE'S EVER TAKEN A PICTURE OF IT -- BUT HE'S GOING TO.
A BIRD?
A BIRD IN FLIGHT.
SEE YOU AND RAISE YOU.
I FOLD.
I FOLD TOO.
SO HE GOES INTO THE JUNGLE. THE DEEP, DEEP JUNGLE. HE SITS UP IN THIS TREE. AND HE WAITS THERE -- JUST SITS THERE AND WAITS UNTIL THIS SHY SON OF A $%#@ BIRD DECIDES TO GO FOR A SPIN.
I SEE IT AND RAISE IT.
AND HE JUST SITS IN THIS TREE EVERY DAY, ALL DAY -- FOR THREE WEEKS.
NO JOKE. THREE WEEKS.
WHO DID THIS?
ALL DAY HE SITS.
'TIL -- 'TIL ALL THE WAY TILL NIGHT TIME.
HE JUST WOULD SIT UP THERE AND WAIT.
OH SURE -- THE GUY HAD DOUBTS AND ALL.
BUT YOU KNOW WHAT?
HE GOT THE PICTURE?
HE GOT THE PICTURE.

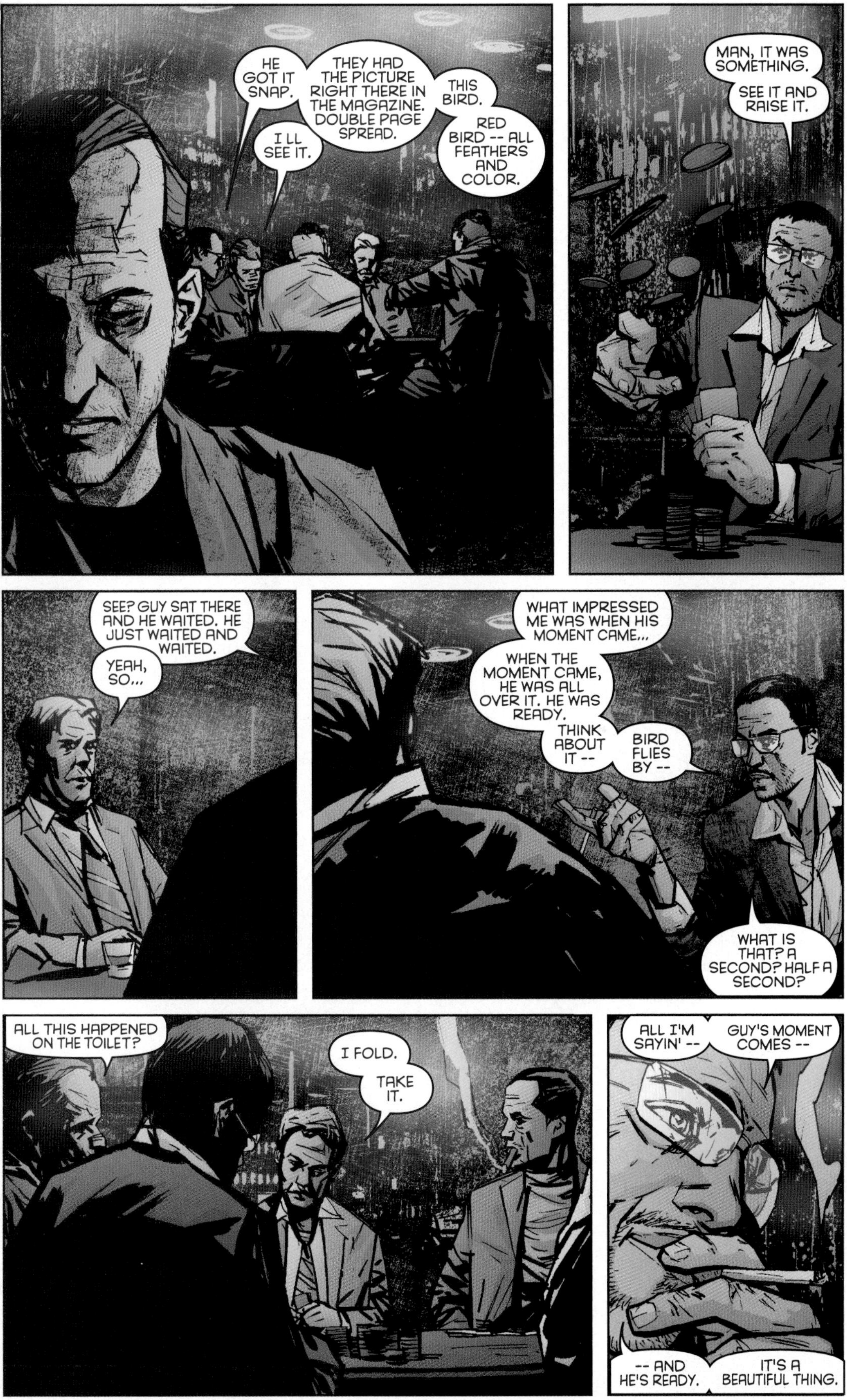
HE GOT IT SNAP.
THEY HAD THE PICTURE RIGHT THERE IN THE MAGAZINE. DOUBLE PAGE SPREAD.
THIS BIRD.
RED BIRD -- ALL FEATHERS AND COLOR.
I LL SEE IT.
MAN, IT WAS SOMETHING.
SEE IT AND RAISE IT.
SEE? GUY SAT THERE AND HE WAITED. HE JUST WAITED AND WAITED.
YEAH, SO...
WHAT IMPRESSED ME WAS WHEN HIS MOMENT CAME...
WHEN THE MOMENT CAME, HE WAS ALL OVER IT. HE WAS READY.
THINK ABOUT IT --
BIRD FLIES BY --
WHAT IS THAT? A SECOND? HALF A SECOND?
ALL THIS HAPPENED ON THE TOILET?
I FOLD.
TAKE IT.
ALL I'M SAYIN' --
GUY'S MOMENT COMES --
-- AND HE'S READY.
IT'S A BEAUTIFUL THING.

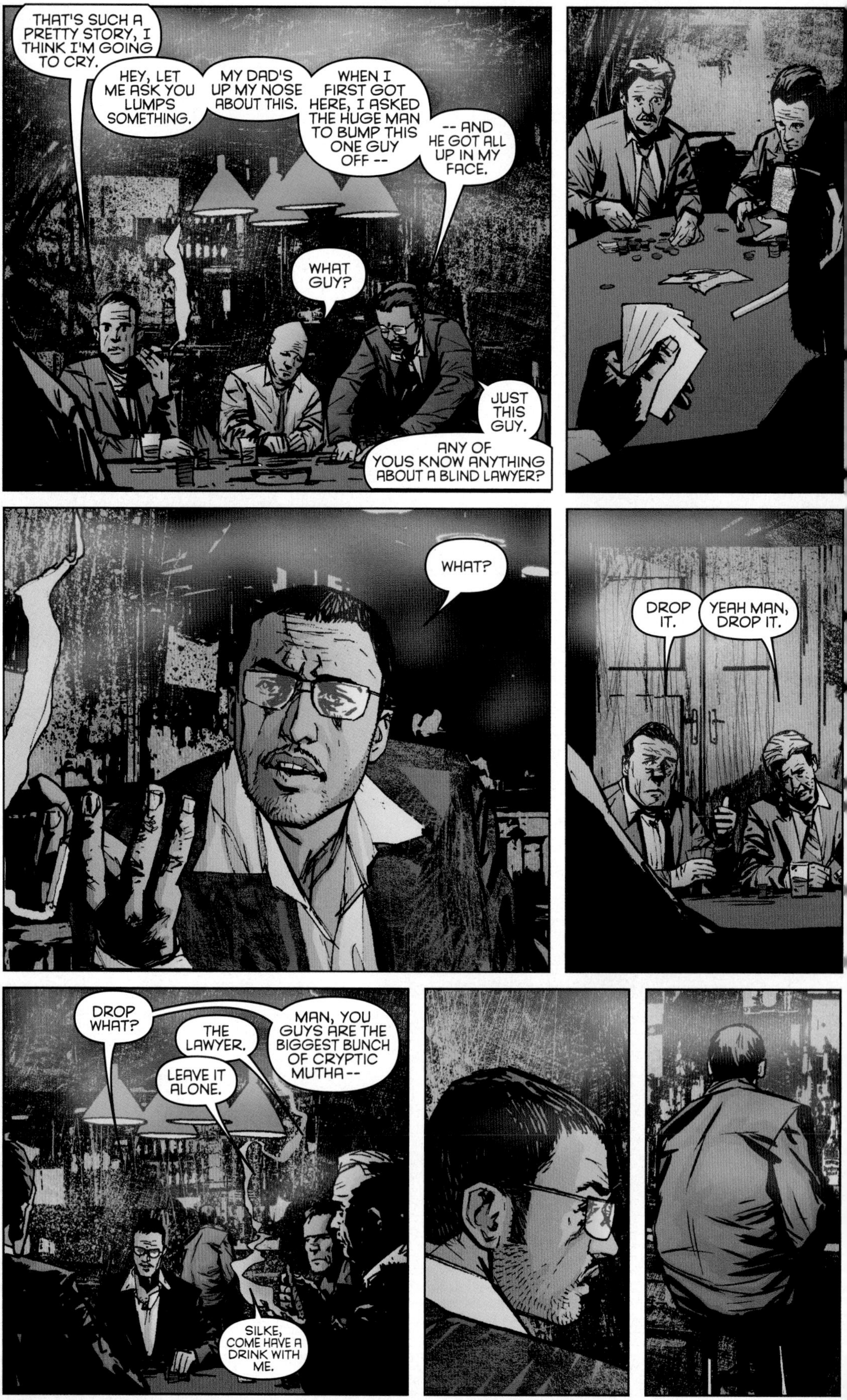
THAT'S SUCH A PRETTY STORY, I THINK I'M GOING TO CRY.
HEY, LET ME ASK YOU LUMPS SOMETHING.
MY DAD'S UP MY NOSE ABOUT THIS.
WHEN I FIRST GOT HERE, I ASKED THE HUGE MAN TO BUMP THIS ONE GUY OFF --
-- AND HE GOT ALL UP IN MY FACE.
WHAT GUY?
JUST THIS GUY.
ANY OF YOUS KNOW ANYTHING ABOUT A BLIND LAWYER?
WHAT?
DROP IT.
YEAH MAN, DROP IT.
DROP WHAT?
THE LAWYER.
LEAVE IT ALONE.
MAN, YOU GUYS ARE THE BIGGEST BUNCH OF CRYPTIC MUTHA --
SILKE, COME HAVE A DRINK WITH ME.

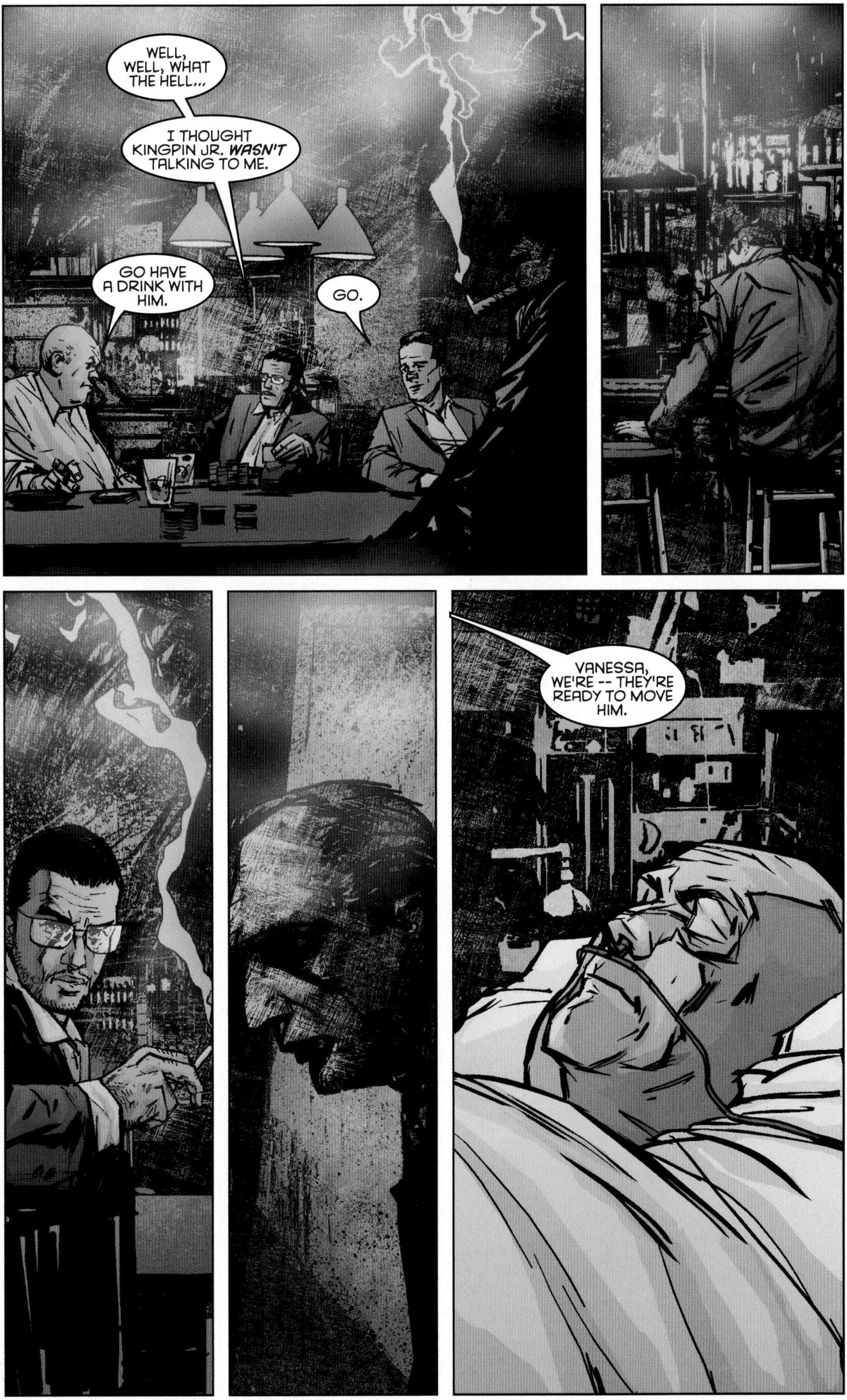
WELL, WELL, WHAT THE HELL...
I THOUGHT KINGPIN JR. WASN'T TALKING TO ME.
GO HAVE A DRINK WITH HIM.
GO.
VANESSA, WE'RE -- THEY'RE READY TO MOVE HIM.

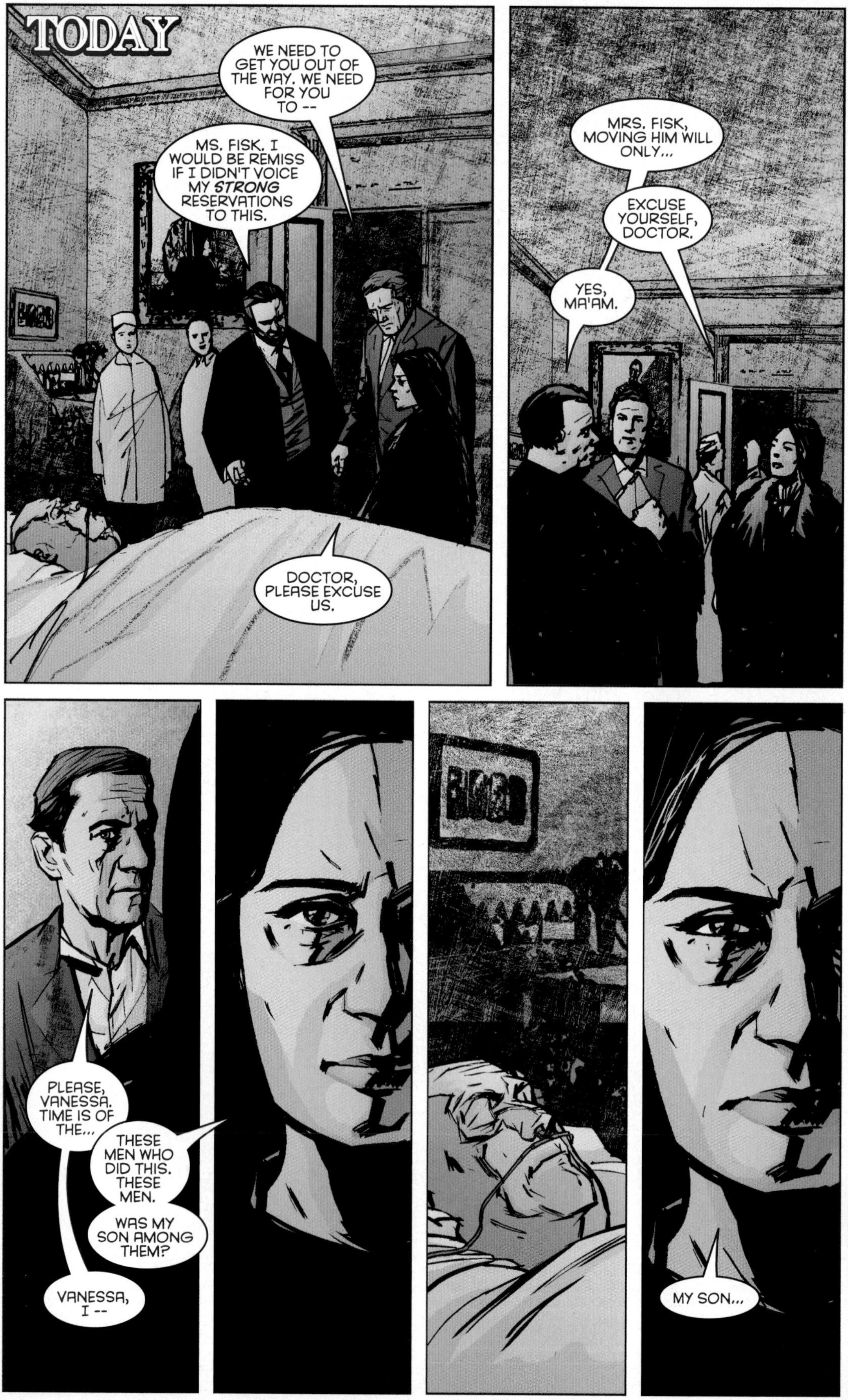
TODAY
WE NEED TO GET YOU OUT OF THE WAY. WE NEED FOR YOU TO --
MS. FISK. I WOULD BE REMISS IF I DIDN'T VOICE MY STRONG RESERVATIONS TO THIS.
DOCTOR, PLEASE EXCUSE US.
MRS. FISK, MOVING HIM WILL ONLY...
EXCUSE YOURSELF, DOCTOR.
YES, MA'AM.
PLEASE, VANESSA. TIME IS OF THE...
THESE MEN WHO DID THIS. THESE MEN.
WAS MY SON AMONG THEM?
VANESSA, I --
MY SON...

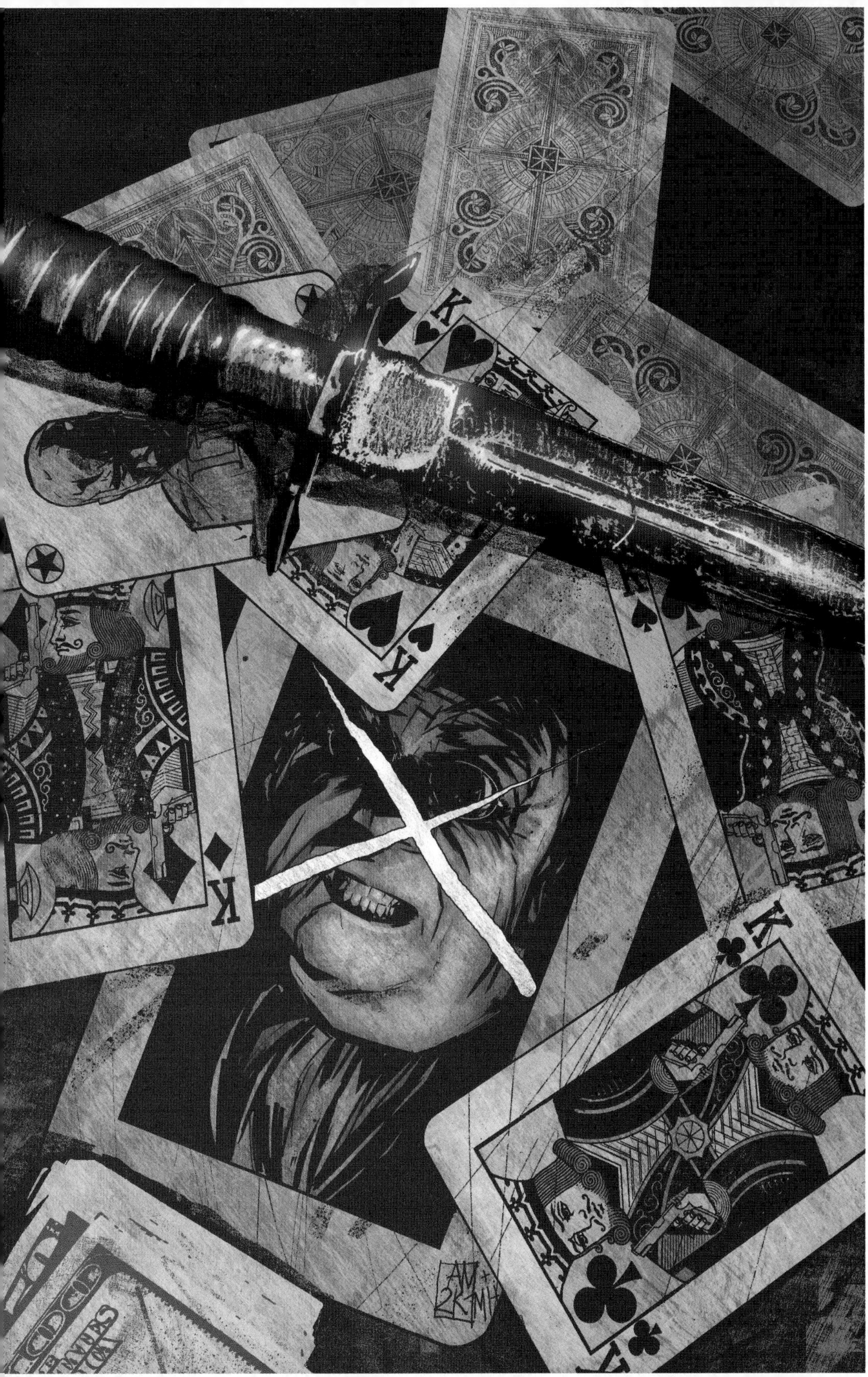

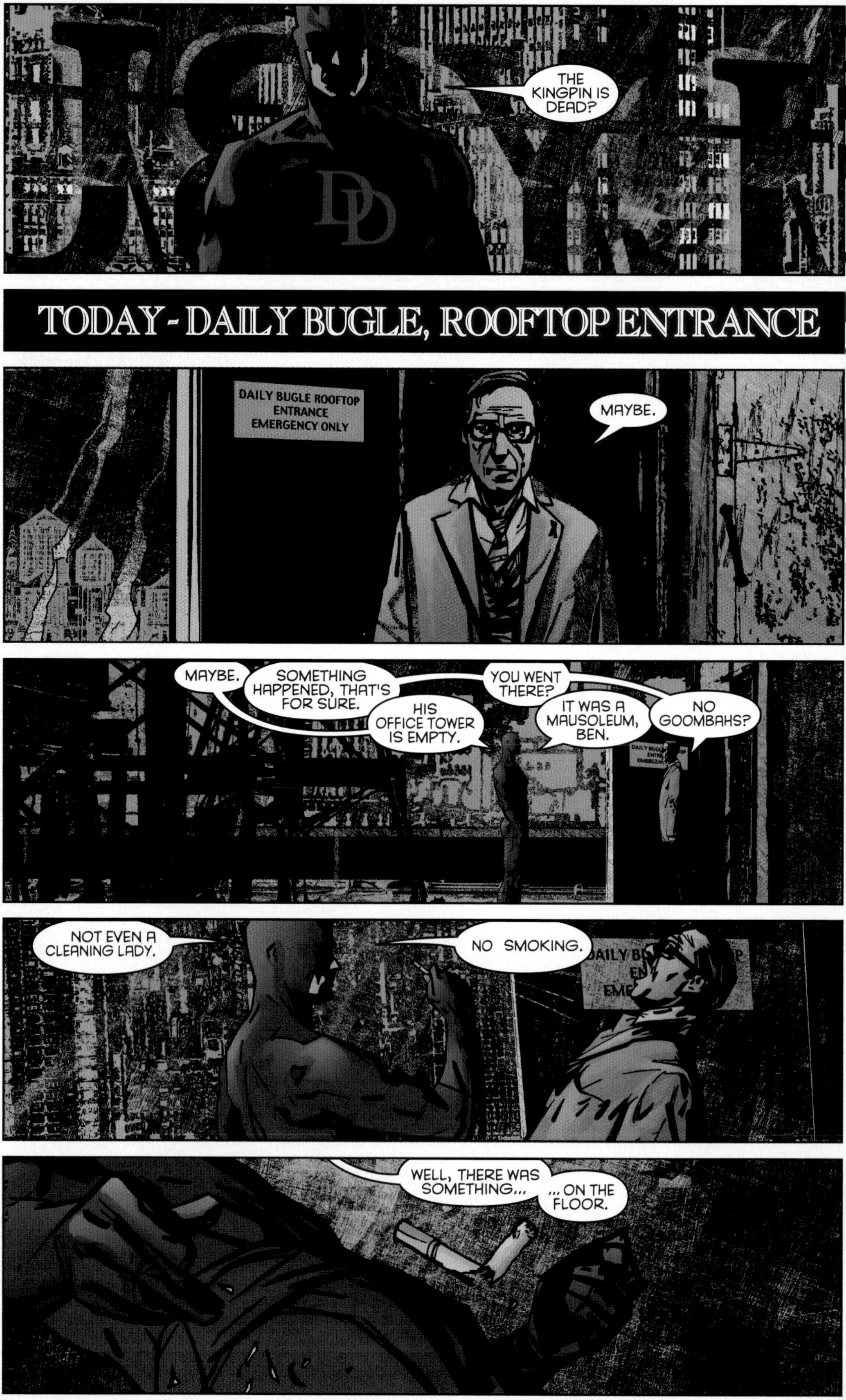
THE KINGPIN IS DEAD?
TODAY - DAILY BUGLE, ROOFTOP ENTRANCE
DAILY BUGLE ROOFTOP ENTRANCE EMERGENCY ONLY
MAYBE.
MAYBE.
SOMETHING HAPPENED, THAT'S FOR SURE.
HIS OFFICE TOWER IS EMPTY.
YOU WENT THERE?
IT WAS A MAUSOLEUM, BEN.
NO GOOMBAHS?
NOT EVEN A CLEANING LADY.
NO SMOKING.
WELL, THERE WAS SOMETHING...
...ON THE FLOOR.

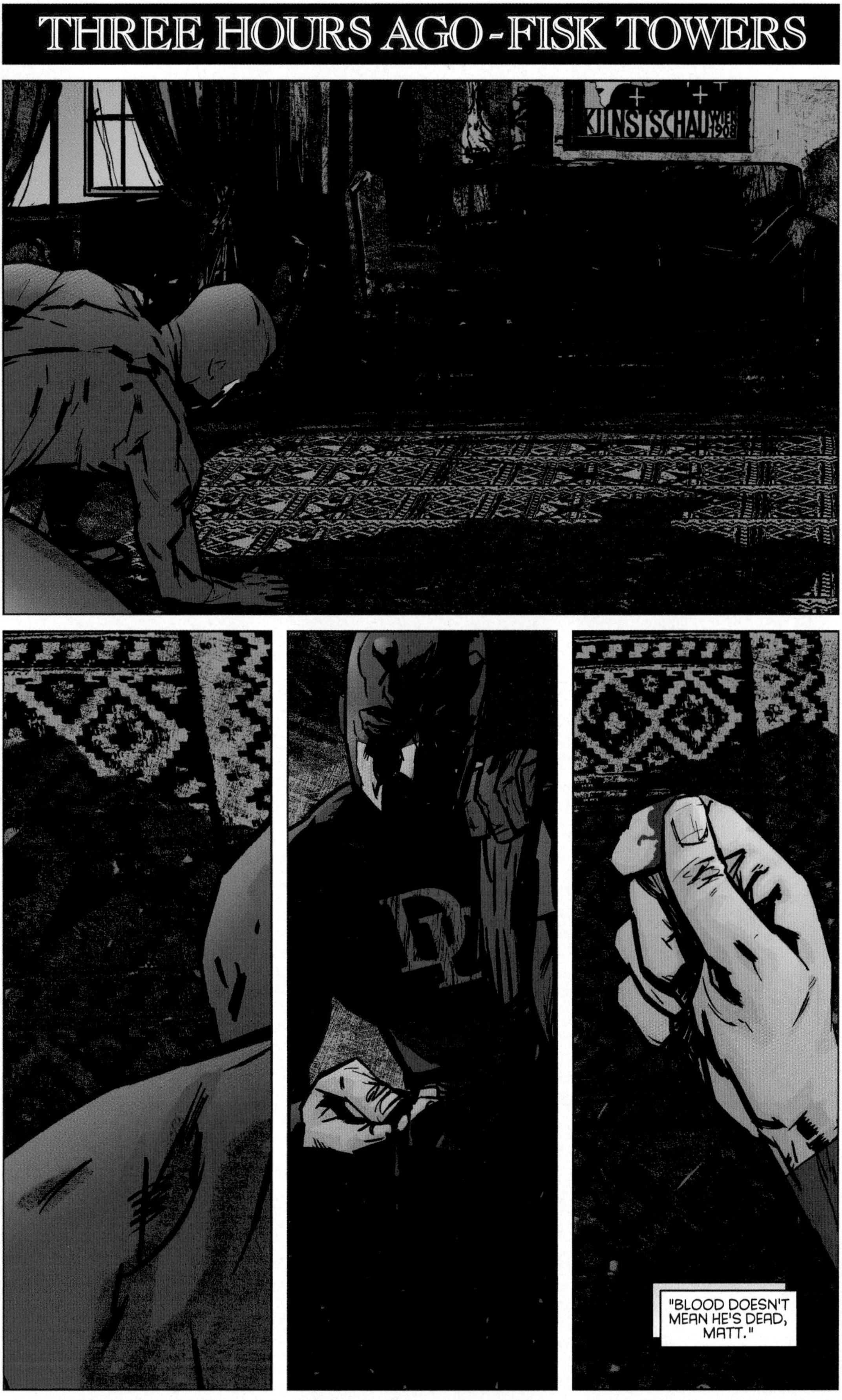
THREE HOURS AGO - FISK TOWERS
KUNSTSCHAU WIEN 1908
"BLOOD DOESN'T MEAN HE'S DEAD, MATT."

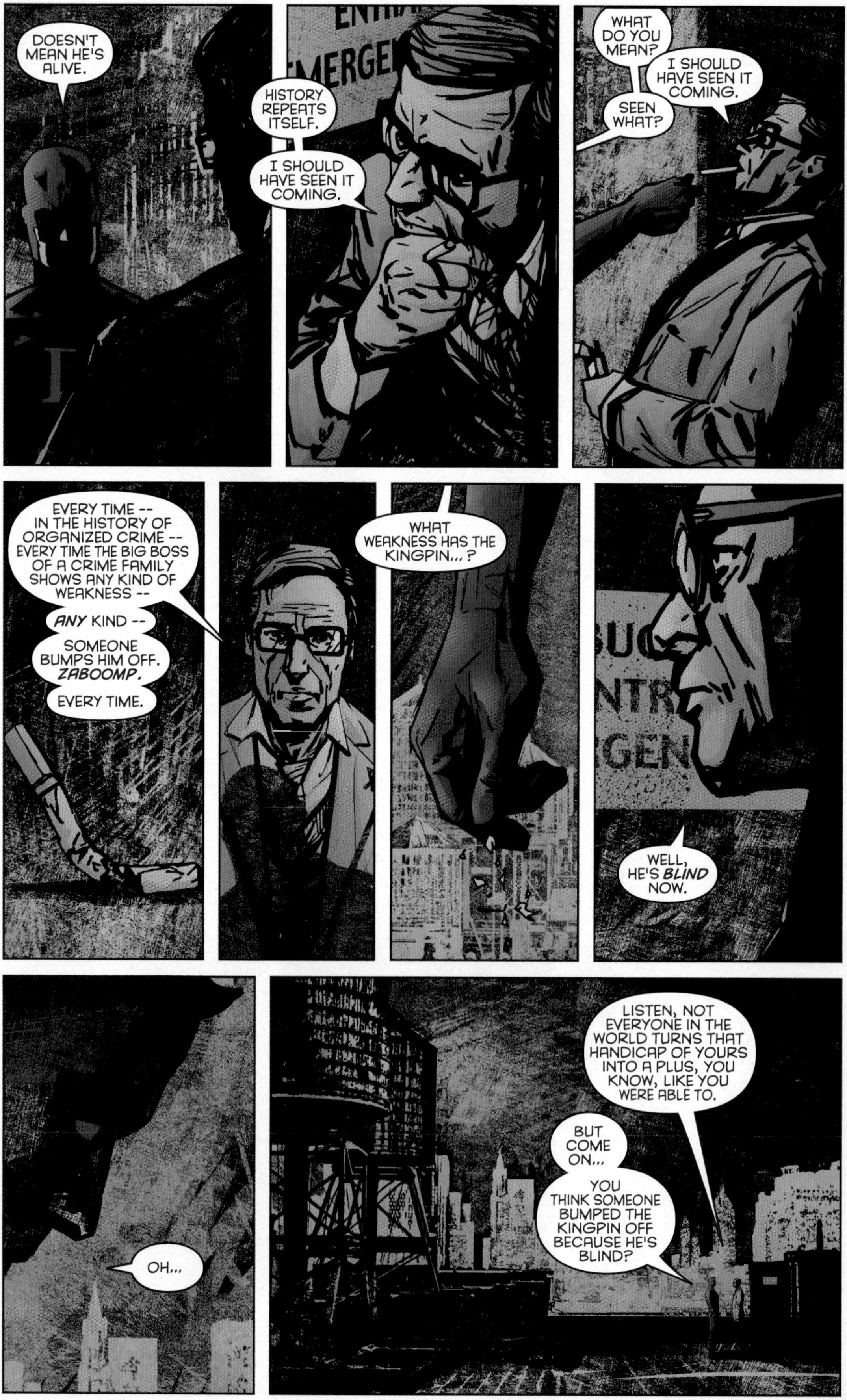
DOESN'T MEAN HE'S ALIVE.
ENTRA
EMERGEN
HISTORY REPEATS ITSELF.
I SHOULD HAVE SEEN IT COMING.
WHAT DO YOU MEAN?
SEEN WHAT?
I SHOULD HAVE SEEN IT COMING.
EVERY TIME -- IN THE HISTORY OF ORGANIZED CRIME -- EVERY TIME THE BIG BOSS OF A CRIME FAMILY SHOWS ANY KIND OF WEAKNESS --
ANY KIND --
SOMEONE BUMPS HIM OFF. *ZABOOMP.*
EVERY TIME.
WHAT WEAKNESS HAS THE KINGPIN...?
WELL, HE'S *BLIND* NOW.
OH...
LISTEN, NOT EVERYONE IN THE WORLD TURNS THAT HANDICAP OF YOURS INTO A PLUS, YOU KNOW, LIKE YOU WERE ABLE TO.
BUT COME ON...
YOU THINK SOMEONE BUMPED THE KINGPIN OFF BECAUSE HE'S BLIND?

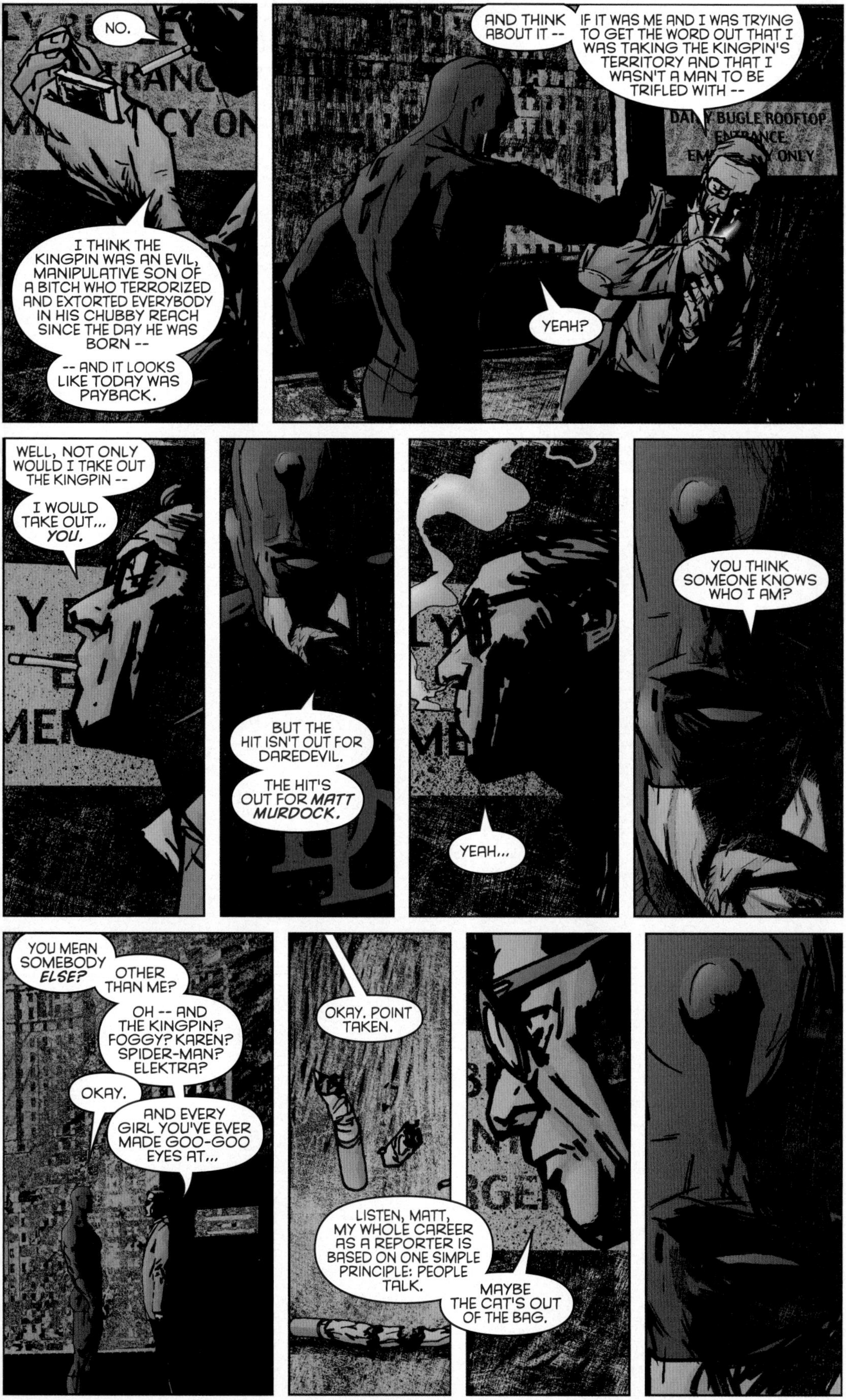

NO.
I THINK THE KINGPIN WAS AN EVIL, MANIPULATIVE SON OF A BITCH WHO TERRORIZED AND EXTORTED EVERYBODY IN HIS CHUBBY REACH SINCE THE DAY HE WAS BORN --
-- AND IT LOOKS LIKE TODAY WAS PAYBACK.
AND THINK ABOUT IT --
IF IT WAS ME AND I WAS TRYING TO GET THE WORD OUT THAT I WAS TAKING THE KINGPIN'S TERRITORY AND THAT I WASN'T A MAN TO BE TRIFLED WITH --
DAILY BUGLE ROOFTOP ENTRANCE EMERGENCY ONLY
YEAH?
WELL, NOT ONLY WOULD I TAKE OUT THE KINGPIN --
I WOULD TAKE OUT... *YOU.*
BUT THE HIT ISN'T OUT FOR DAREDEVIL.
THE HIT'S OUT FOR *MATT MURDOCK.*
YEAH...
YOU THINK SOMEONE KNOWS WHO I AM?
YOU MEAN SOMEBODY *ELSE?*
OTHER THAN ME?
OH -- AND THE KINGPIN? FOGGY? KAREN? SPIDER-MAN? ELEKTRA?
OKAY.
AND EVERY GIRL YOU'VE EVER MADE GOO-GOO EYES AT...
OKAY. POINT TAKEN.
LISTEN, MATT, MY WHOLE CAREER AS A REPORTER IS BASED ON ONE SIMPLE PRINCIPLE: PEOPLE TALK.
MAYBE THE CAT'S OUT OF THE BAG.

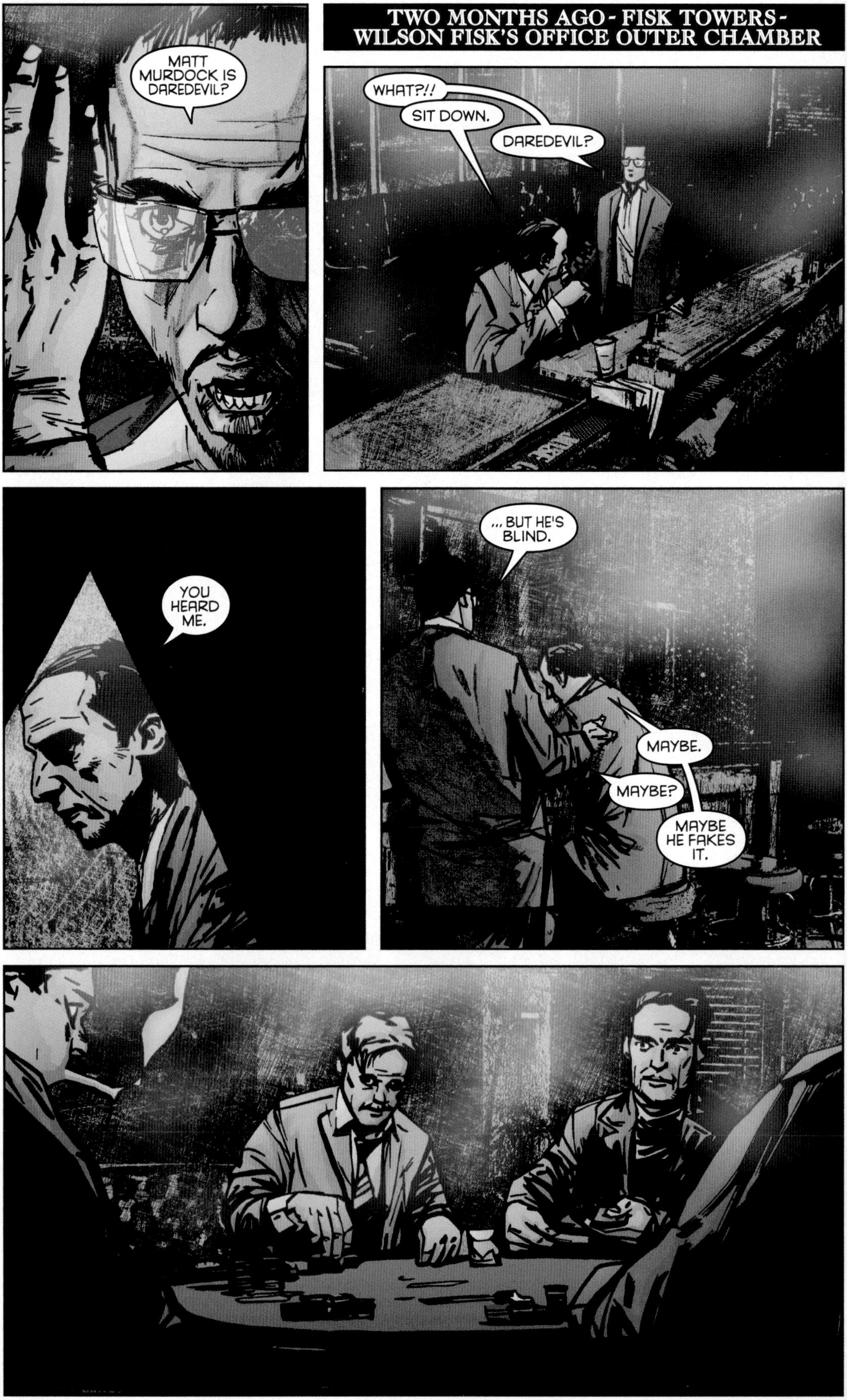
MATT MURDOCK IS DAREDEVIL?
TWO MONTHS AGO- FISK TOWERS- WILSON FISK'S OFFICE OUTER CHAMBER
WHAT?!!
SIT DOWN.
DAREDEVIL?
YOU HEARD ME.
...BUT HE'S BLIND.
MAYBE.
MAYBE?
MAYBE HE FAKES IT.

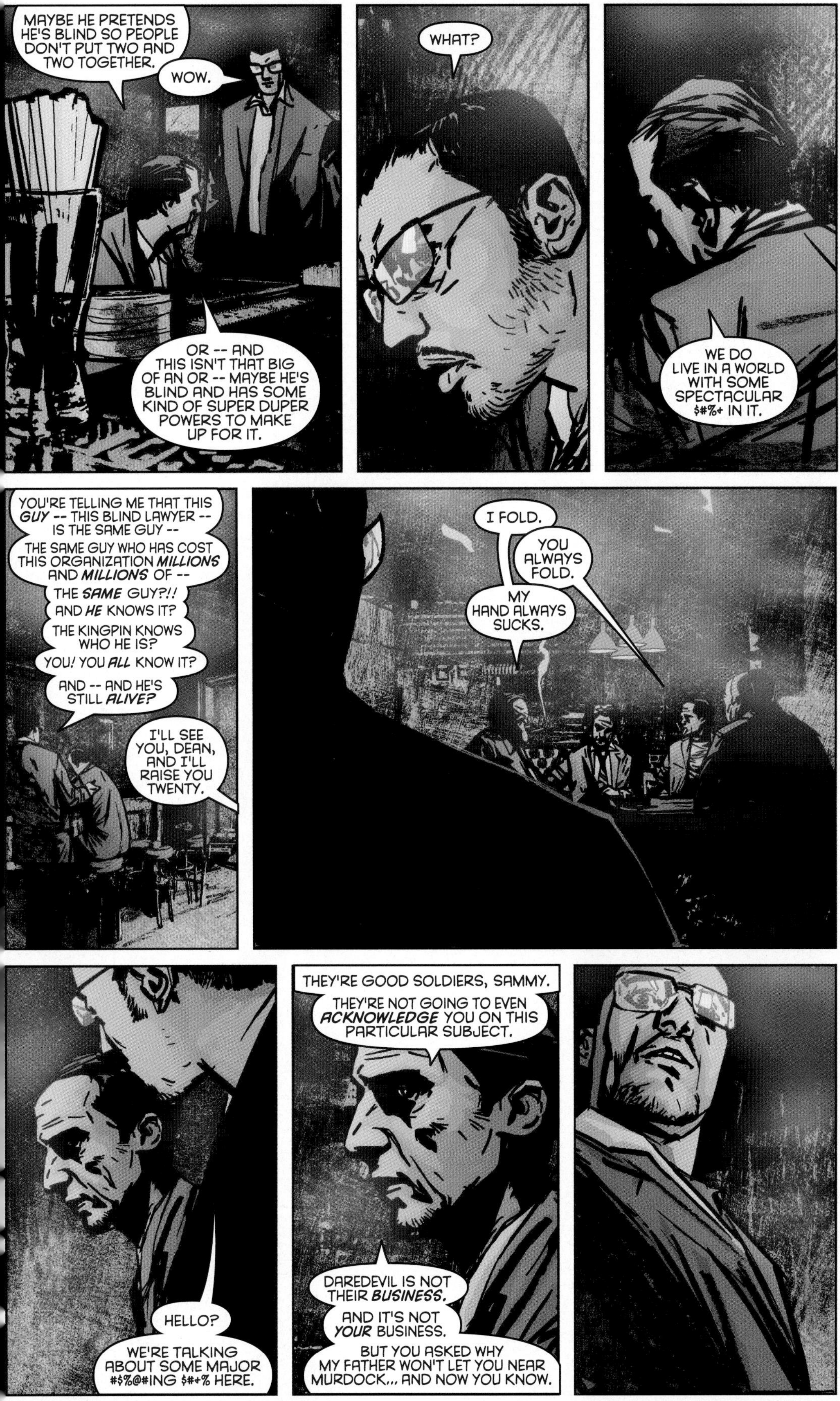

MAYBE HE PRETENDS HE'S BLIND SO PEOPLE DON'T PUT TWO AND TWO TOGETHER.
WOW.
OR -- AND THIS ISN'T THAT BIG OF AN OR -- MAYBE HE'S BLIND AND HAS SOME KIND OF SUPER DUPER POWERS TO MAKE UP FOR IT.
WHAT?
WE DO LIVE IN A WORLD WITH SOME SPECTACULAR $#%+ IN IT.
YOU'RE TELLING ME THAT THIS *GUY* -- THIS BLIND LAWYER -- IS THE SAME GUY --
THE SAME GUY WHO HAS COST THIS ORGANIZATION *MILLIONS* AND *MILLIONS* OF --
THE *SAME* GUY?!!
AND *HE* KNOWS IT?
THE KINGPIN KNOWS WHO HE IS?
YOU! YOU *ALL* KNOW IT?
AND -- AND HE'S STILL *ALIVE?*
I'LL SEE YOU, DEAN, AND I'LL RAISE YOU TWENTY.
I FOLD.
YOU ALWAYS FOLD.
MY HAND ALWAYS SUCKS.
HELLO?
WE'RE TALKING ABOUT SOME MAJOR #$%@#ING $#+% HERE.
THEY'RE GOOD SOLDIERS, SAMMY.
THEY'RE NOT GOING TO EVEN *ACKNOWLEDGE* YOU ON THIS PARTICULAR SUBJECT.
DAREDEVIL IS NOT THEIR *BUSINESS.*
AND IT'S NOT *YOUR* BUSINESS.
BUT YOU ASKED WHY MY FATHER WON'T LET YOU NEAR MURDOCK... AND NOW YOU KNOW.

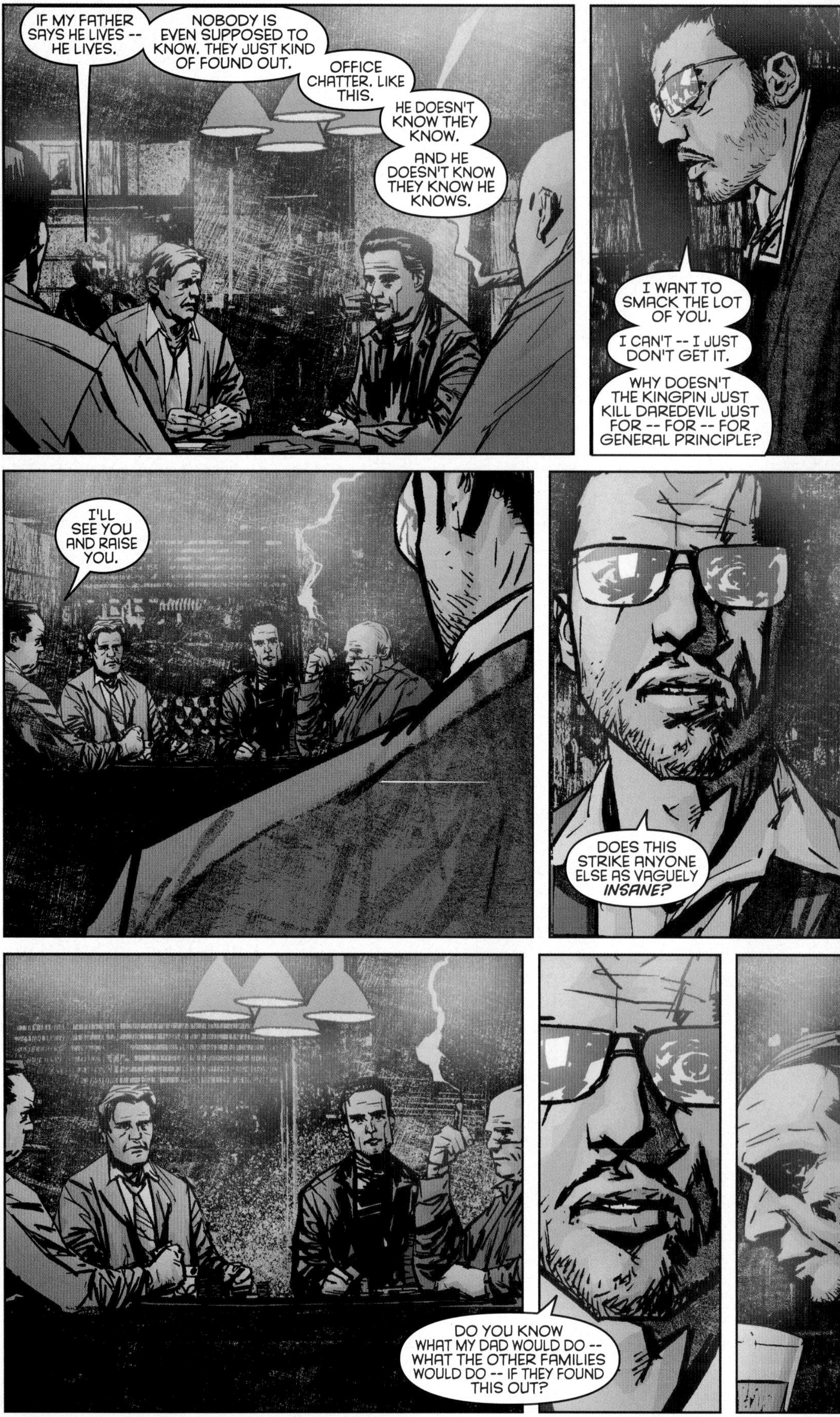
IF MY FATHER SAYS HE LIVES -- HE LIVES.
NOBODY IS EVEN SUPPOSED TO KNOW. THEY JUST KIND OF FOUND OUT.
OFFICE CHATTER. LIKE THIS.
HE DOESN'T KNOW THEY KNOW.
AND HE DOESN'T KNOW THEY KNOW HE KNOWS.
I WANT TO SMACK THE LOT OF YOU.
I CAN'T -- I JUST DON'T GET IT.
WHY DOESN'T THE KINGPIN JUST KILL DAREDEVIL JUST FOR -- FOR -- FOR GENERAL PRINCIPLE?
I'LL SEE YOU AND RAISE YOU.
DOES THIS STRIKE ANYONE ELSE AS VAGUELY *INSANE?*
DO YOU KNOW WHAT MY DAD WOULD DO -- WHAT THE OTHER FAMILIES WOULD DO -- IF THEY FOUND THIS OUT?

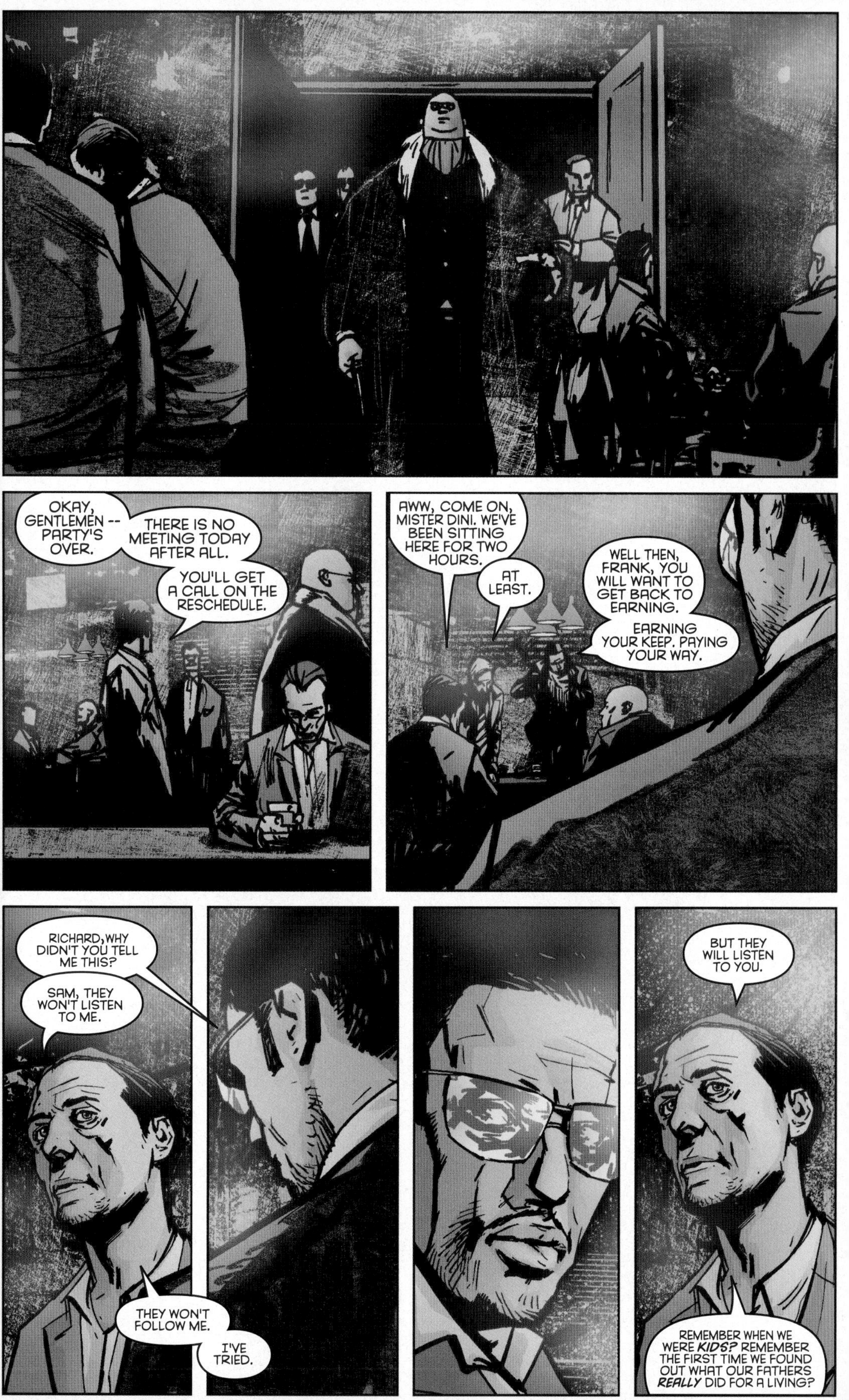
OKAY, GENTLEMEN -- PARTY'S OVER.
THERE IS NO MEETING TODAY AFTER ALL.
YOU'LL GET A CALL ON THE RESCHEDULE.
AWW, COME ON, MISTER DINI. WE'VE BEEN SITTING HERE FOR TWO HOURS.
AT LEAST.
WELL THEN, FRANK, YOU WILL WANT TO GET BACK TO EARNING.
EARNING YOUR KEEP. PAYING YOUR WAY.
RICHARD, WHY DIDN'T YOU TELL ME THIS?
SAM, THEY WON'T LISTEN TO ME.
THEY WON'T FOLLOW ME.
I'VE TRIED.
BUT THEY WILL LISTEN TO YOU.
REMEMBER WHEN WE WERE *KIDS?* REMEMBER THE FIRST TIME WE FOUND OUT WHAT OUR FATHERS *REALLY* DID FOR A LIVING?

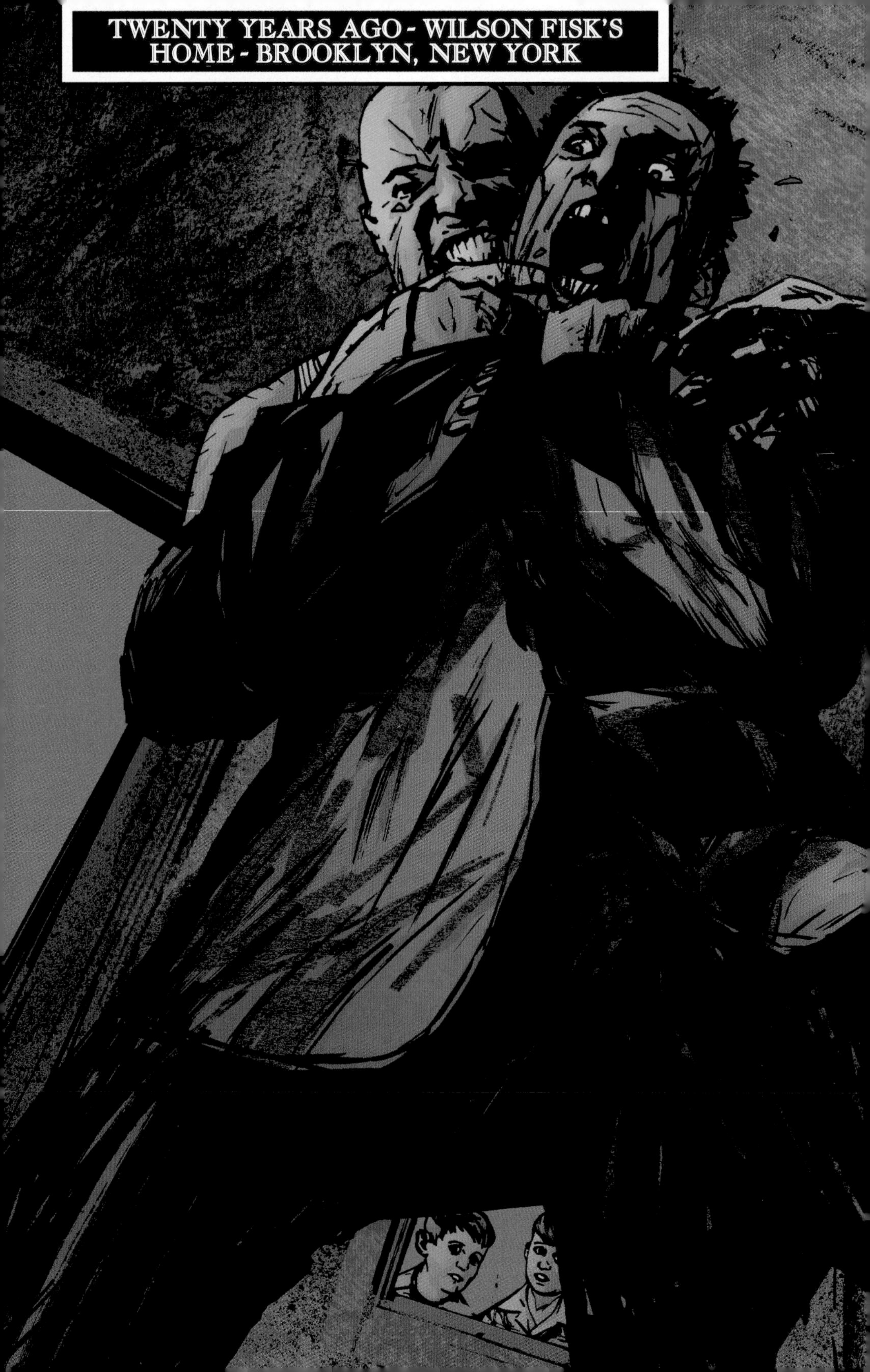
TWENTY YEARS AGO - WILSON FISK'S HOME - BROOKLYN, NEW YORK

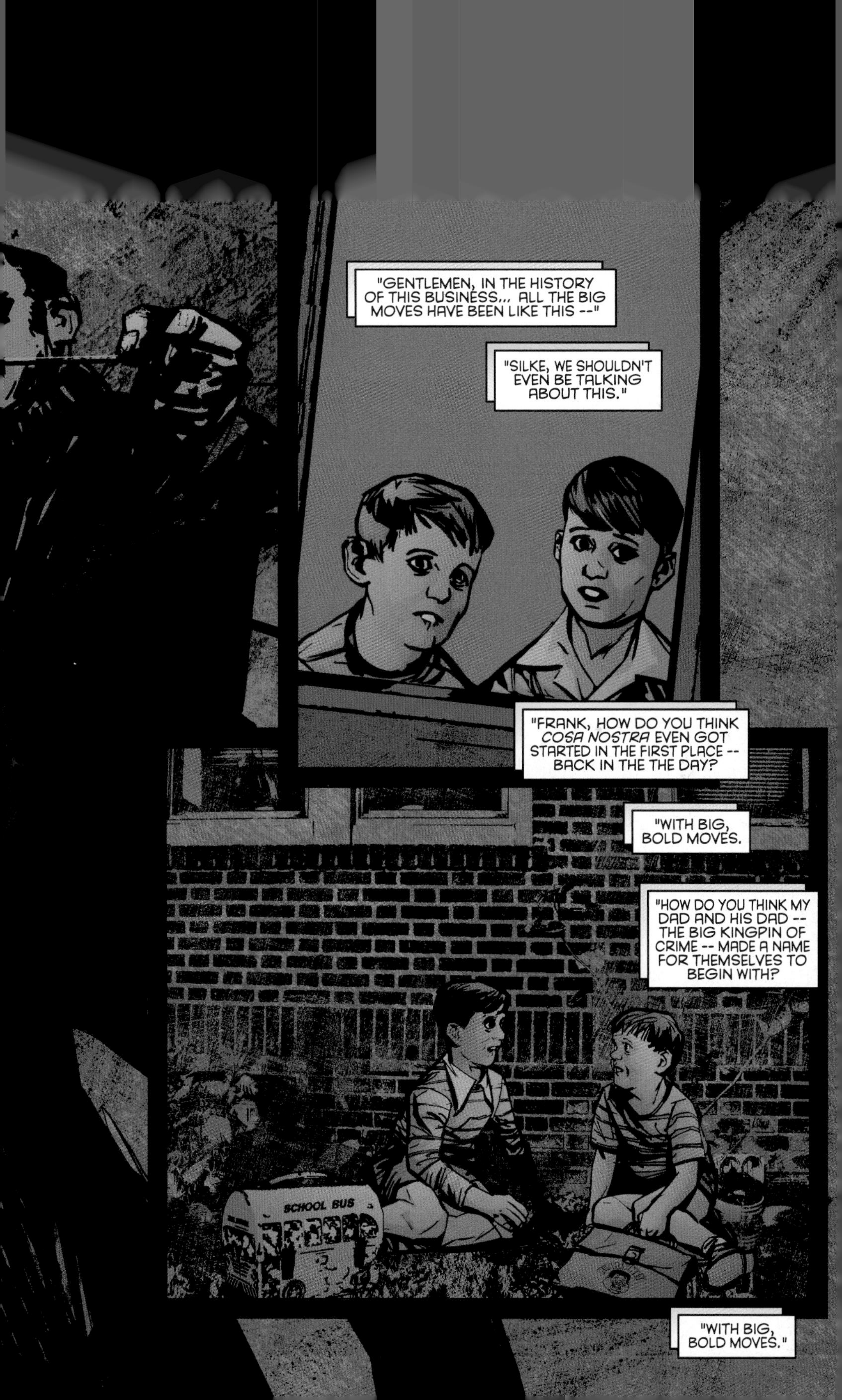

"GENTLEMEN, IN THE HISTORY OF THIS BUSINESS... ALL THE BIG MOVES HAVE BEEN LIKE THIS --"
"SILKE, WE SHOULDN'T EVEN BE TALKING ABOUT THIS."
"FRANK, HOW DO YOU THINK *COSA NOSTRA* EVEN GOT STARTED IN THE FIRST PLACE -- BACK IN THE THE DAY?
"WITH BIG, BOLD MOVES.
"HOW DO YOU THINK MY DAD AND HIS DAD -- THE BIG KINGPIN OF CRIME -- MADE A NAME FOR THEMSELVES TO BEGIN WITH?
SCHOOL BUS
"WITH BIG, BOLD MOVES."

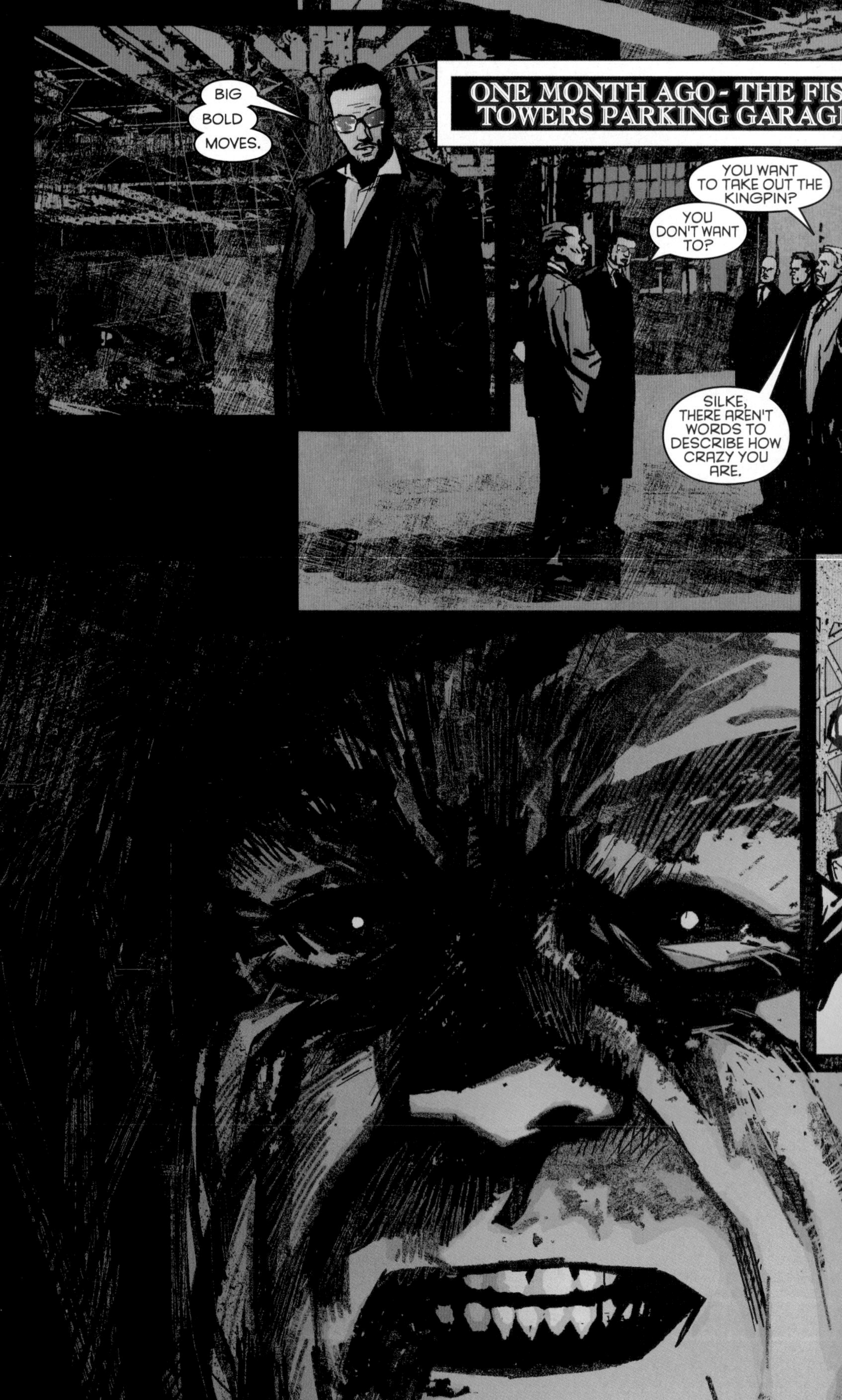
ONE MONTH AGO- THE FIS
TOWERS PARKING GARAG
BIG BOLD MOVES.
YOU WANT TO TAKE OUT THE KINGPIN?
YOU DON'T WANT TO?
SILKE, THERE AREN'T WORDS TO DESCRIBE HOW CRAZY YOU ARE.

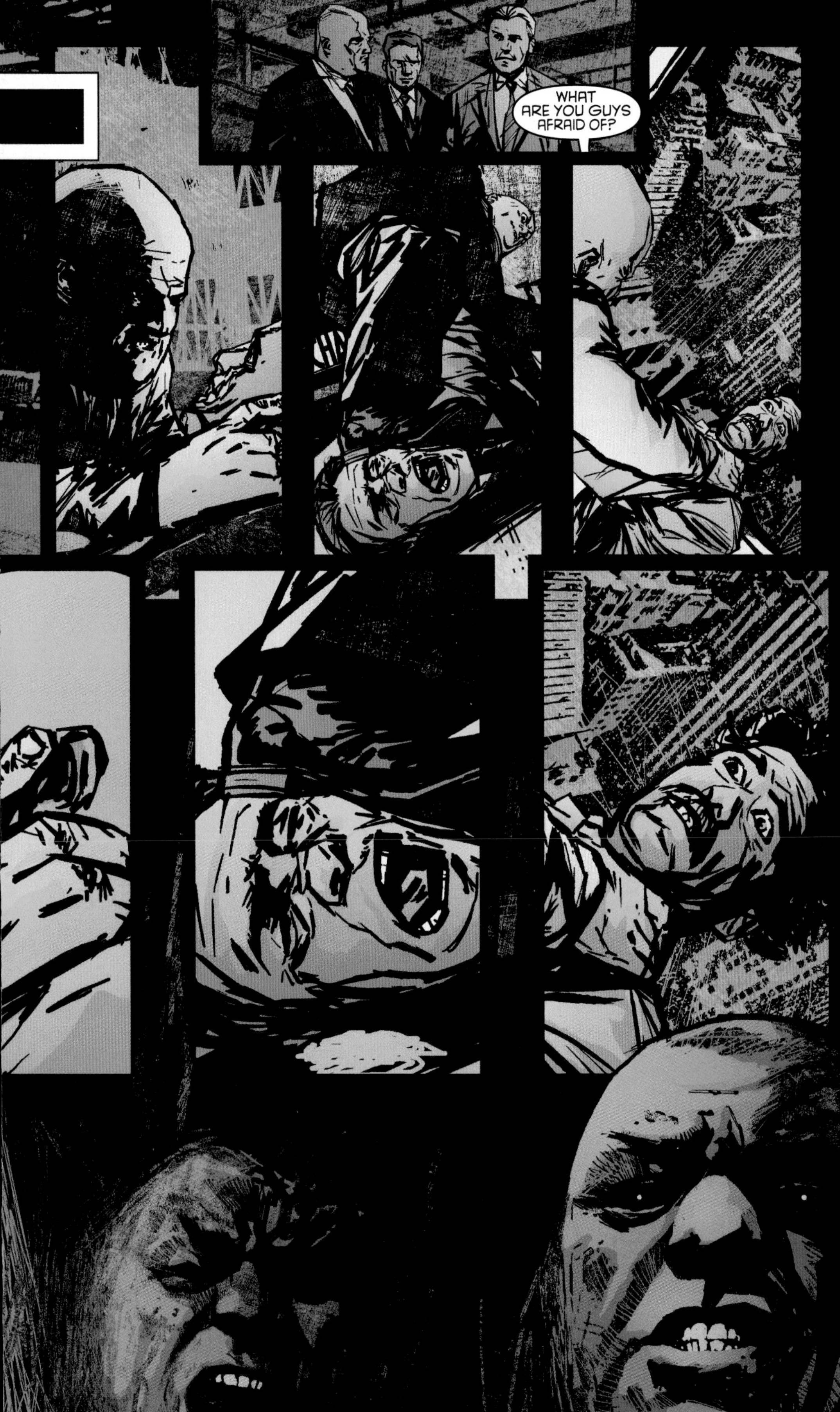
WHAT ARE YOU GUYS AFRAID OF?

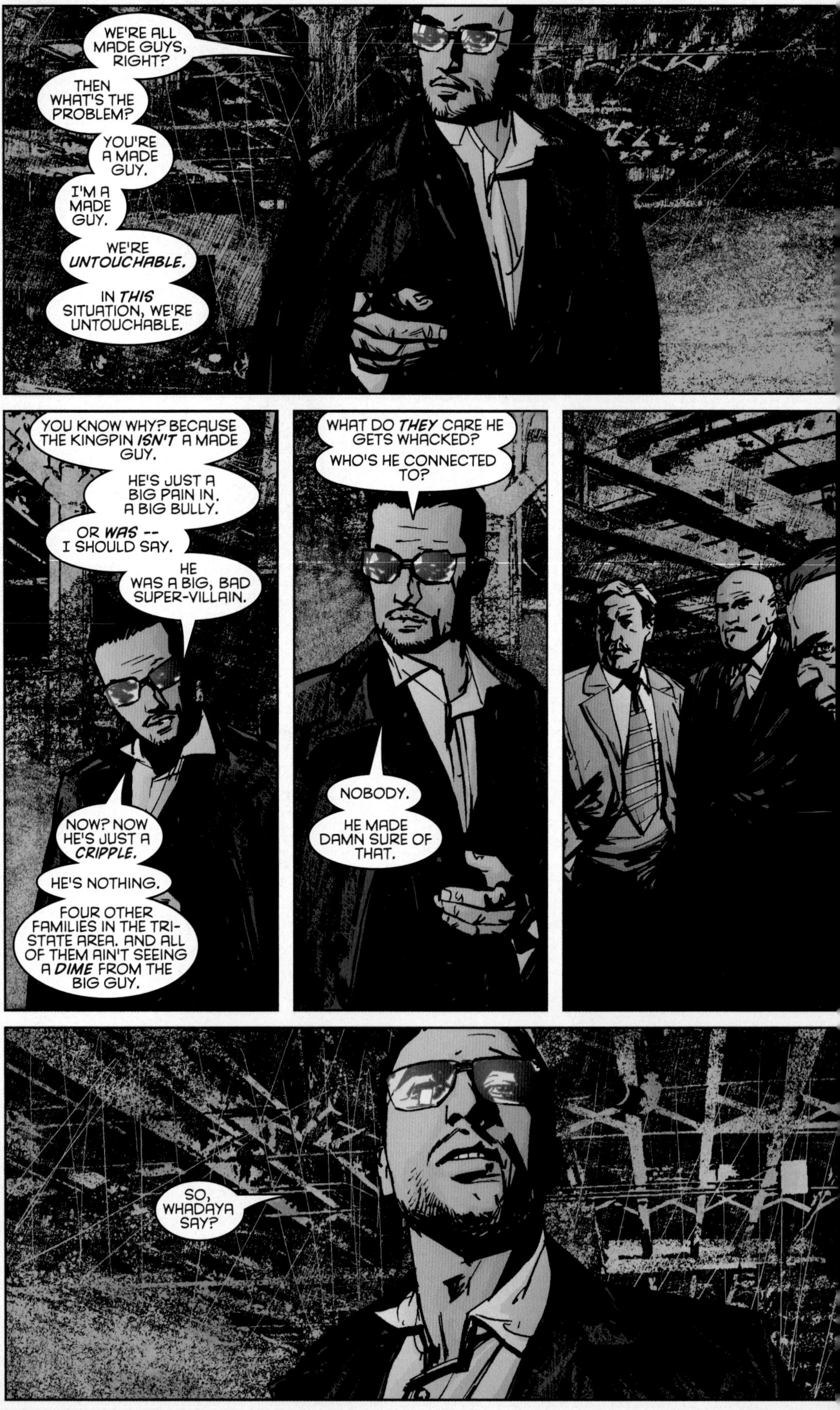
WE'RE ALL MADE GUYS, RIGHT?
THEN WHAT'S THE PROBLEM?
YOU'RE A MADE GUY.
I'M A MADE GUY.
WE'RE UNTOUCHABLE.
IN THIS SITUATION, WE'RE UNTOUCHABLE.
YOU KNOW WHY? BECAUSE THE KINGPIN ISN'T A MADE GUY.
HE'S JUST A BIG PAIN IN. A BIG BULLY.
OR WAS -- I SHOULD SAY.
HE WAS A BIG, BAD SUPER-VILLAIN.
NOW? NOW HE'S JUST A CRIPPLE.
HE'S NOTHING.
FOUR OTHER FAMILIES IN THE TRI-STATE AREA. AND ALL OF THEM AIN'T SEEING A DIME FROM THE BIG GUY.
WHAT DO THEY CARE HE GETS WHACKED?
WHO'S HE CONNECTED TO?
NOBODY.
HE MADE DAMN SURE OF THAT.
SO, WHADAYA SAY?

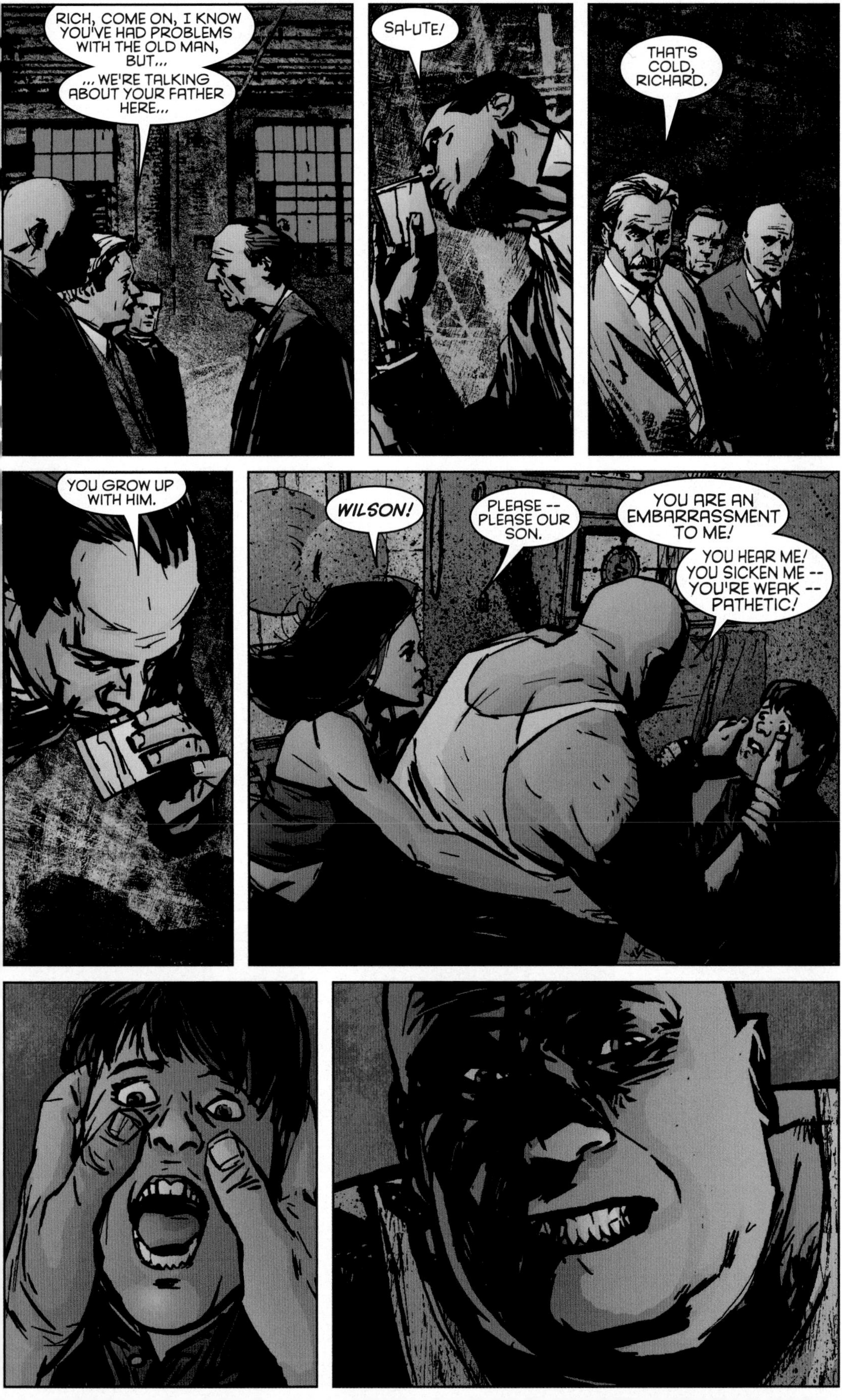
RICH, COME ON, I KNOW YOU'VE HAD PROBLEMS WITH THE OLD MAN, BUT...
... WE'RE TALKING ABOUT YOUR FATHER HERE...
SALUTE!
THAT'S COLD, RICHARD.
YOU GROW UP WITH HIM.
WILSON!
PLEASE -- PLEASE OUR SON.
YOU ARE AN EMBARRASSMENT TO ME!
YOU HEAR ME! YOU SICKEN ME -- YOU'RE WEAK -- PATHETIC!

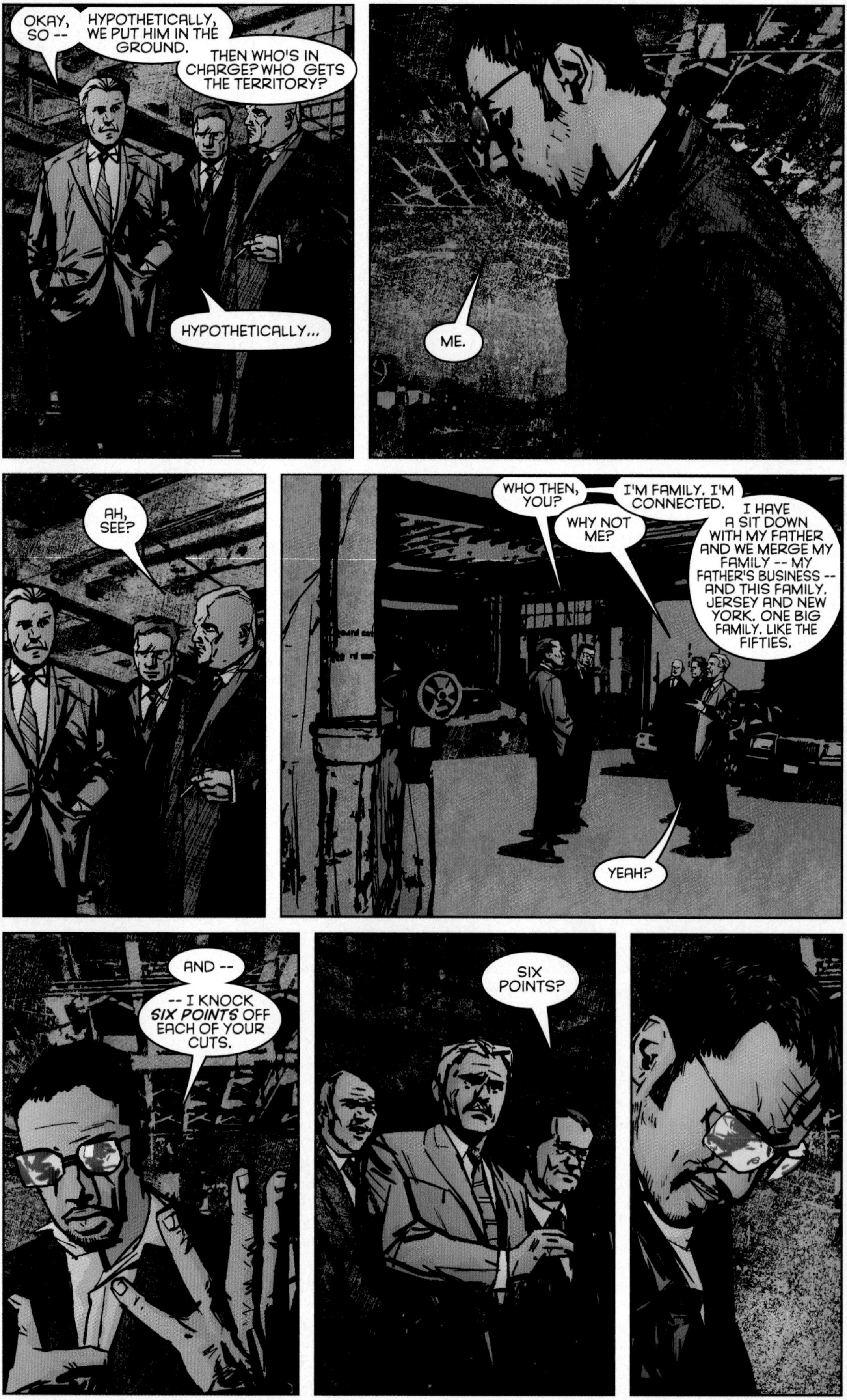

OKAY, SO --
HYPOTHETICALLY, WE PUT HIM IN THE GROUND.
THEN WHO'S IN CHARGE? WHO GETS THE TERRITORY?
HYPOTHETICALLY...
ME.
AH, SEE?
WHO THEN, YOU?
WHY NOT ME?
I'M FAMILY. I'M CONNECTED.
I HAVE A SIT DOWN WITH MY FATHER AND WE MERGE MY FAMILY -- MY FATHER'S BUSINESS -- AND THIS FAMILY. JERSEY AND NEW YORK. ONE BIG FAMILY. LIKE THE FIFTIES.
YEAH?
AND --
-- I KNOCK *SIX POINTS* OFF EACH OF YOUR CUTS.
SIX POINTS?

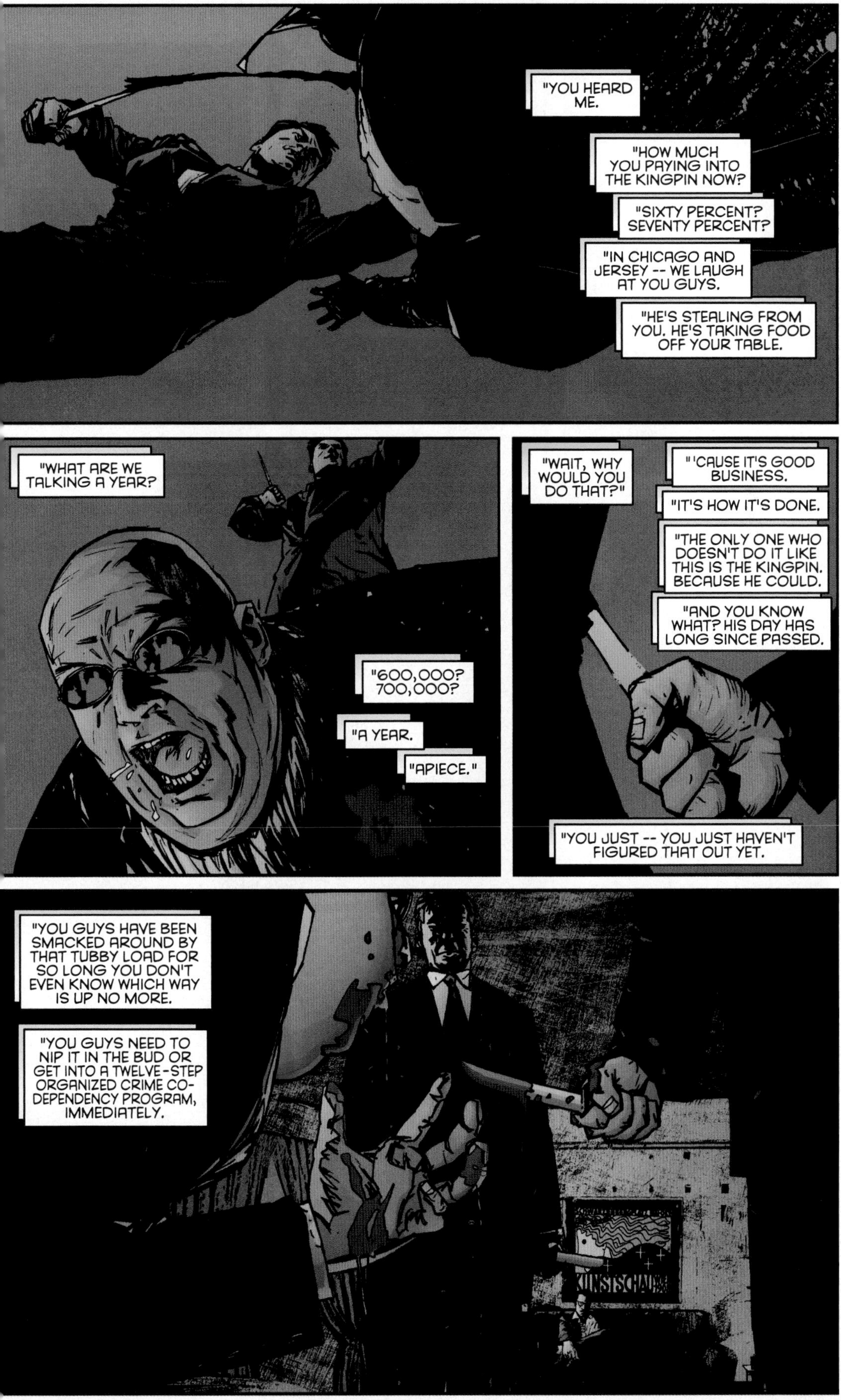
"YOU HEARD ME.
"HOW MUCH YOU PAYING INTO THE KINGPIN NOW?
"SIXTY PERCENT? SEVENTY PERCENT?
"IN CHICAGO AND JERSEY -- WE LAUGH AT YOU GUYS.
"HE'S STEALING FROM YOU. HE'S TAKING FOOD OFF YOUR TABLE.
"WHAT ARE WE TALKING A YEAR?
"600,000? 700,000?
"A YEAR.
"APIECE."
"WAIT, WHY WOULD YOU DO THAT?"
"'CAUSE IT'S GOOD BUSINESS.
"IT'S HOW IT'S DONE.
"THE ONLY ONE WHO DOESN'T DO IT LIKE THIS IS THE KINGPIN. BECAUSE HE COULD.
"AND YOU KNOW WHAT? HIS DAY HAS LONG SINCE PASSED.
"YOU JUST -- YOU JUST HAVEN'T FIGURED THAT OUT YET.
"YOU GUYS HAVE BEEN SMACKED AROUND BY THAT TUBBY LOAD FOR SO LONG YOU DON'T EVEN KNOW WHICH WAY IS UP NO MORE.
"YOU GUYS NEED TO NIP IT IN THE BUD OR GET INTO A TWELVE-STEP ORGANIZED CRIME CO-DEPENDENCY PROGRAM, IMMEDIATELY.

"SIXTY PERCENT?"

"YEAH, THAT'S RIGHT.

"LISTEN, I'M DOING ALL RIGHT.

"I GOT A NICE HOUSE.

"A COUPLE OF KIDS. A WIFE. A GIRLFRIEND.

"WHAT I NEED I GOTTA LIVE UP IN SOME IVORY TOWER IN THE MIDDLE OF MANHATTAN?

"WHO NEEDS ALL THIS? WHY ARE WE PAYING FOR IT?

"ALL I NEED IS A CREW WHO'S GONNA HUSTLE.

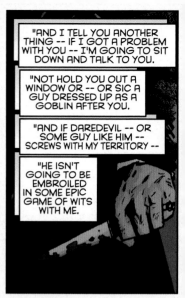

"AND I TELL YOU ANOTHER THING -- IF I GOT A PROBLEM WITH YOU -- I'M GOING TO SIT DOWN AND TALK TO YOU.

"NOT HOLD YOU OUT A WINDOW OR -- OR SIC A GUY DRESSED UP AS A GOBLIN AFTER YOU.

"AND IF DAREDEVIL -- OR SOME GUY LIKE HIM -- SCREWS WITH MY TERRITORY --

"HE ISN'T GOING TO BE EMBROILED IN SOME EPIC GAME OF WITS WITH ME.

"HE'S GOING TO WAKE UP ONE MORNING AND HIS LIVER WILL BE GONE -- WITH A NOTE THAT SAYS 'YOU DON'T MESS WITH MR. SILKE AND YOU DON'T MESS WITH HIS GUYS.'

"BECAUSE ANY ONE OF YOU WHO ARE MAN ENOUGH TO JOIN RICHARD AND ME ARE MY PAIZANS TILL THE END OF TIME...

"YOU ARE MEN OF HONOR WHO STOOD UP FOR YOURSELVES.

"YOU ARE MEN."

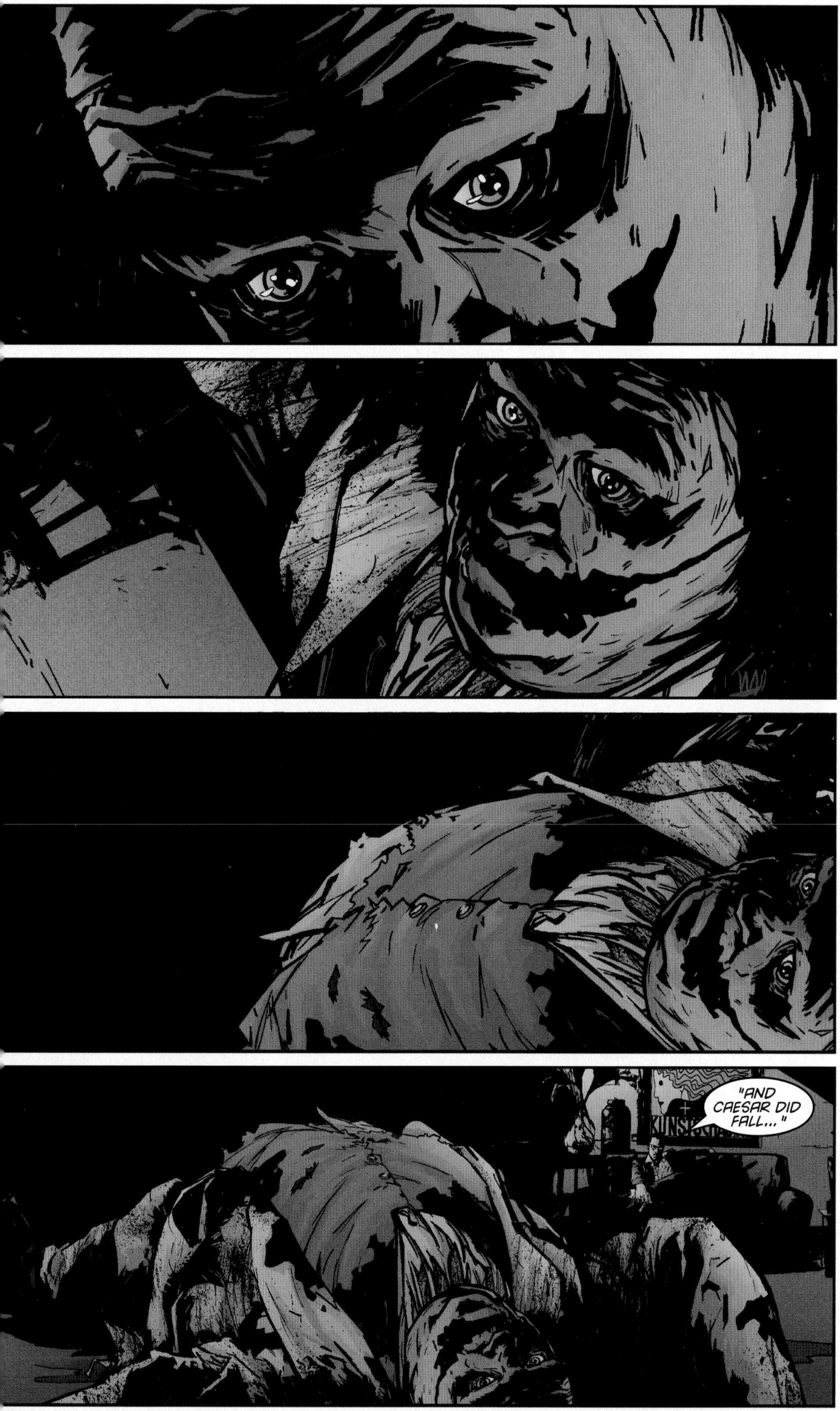
"AND CAESAR DID FALL..."

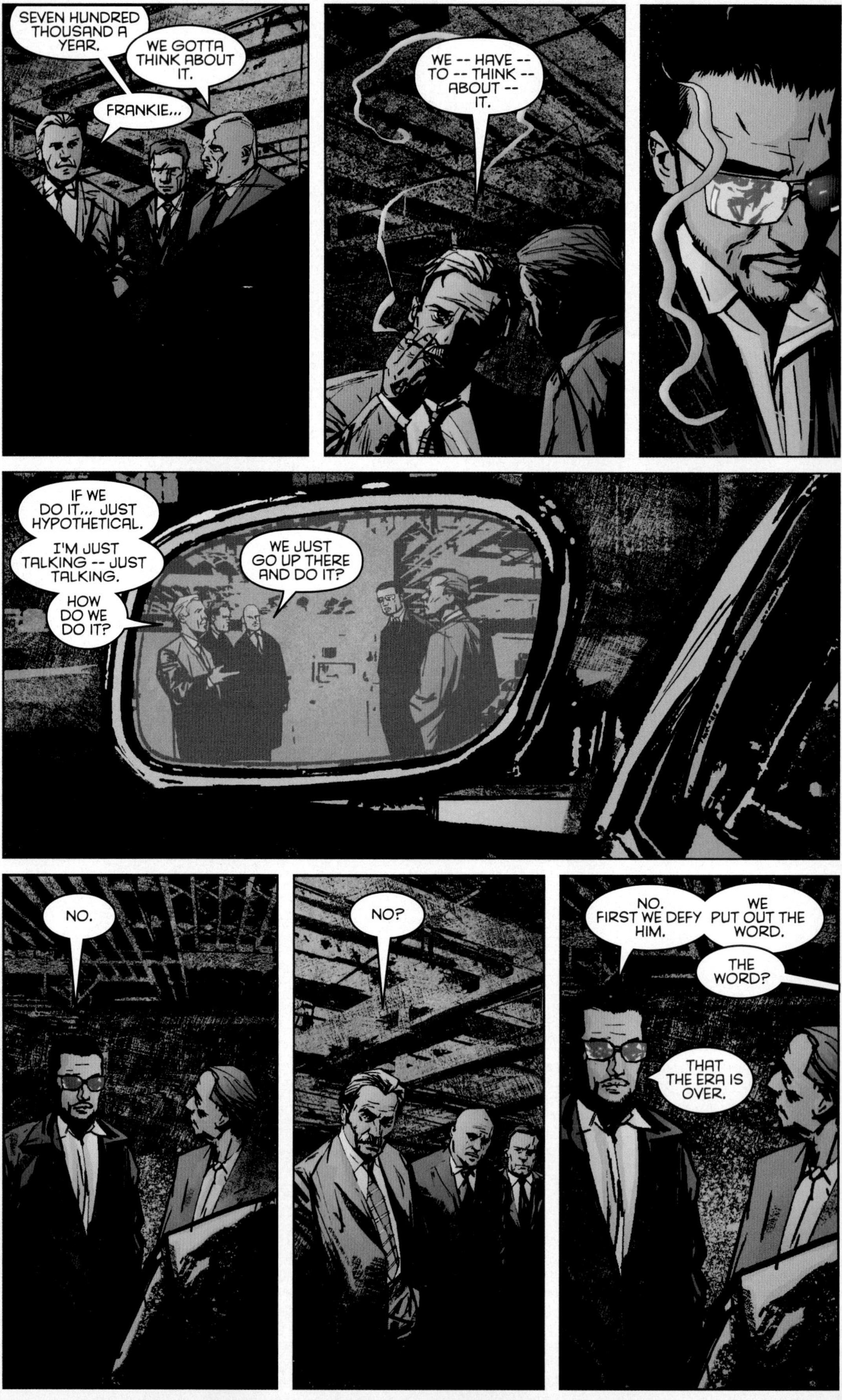
SEVEN HUNDRED THOUSAND A YEAR.
WE GOTTA THINK ABOUT IT.
FRANKIE...
WE -- HAVE -- TO -- THINK -- ABOUT -- IT.
IF WE DO IT... JUST HYPOTHETICAL.
I'M JUST TALKING -- JUST TALKING.
HOW DO WE DO IT?
WE JUST GO UP THERE AND DO IT?
NO.
NO?
NO. FIRST WE DEFY HIM.
WE PUT OUT THE WORD.
THE WORD?
THAT THE ERA IS OVER.

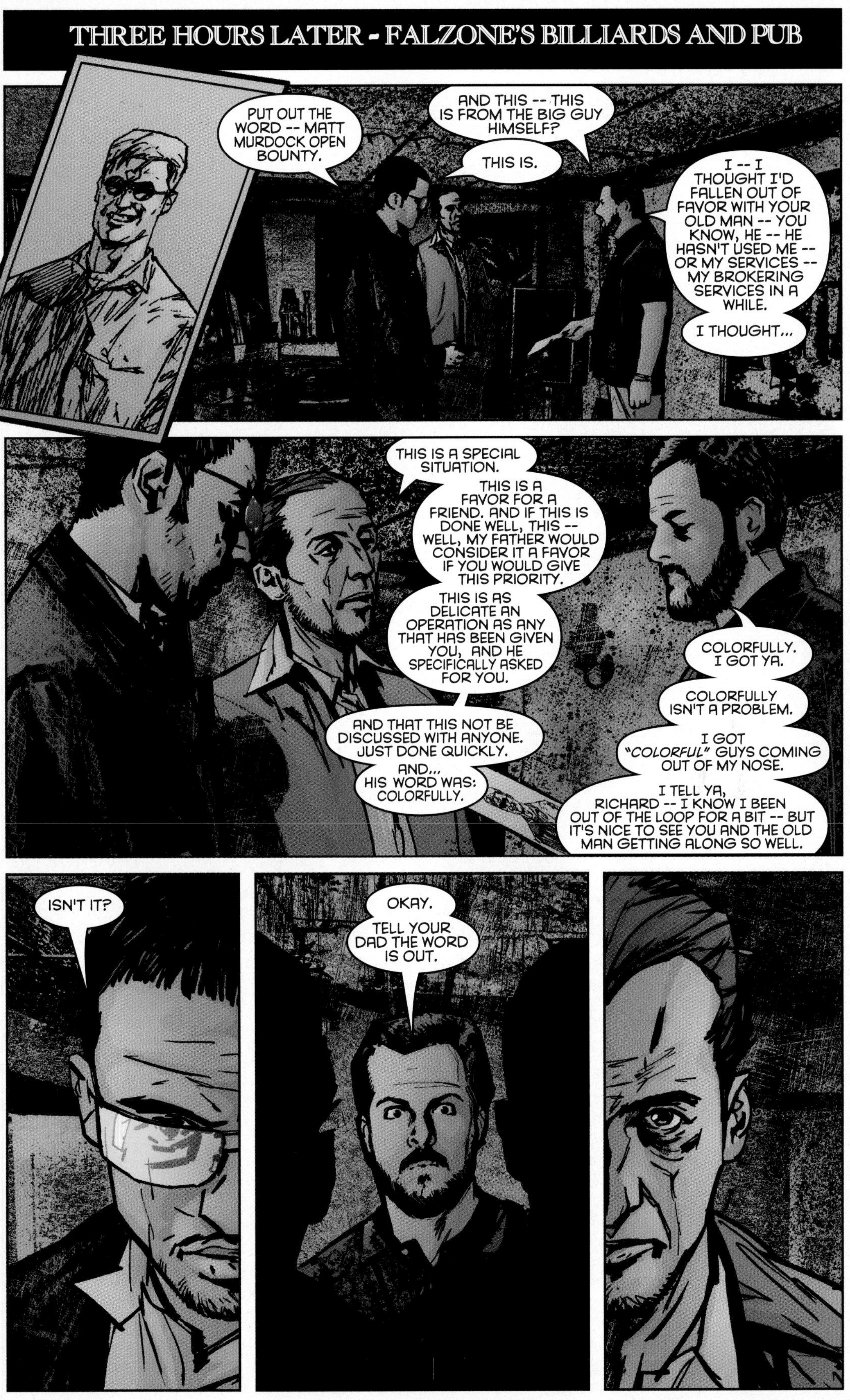

THREE HOURS LATER - FALZONE'S BILLIARDS AND PUB
PUT OUT THE WORD -- MATT MURDOCK OPEN BOUNTY.
AND THIS -- THIS IS FROM THE BIG GUY HIMSELF?
THIS IS.
I -- I THOUGHT I'D FALLEN OUT OF FAVOR WITH YOUR OLD MAN -- YOU KNOW, HE -- HE HASN'T USED ME -- OR MY SERVICES -- MY BROKERING SERVICES IN A WHILE.
I THOUGHT...
THIS IS A SPECIAL SITUATION.
THIS IS A FAVOR FOR A FRIEND. AND IF THIS IS DONE WELL, THIS -- WELL, MY FATHER WOULD CONSIDER IT A FAVOR IF YOU WOULD GIVE THIS PRIORITY.
THIS IS AS DELICATE AN OPERATION AS ANY THAT HAS BEEN GIVEN YOU, AND HE SPECIFICALLY ASKED FOR YOU.
AND THAT THIS NOT BE DISCUSSED WITH ANYONE. JUST DONE QUICKLY.
AND... HIS WORD WAS: COLORFULLY.
COLORFULLY. I GOT YA.
COLORFULLY ISN'T A PROBLEM.
I GOT "COLORFUL" GUYS COMING OUT OF MY NOSE.
I TELL YA, RICHARD -- I KNOW I BEEN OUT OF THE LOOP FOR A BIT -- BUT IT'S NICE TO SEE YOU AND THE OLD MAN GETTING ALONG SO WELL.
ISN'T IT?
OKAY.
TELL YOUR DAD THE WORD IS OUT.

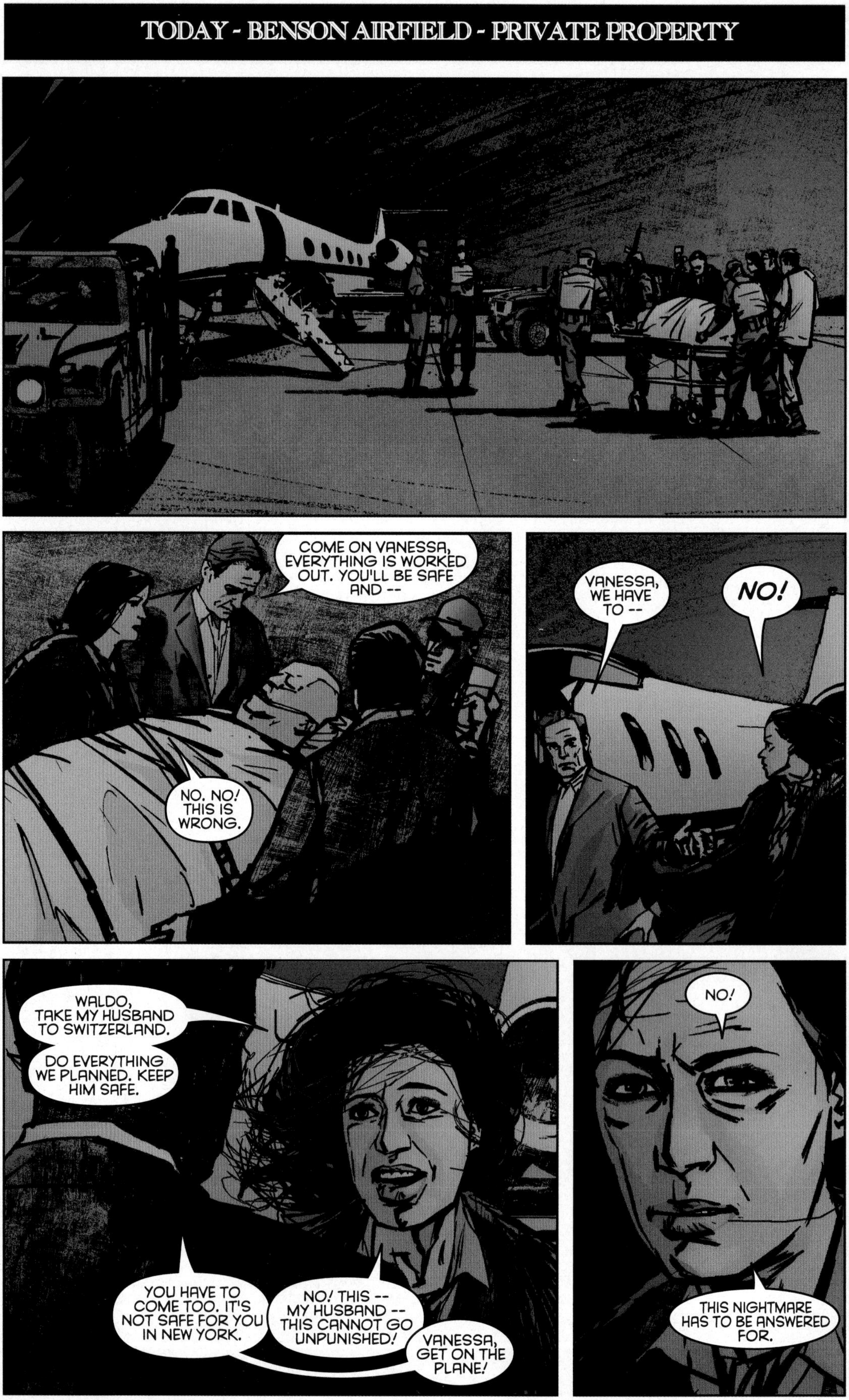
TODAY - BENSON AIRFIELD - PRIVATE PROPERTY
COME ON VANESSA, EVERYTHING IS WORKED OUT. YOU'LL BE SAFE AND --
NO. NO! THIS IS WRONG.
VANESSA, WE HAVE TO --
NO!
WALDO, TAKE MY HUSBAND TO SWITZERLAND.
DO EVERYTHING WE PLANNED. KEEP HIM SAFE.
YOU HAVE TO COME TOO. IT'S NOT SAFE FOR YOU IN NEW YORK.
NO! THIS -- MY HUSBAND -- THIS CANNOT GO UNPUNISHED!
VANESSA, GET ON THE PLANE!
NO!
THIS NIGHTMARE HAS TO BE ANSWERED FOR.

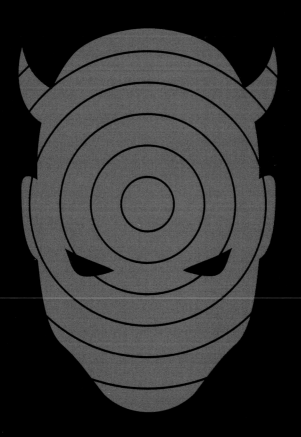

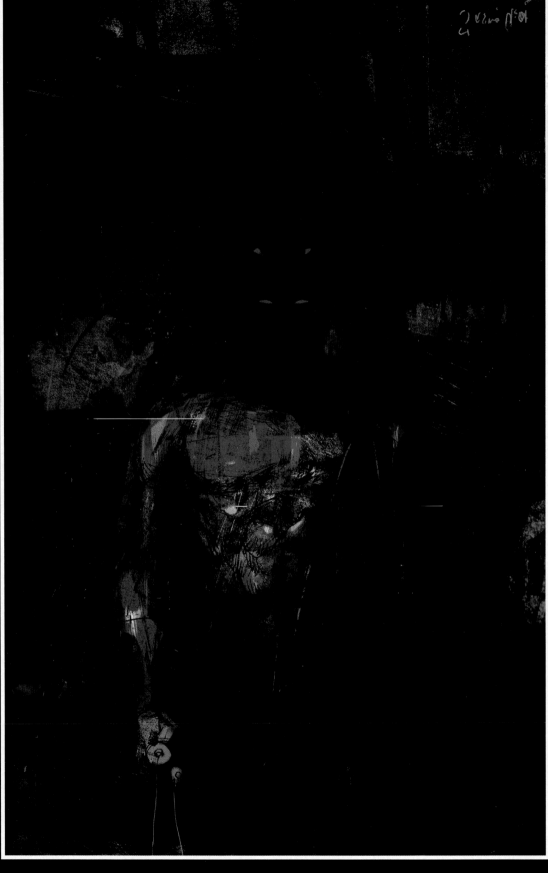

31

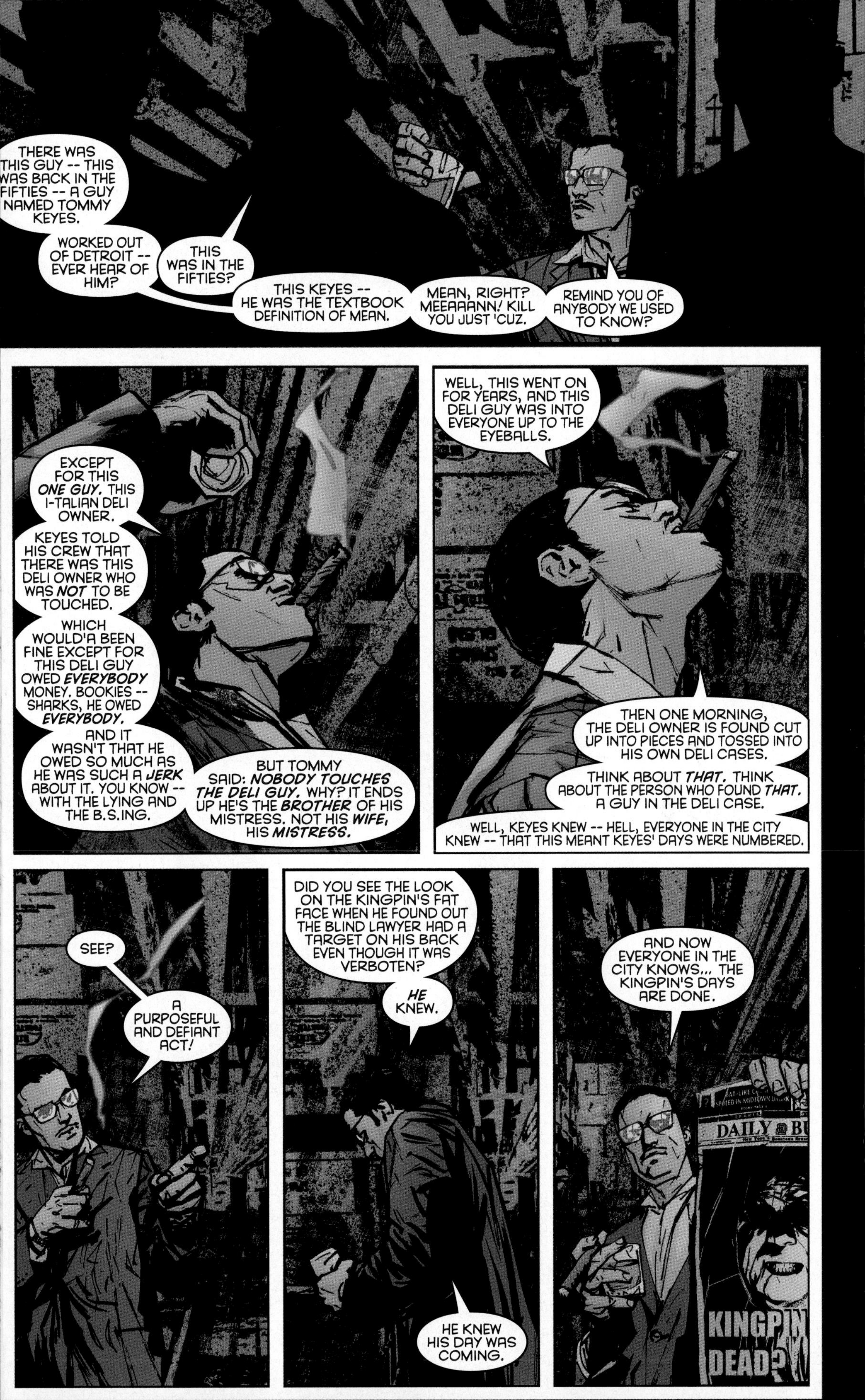

THERE WAS THIS GUY -- THIS WAS BACK IN THE FIFTIES -- A GUY NAMED TOMMY KEYES.
WORKED OUT OF DETROIT -- EVER HEAR OF HIM?
THIS WAS IN THE FIFTIES?
THIS KEYES -- HE WAS THE TEXTBOOK DEFINITION OF MEAN.
MEAN, RIGHT? MEEAAAANN! KILL YOU JUST 'CUZ.
REMIND YOU OF ANYBODY WE USED TO KNOW?
EXCEPT FOR THIS ONE GUY. THIS I-TALIAN DELI OWNER.
KEYES TOLD HIS CREW THAT THERE WAS THIS DELI OWNER WHO WAS NOT TO BE TOUCHED.
WHICH WOULD'A BEEN FINE EXCEPT FOR THIS DELI GUY OWED EVERYBODY MONEY. BOOKIES -- SHARKS, HE OWED EVERYBODY.
AND IT WASN'T THAT HE OWED SO MUCH AS HE WAS SUCH A JERK ABOUT IT. YOU KNOW -- WITH THE LYING AND THE B.S.ING.
BUT TOMMY SAID: NOBODY TOUCHES THE DELI GUY. WHY? IT ENDS UP HE'S THE BROTHER OF HIS MISTRESS. NOT HIS WIFE, HIS MISTRESS.
WELL, THIS WENT ON FOR YEARS, AND THIS DELI GUY WAS INTO EVERYONE UP TO THE EYEBALLS.
THEN ONE MORNING, THE DELI OWNER IS FOUND CUT UP INTO PIECES AND TOSSED INTO HIS OWN DELI CASES.
THINK ABOUT THAT. THINK ABOUT THE PERSON WHO FOUND THAT. A GUY IN THE DELI CASE.
WELL, KEYES KNEW -- HELL, EVERYONE IN THE CITY KNEW -- THAT THIS MEANT KEYES' DAYS WERE NUMBERED.
SEE?
A PURPOSEFUL AND DEFIANT ACT!
DID YOU SEE THE LOOK ON THE KINGPIN'S FAT FACE WHEN HE FOUND OUT THE BLIND LAWYER HAD A TARGET ON HIS BACK EVEN THOUGH IT WAS VERBOTEN?
HE KNEW.
HE KNEW HIS DAY WAS COMING.
AND NOW EVERYONE IN THE CITY KNOWS... THE KINGPIN'S DAYS ARE DONE.
DAILY BU
KINGPIN DEAD?

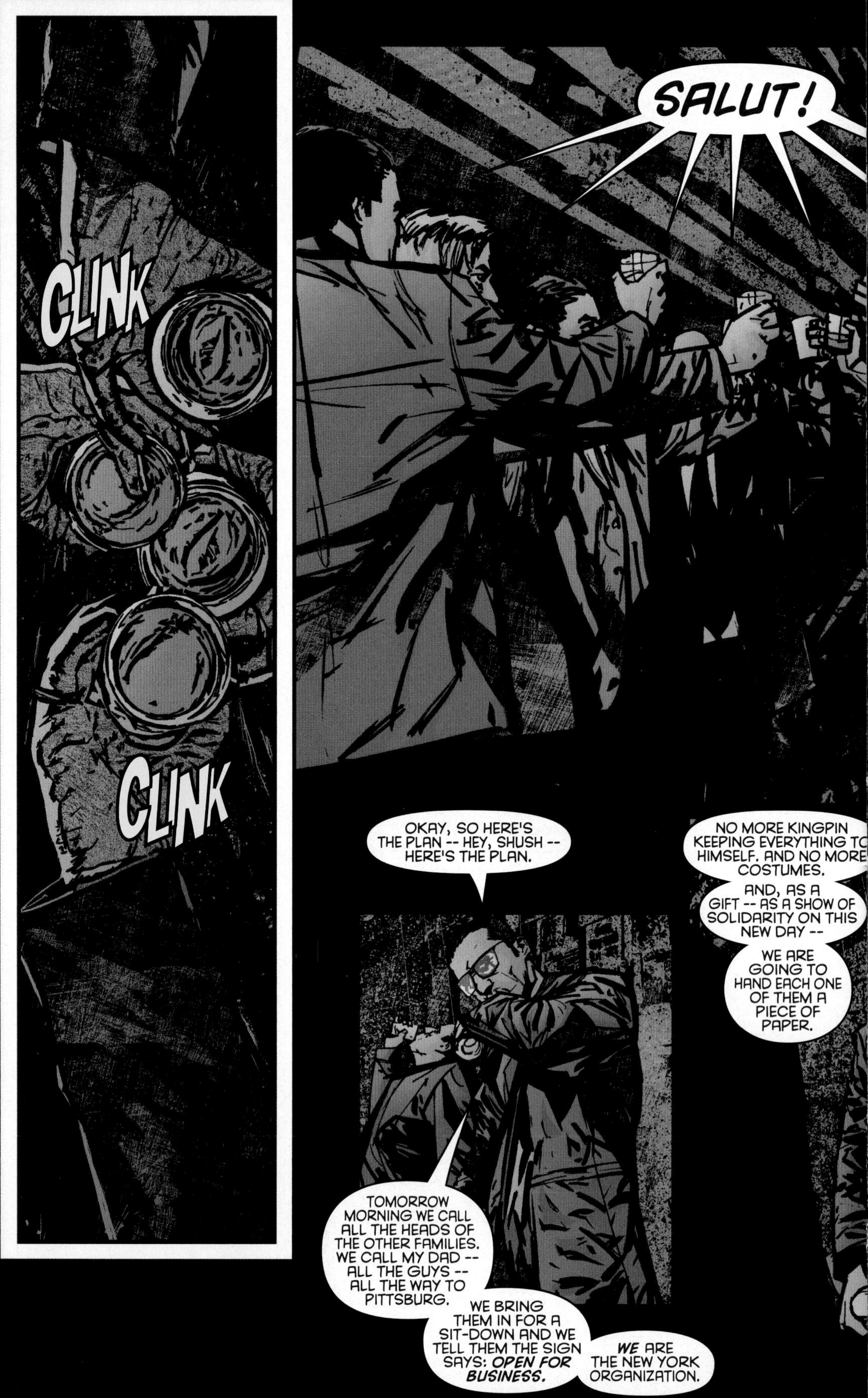
CLINK
CLINK
SALUT!
OKAY, SO HERE'S THE PLAN -- HEY, SHUSH -- HERE'S THE PLAN.
TOMORROW MORNING WE CALL ALL THE HEADS OF THE OTHER FAMILIES. WE CALL MY DAD -- ALL THE GUYS -- ALL THE WAY TO PITTSBURG.
WE BRING THEM IN FOR A SIT-DOWN AND WE TELL THEM THE SIGN SAYS: OPEN FOR BUSINESS.
WE ARE THE NEW YORK ORGANIZATION.
NO MORE KINGPIN KEEPING EVERYTHING TO HIMSELF. AND NO MORE COSTUMES.
AND, AS A GIFT -- AS A SHOW OF SOLIDARITY ON THIS NEW DAY --
WE ARE GOING TO HAND EACH ONE OF THEM A PIECE OF PAPER.

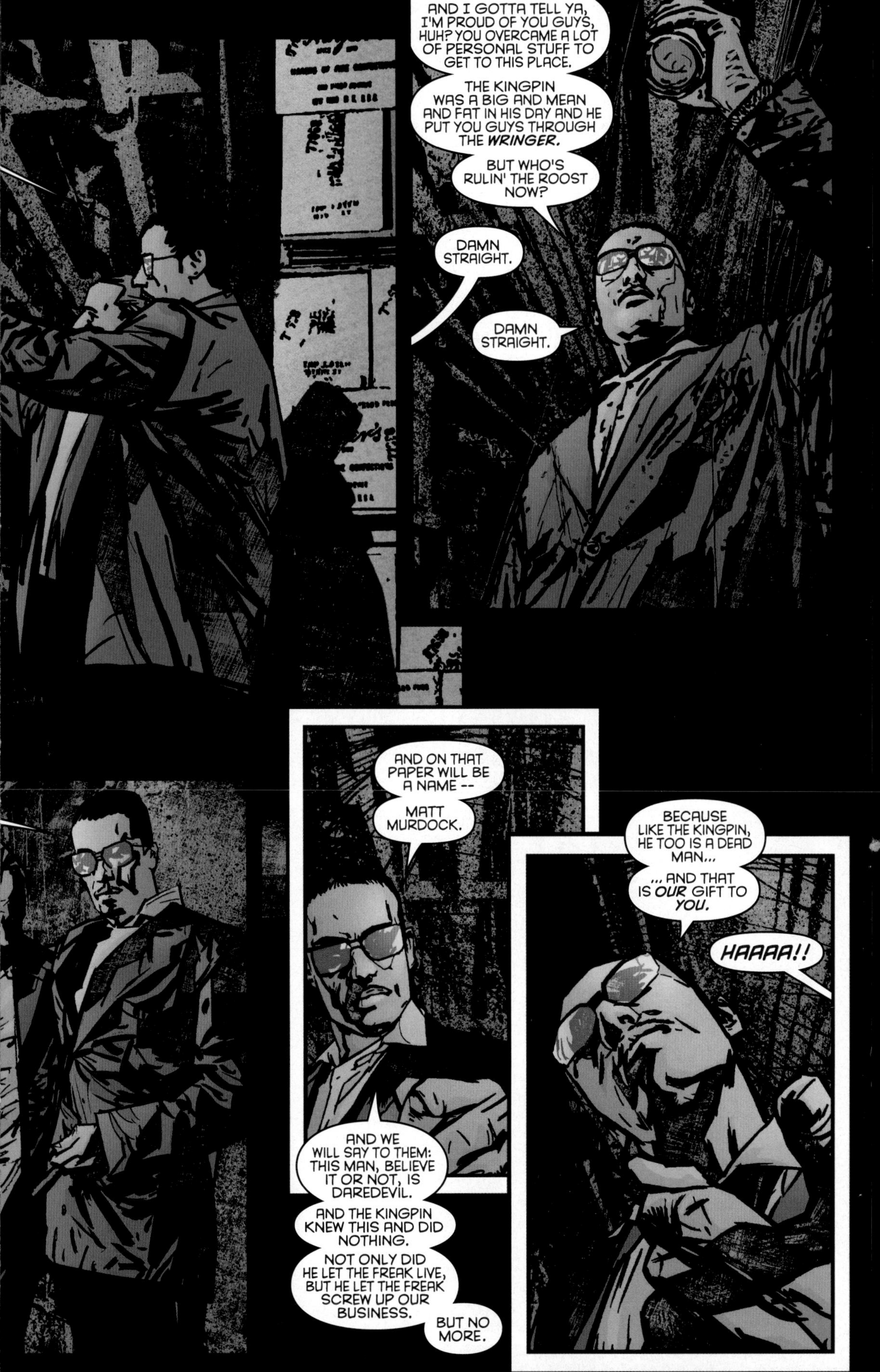
AND I GOTTA TELL YA, I'M PROUD OF YOU GUYS, HUH? YOU OVERCAME A LOT OF PERSONAL STUFF TO GET TO THIS PLACE.
THE KINGPIN WAS A BIG AND MEAN AND FAT IN HIS DAY AND HE PUT YOU GUYS THROUGH THE WRINGER.
BUT WHO'S RULIN' THE ROOST NOW?
DAMN STRAIGHT.
DAMN STRAIGHT.
AND ON THAT PAPER WILL BE A NAME --
MATT MURDOCK.
AND WE WILL SAY TO THEM: THIS MAN, BELIEVE IT OR NOT, IS DAREDEVIL.
AND THE KINGPIN KNEW THIS AND DID NOTHING.
NOT ONLY DID HE LET THE FREAK LIVE, BUT HE LET THE FREAK SCREW UP OUR BUSINESS.
BUT NO MORE.
BECAUSE LIKE THE KINGPIN, HE TOO IS A DEAD MAN...
...AND THAT IS OUR GIFT TO YOU.
HAAAA!!

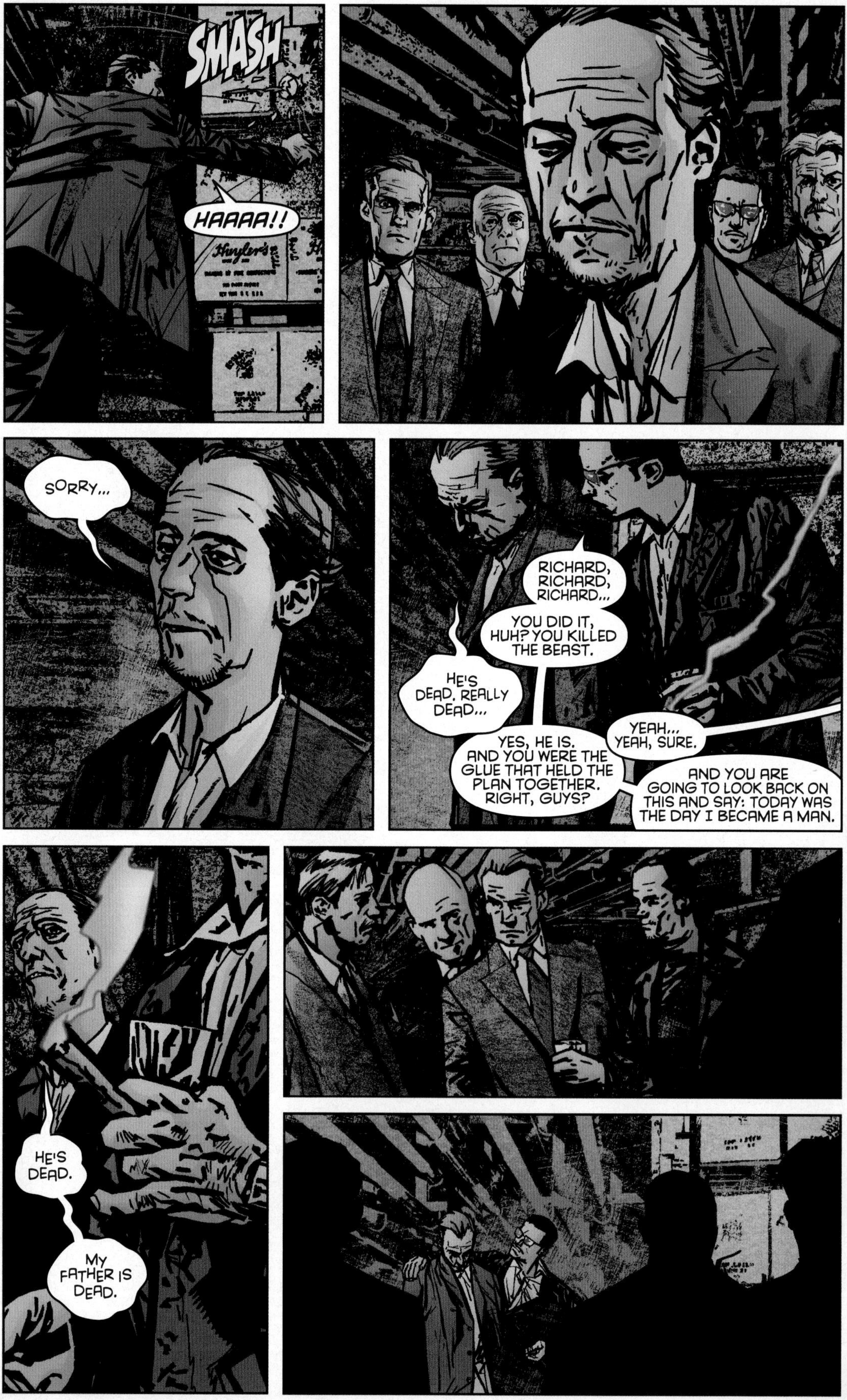
SMASH
HAAAA!!
SORRY...
RICHARD, RICHARD, RICHARD...
YOU DID IT, HUH? YOU KILLED THE BEAST.
HE'S DEAD. REALLY DEAD...
YES, HE IS. AND YOU WERE THE GLUE THAT HELD THE PLAN TOGETHER. RIGHT, GUYS?
YEAH... YEAH, SURE.
AND YOU ARE GOING TO LOOK BACK ON THIS AND SAY: TODAY WAS THE DAY I BECAME A MAN.
HE'S DEAD.
MY FATHER IS DEAD.

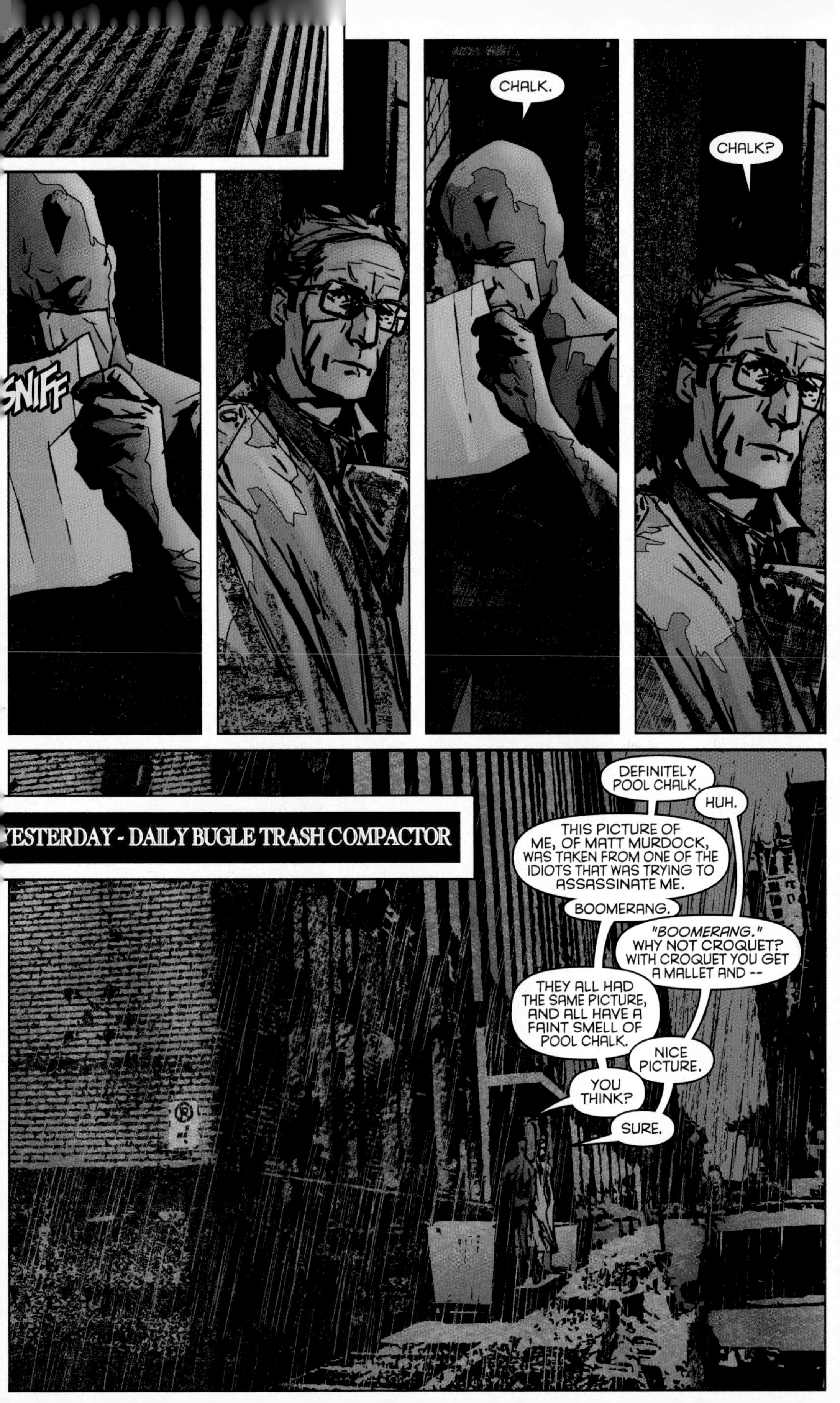
SNIFF
CHALK.
CHALK?
YESTERDAY - DAILY BUGLE TRASH COMPACTOR
DEFINITELY POOL CHALK.
HUH.
THIS PICTURE OF ME, OF MATT MURDOCK, WAS TAKEN FROM ONE OF THE IDIOTS THAT WAS TRYING TO ASSASSINATE ME.
BOOMERANG.
"BOOMERANG." WHY NOT CROQUET? WITH CROQUET YOU GET A MALLET AND --
THEY ALL HAD THE SAME PICTURE, AND ALL HAVE A FAINT SMELL OF POOL CHALK.
NICE PICTURE.
YOU THINK?
SURE.

POOL CHALK.

HIRED KILLERS...

OH, DUH, HEY. FALZONE.

FALZONE?

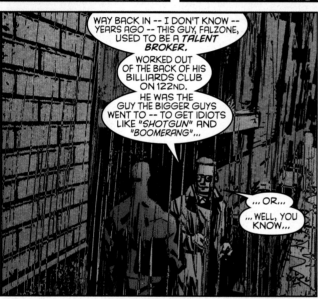

WAY BACK IN -- I DON'T KNOW -- YEARS AGO -- THIS GUY, FALZONE, USED TO BE A *TALENT BROKER.*

WORKED OUT OF THE BACK OF HIS BILLIARDS CLUB ON 122ND.

HE WAS THE GUY THE BIGGER GUYS WENT TO -- TO GET IDIOTS LIKE *"SHOTGUN"* AND *"BOOMERANG"*...

... OR...

... WELL, YOU KNOW...

YOU CAN SAY IT...

... OR *"ELEKTRA."*

IF YOU WANTED SOMEONE BUMPED OFF BY A GUY IN AN OUTFIT -- A SPECIALTY ACT -- YOU'D GO TO FALZONE.

AND THEN HE'D GO TO THE GUY WHO'D GO TO THEIR GUY.

BUT THIS WAS YEEEEARS AGO. GUY HAD A FALL FROM GRACE.

I NEVER HEARD OF THIS GUY.

THERE'S FOUR BILLION GUYS LIKE THIS IN JERSEY ALONE -- SO ONE YOU DON'T KNOW.

HOW DO *YOU* KNOW ABOUT HIM?

I'M A REPORTER FOR A MAJOR METROPOLITAN NEWSPAPER. I FOUND OUT.

I FOUND OUT YOUR SECRET IDENTITY, DIDN'T I?

AND THIS FALZONE?

I'M SURE IT'S UPSTAIRS IN THE COMPUTER.

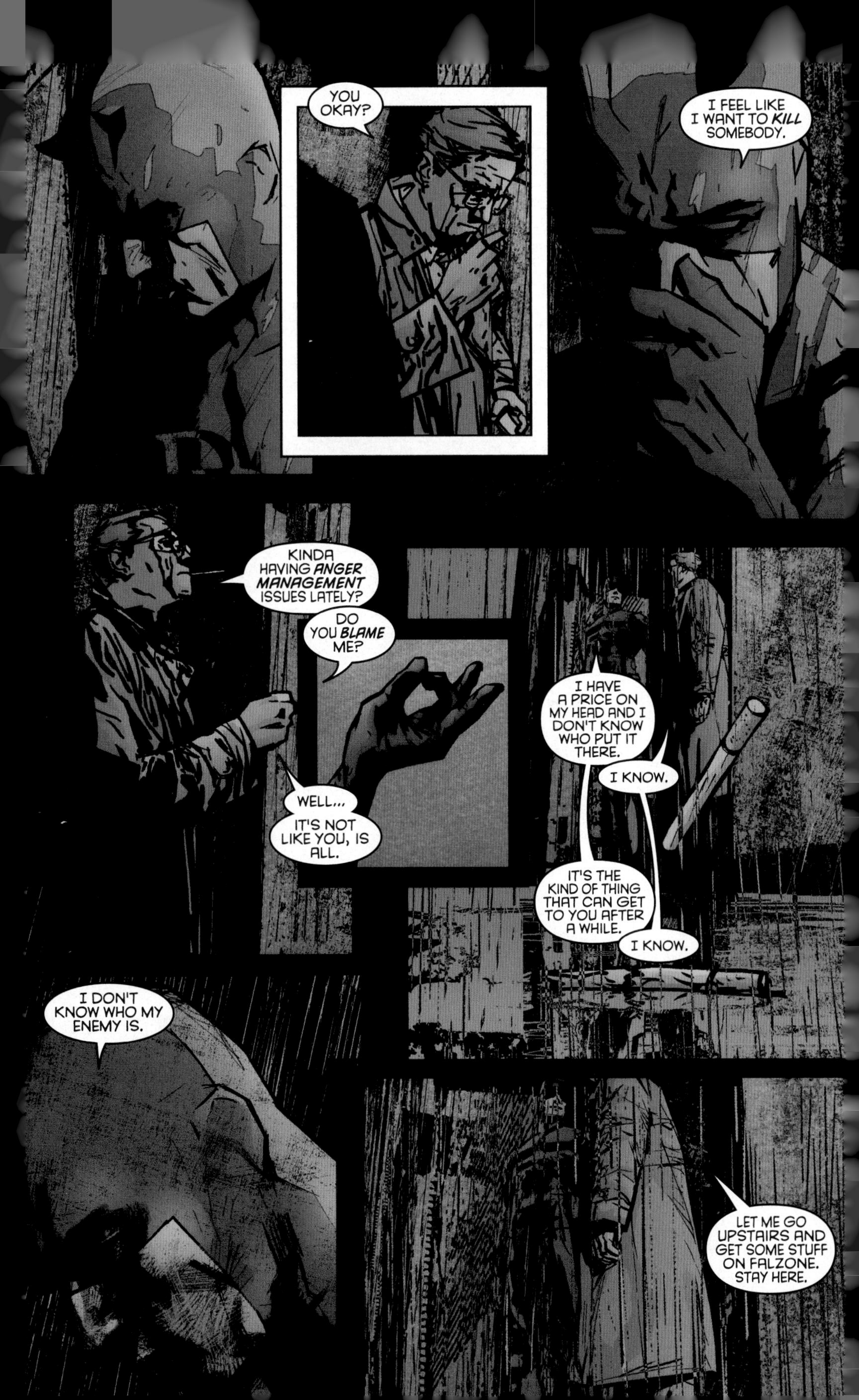
YOU OKAY?
I FEEL LIKE I WANT TO KILL SOMEBODY.
KINDA HAVING ANGER MANAGEMENT ISSUES LATELY?
DO YOU BLAME ME?
WELL...
IT'S NOT LIKE YOU, IS ALL.
I HAVE A PRICE ON MY HEAD AND I DON'T KNOW WHO PUT IT THERE.
I KNOW.
IT'S THE KIND OF THING THAT CAN GET TO YOU AFTER A WHILE.
I KNOW.
I DON'T KNOW WHO MY ENEMY IS.
LET ME GO UPSTAIRS AND GET SOME STUFF ON FALZONE. STAY HERE.

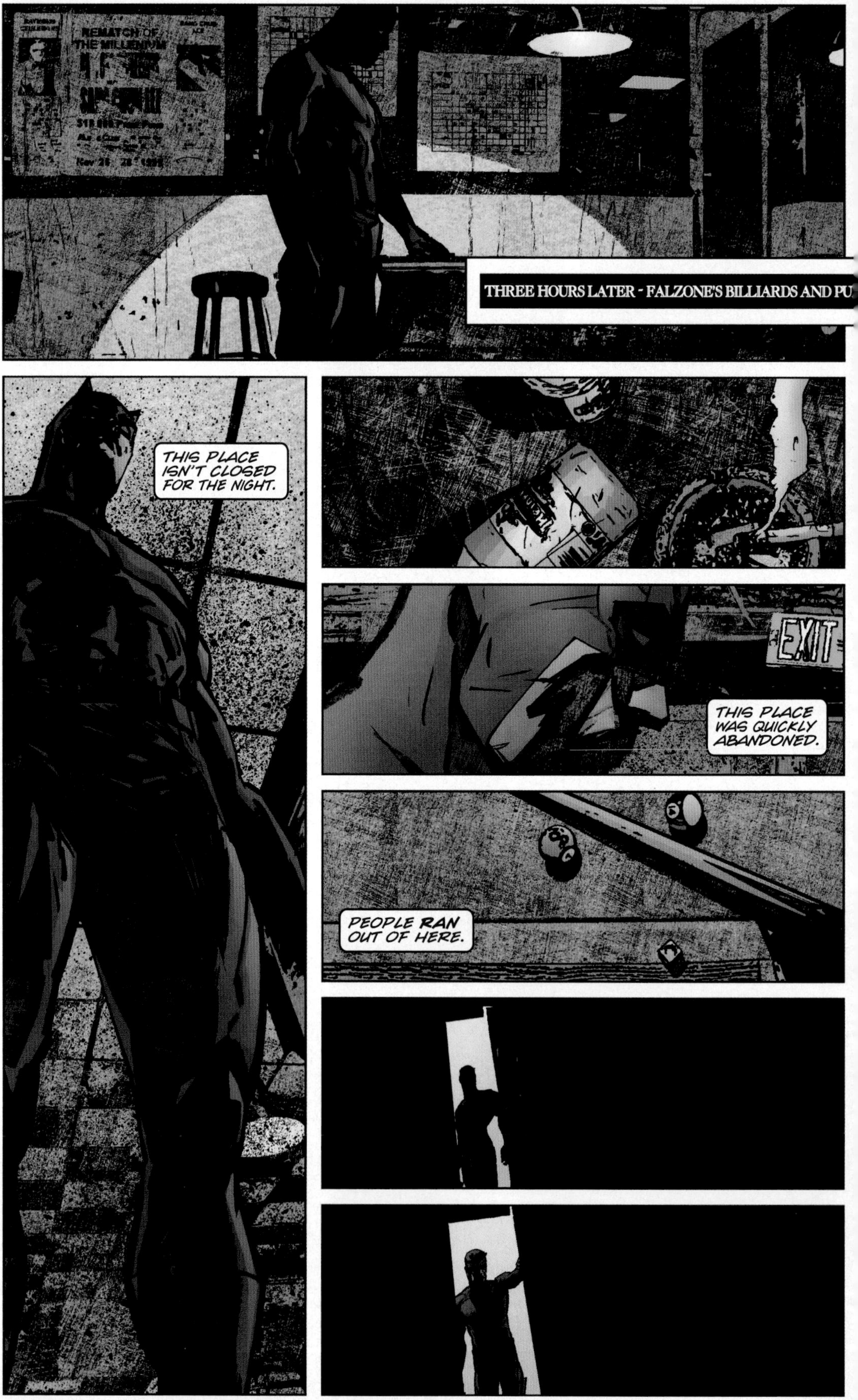
REMATCH OF THE MILLENNIUM
THREE HOURS LATER - FALZONE'S BILLIARDS AND PU
THIS PLACE ISN'T CLOSED FOR THE NIGHT.
THIS PLACE WAS QUICKLY ABANDONED.
EXIT
PEOPLE RAN OUT OF HERE.

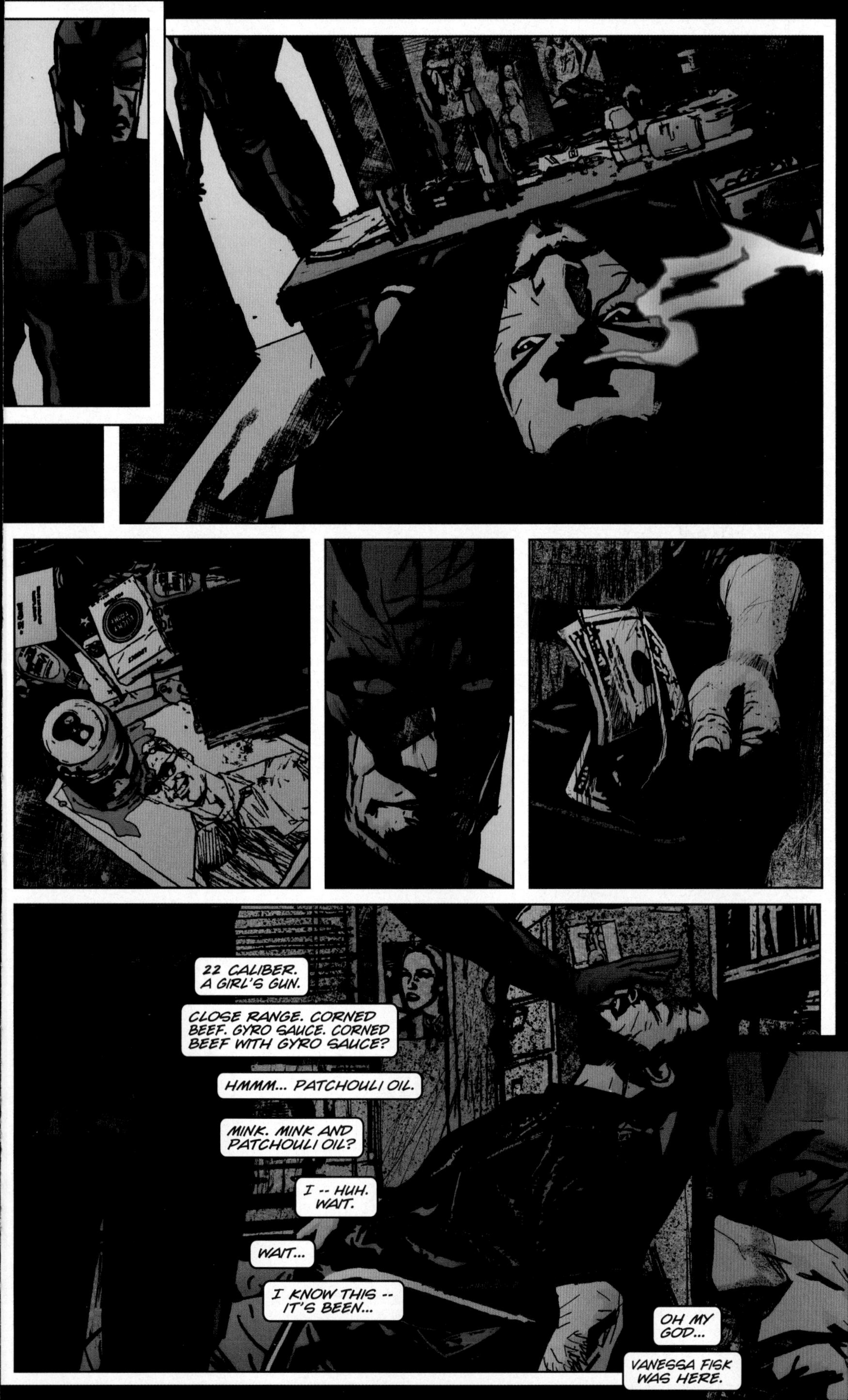
22 CALIBER. A GIRL'S GUN.
CLOSE RANGE. CORNED BEEF. GYRO SAUCE. CORNED BEEF WITH GYRO SAUCE?
HMMM... PATCHOULI OIL.
MINK. MINK AND PATCHOULI OIL?
I -- HUH. WAIT.
WAIT...
I KNOW THIS -- IT'S BEEN...
OH MY GOD...
VANESSA FISK WAS HERE.

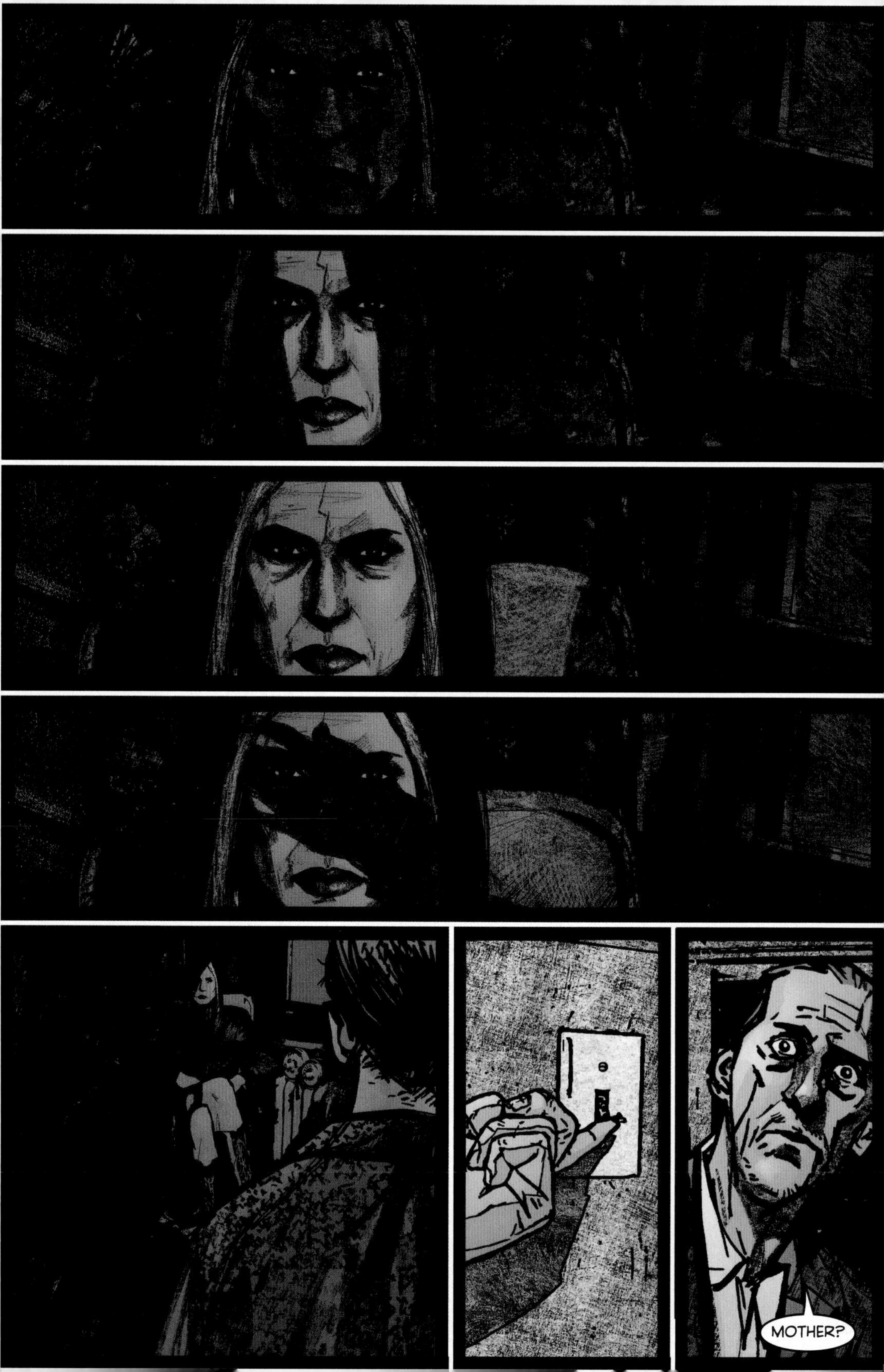
MOTHER?

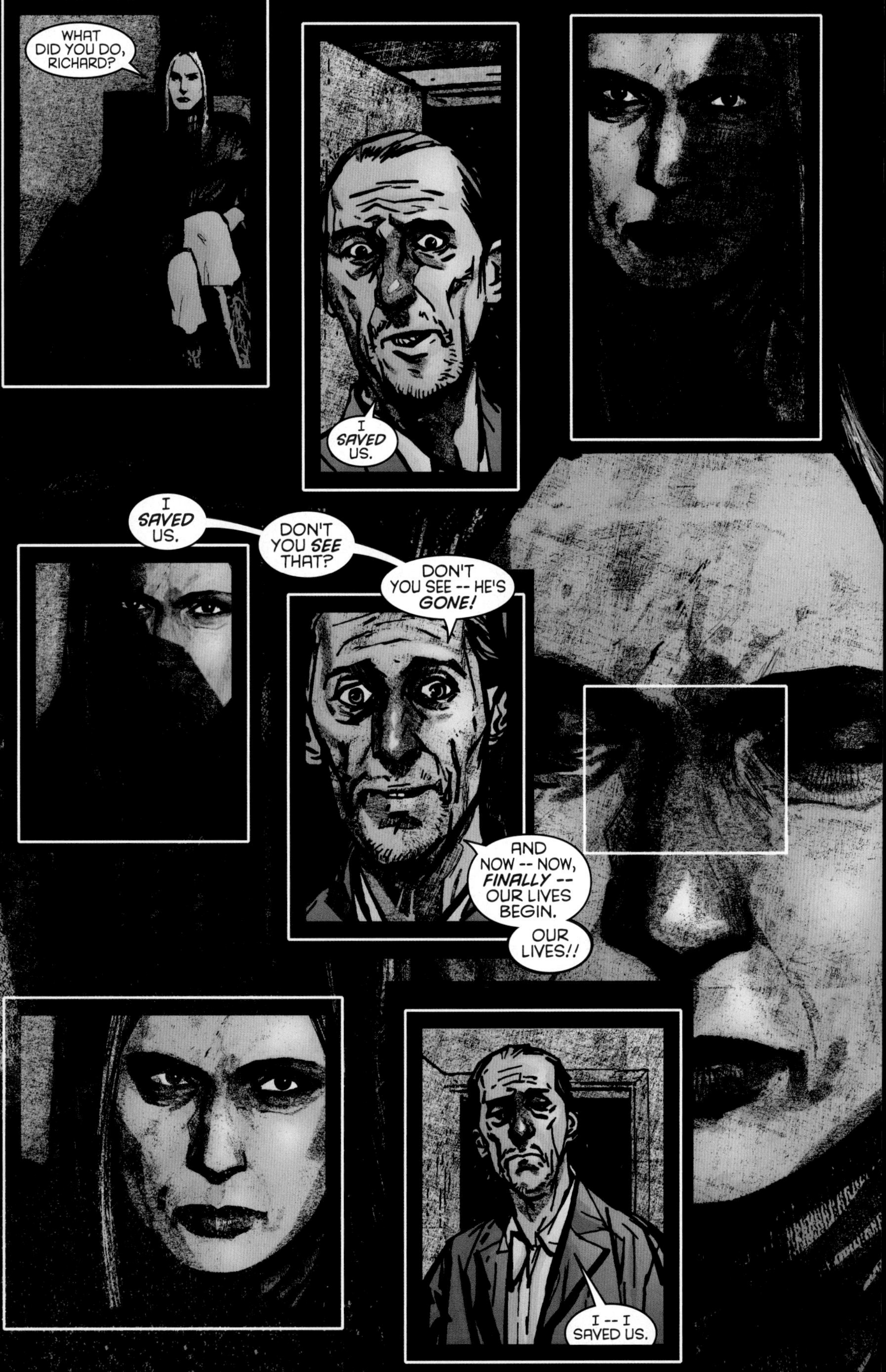
WHAT DID YOU DO, RICHARD?
I SAVED US.
I SAVED US.
DON'T YOU SEE THAT?
DON'T YOU SEE -- HE'S GONE!
AND NOW -- NOW, FINALLY -- OUR LIVES BEGIN.
OUR LIVES!!
I -- I SAVED US.

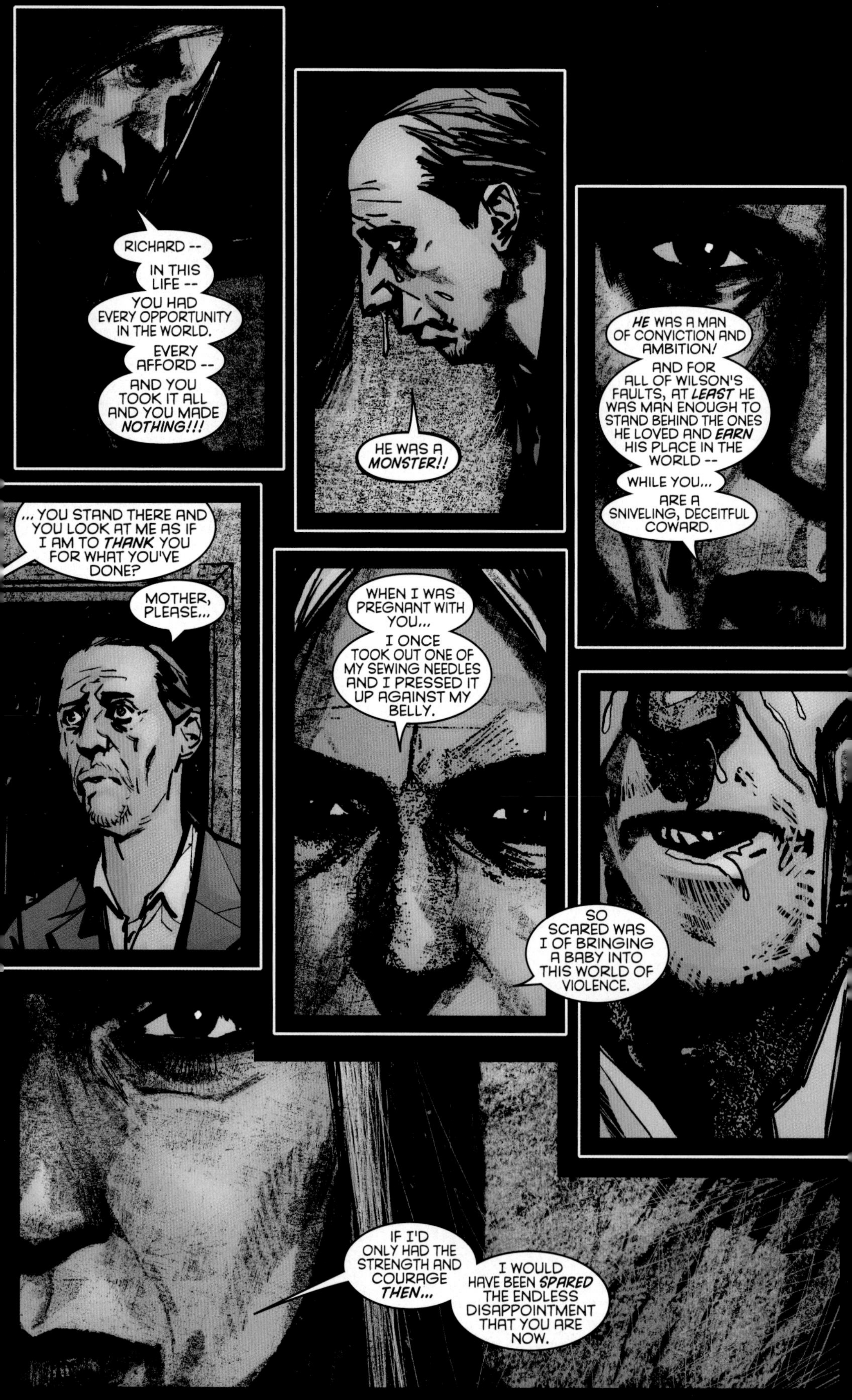
RICHARD --
IN THIS LIFE --
YOU HAD EVERY OPPORTUNITY IN THE WORLD.
EVERY AFFORD --
AND YOU TOOK IT ALL AND YOU MADE *NOTHING!!!*
HE WAS A *MONSTER!!*
HE WAS A MAN OF CONVICTION AND AMBITION!
AND FOR ALL OF WILSON'S FAULTS, AT *LEAST* HE WAS MAN ENOUGH TO STAND BEHIND THE ONES HE LOVED AND *EARN* HIS PLACE IN THE WORLD --
WHILE YOU...
ARE A SNIVELING, DECEITFUL COWARD.
...YOU STAND THERE AND YOU LOOK AT ME AS IF I AM TO *THANK* YOU FOR WHAT YOU'VE DONE?
MOTHER, PLEASE...
WHEN I WAS PREGNANT WITH YOU...
I ONCE TOOK OUT ONE OF MY SEWING NEEDLES AND I PRESSED IT UP AGAINST MY BELLY.
SO SCARED WAS I OF BRINGING A BABY INTO THIS WORLD OF VIOLENCE.
IF I'D ONLY HAD THE STRENGTH AND COURAGE *THEN...*
I WOULD HAVE BEEN *SPARED* THE ENDLESS DISAPPOINTMENT THAT YOU ARE NOW.

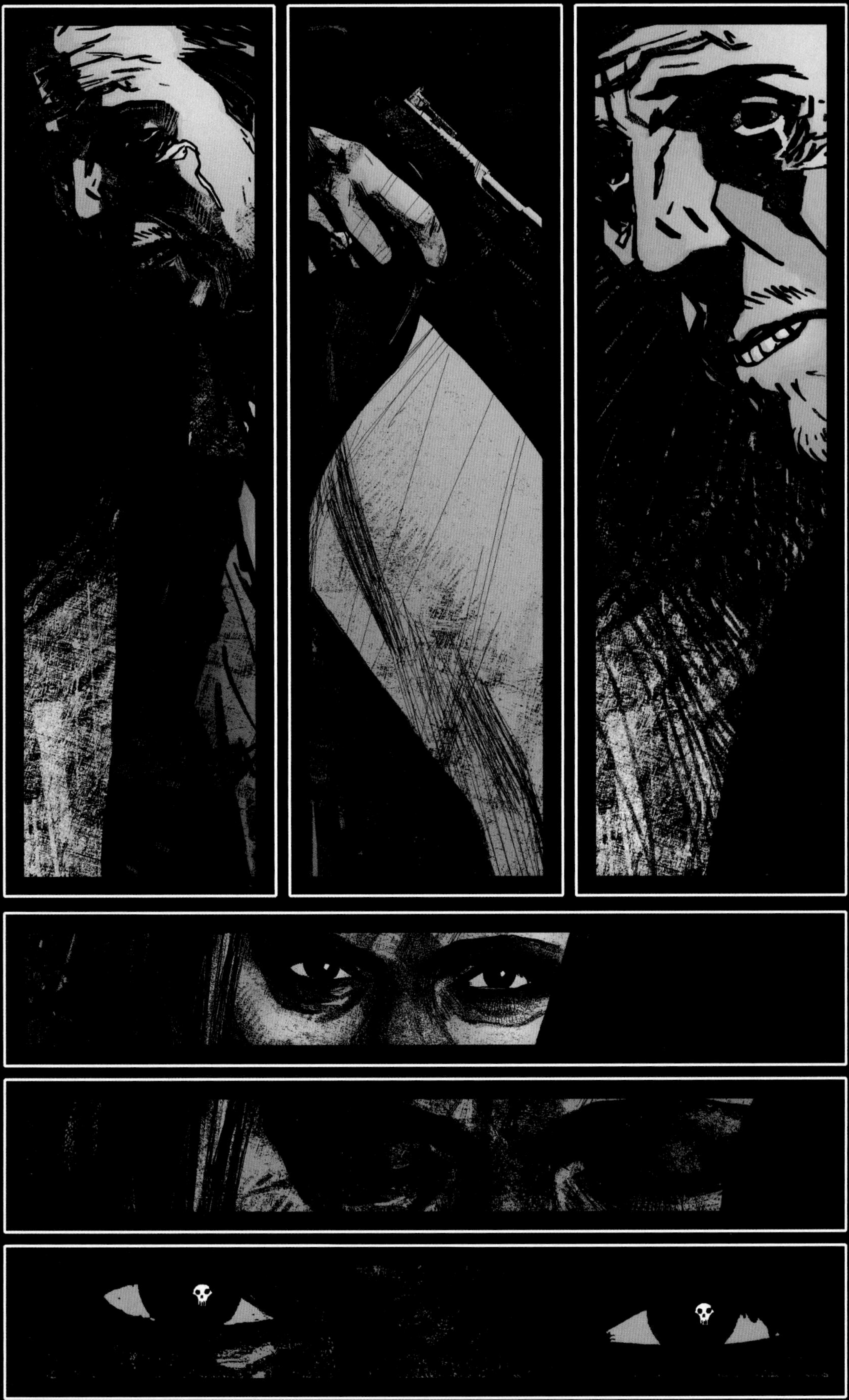

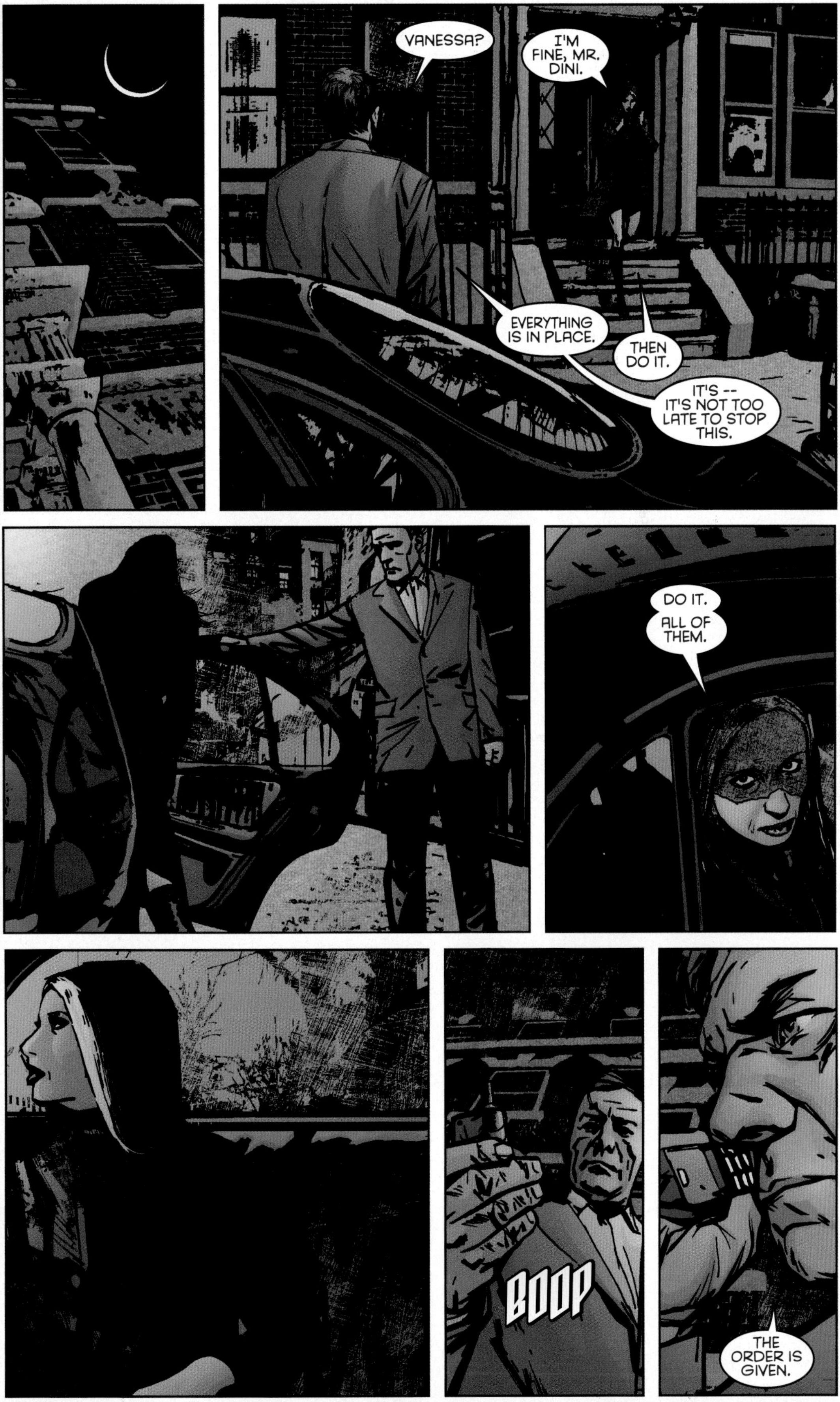
VANESSA?
I'M FINE, MR. DINI.
EVERYTHING IS IN PLACE.
THEN DO IT.
IT'S -- IT'S NOT TOO LATE TO STOP THIS.
DO IT.
ALL OF THEM.
BOOP
THE ORDER IS GIVEN.

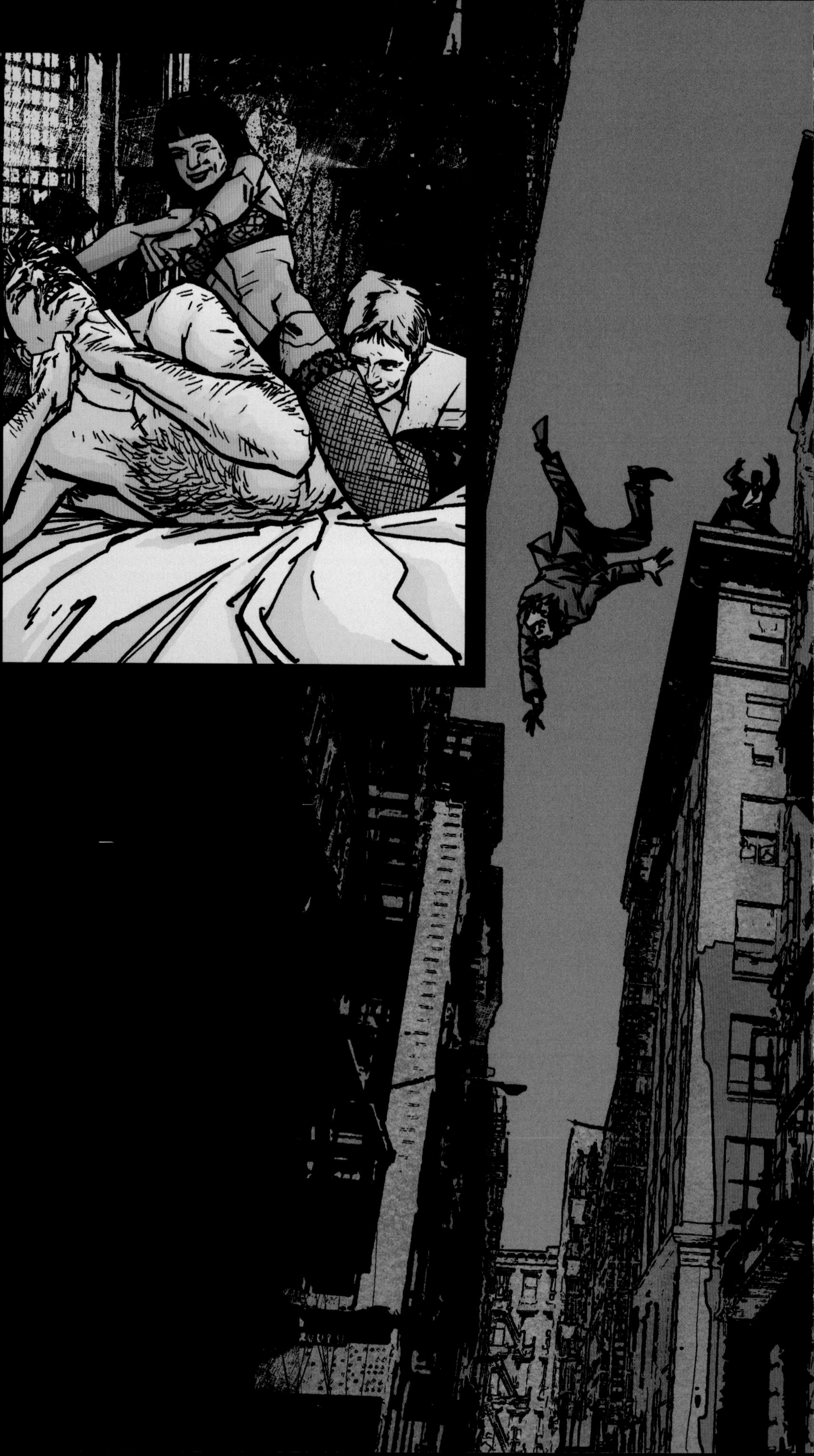

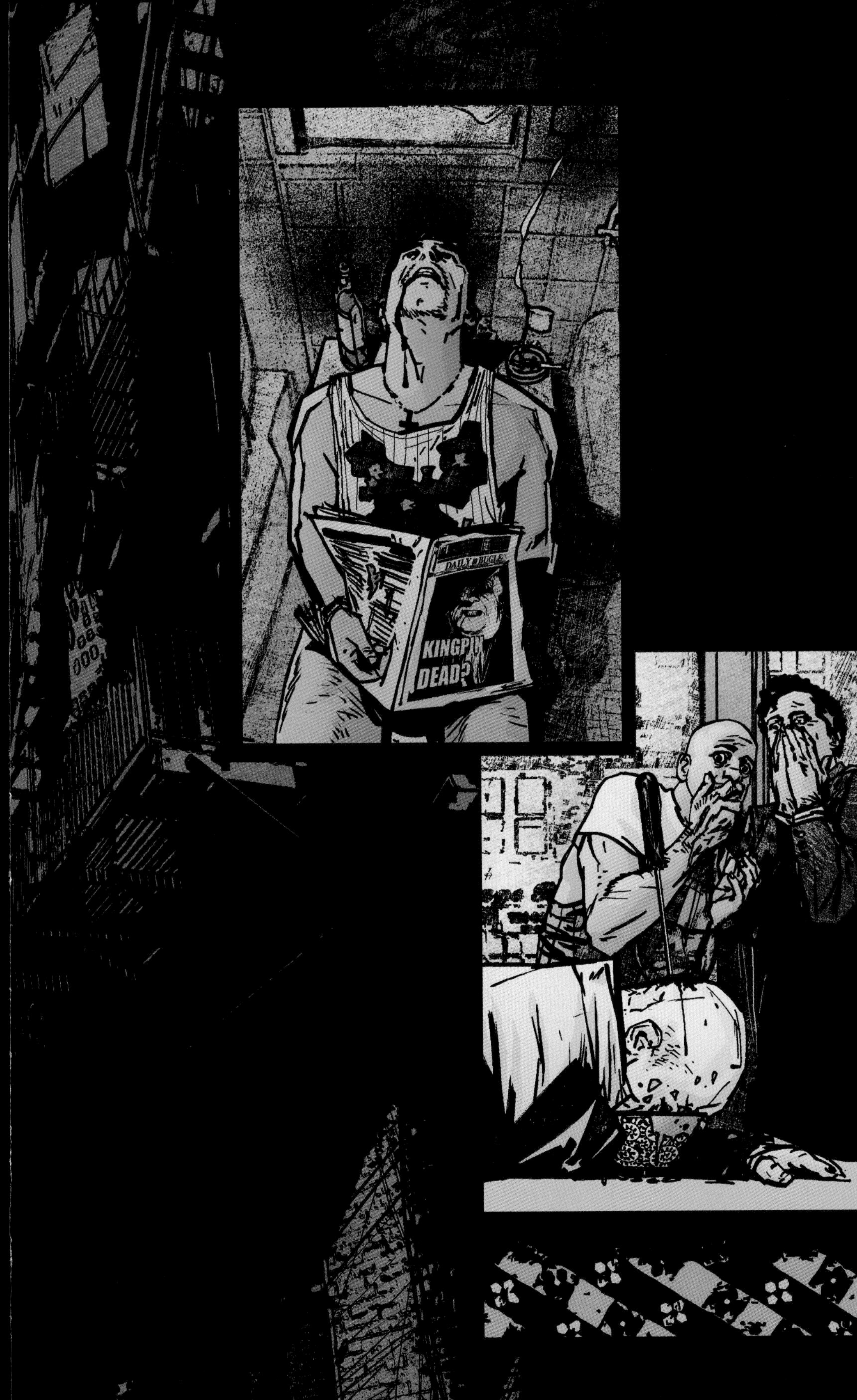
DAILY BUGLE
KINGPIN DEAD?

JUST UNTIL I CAN AFFORD TO PUT MYSELF THROUGH MEDICAL SCHOOL.

UH-HUH.

I'M GOING TO BE A MASSAGE THERAPIST. DO YOU KNOW WHAT THAT IS?

LISTEN, TOOTS, WHEN WE GET IN THE ROOM, LET'S KEEP THE CHIT-CHAT TO A MIN...

CLUMP

...IMUM...

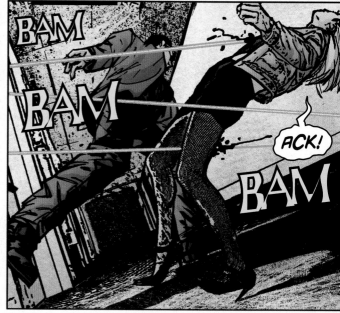

BAM

BAM

ACK!

BAM

BAM BAM

BAM BAM

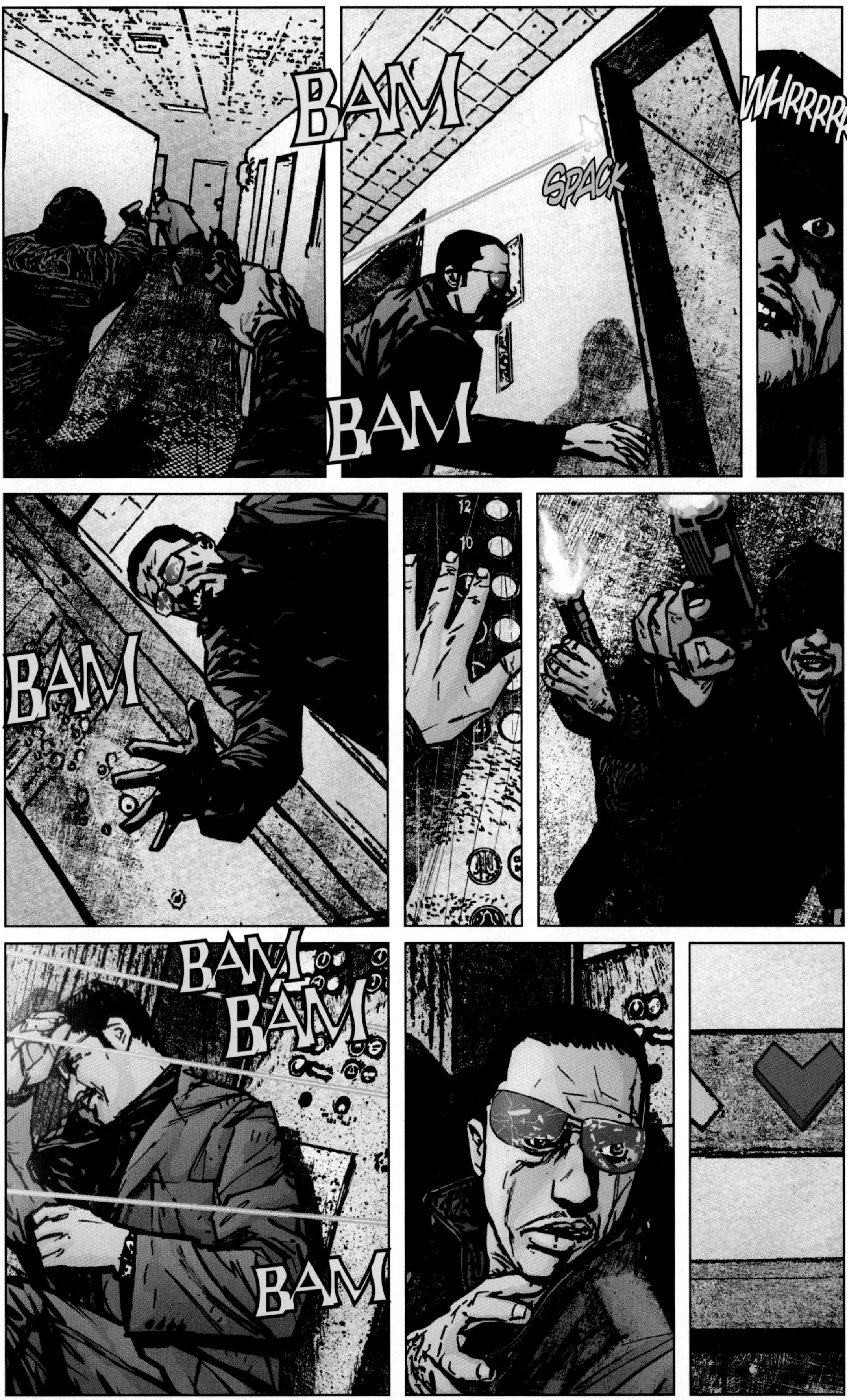
BAM
SPACK
BAM
WHRRRRR
BAM
BAM
BAM
BAM

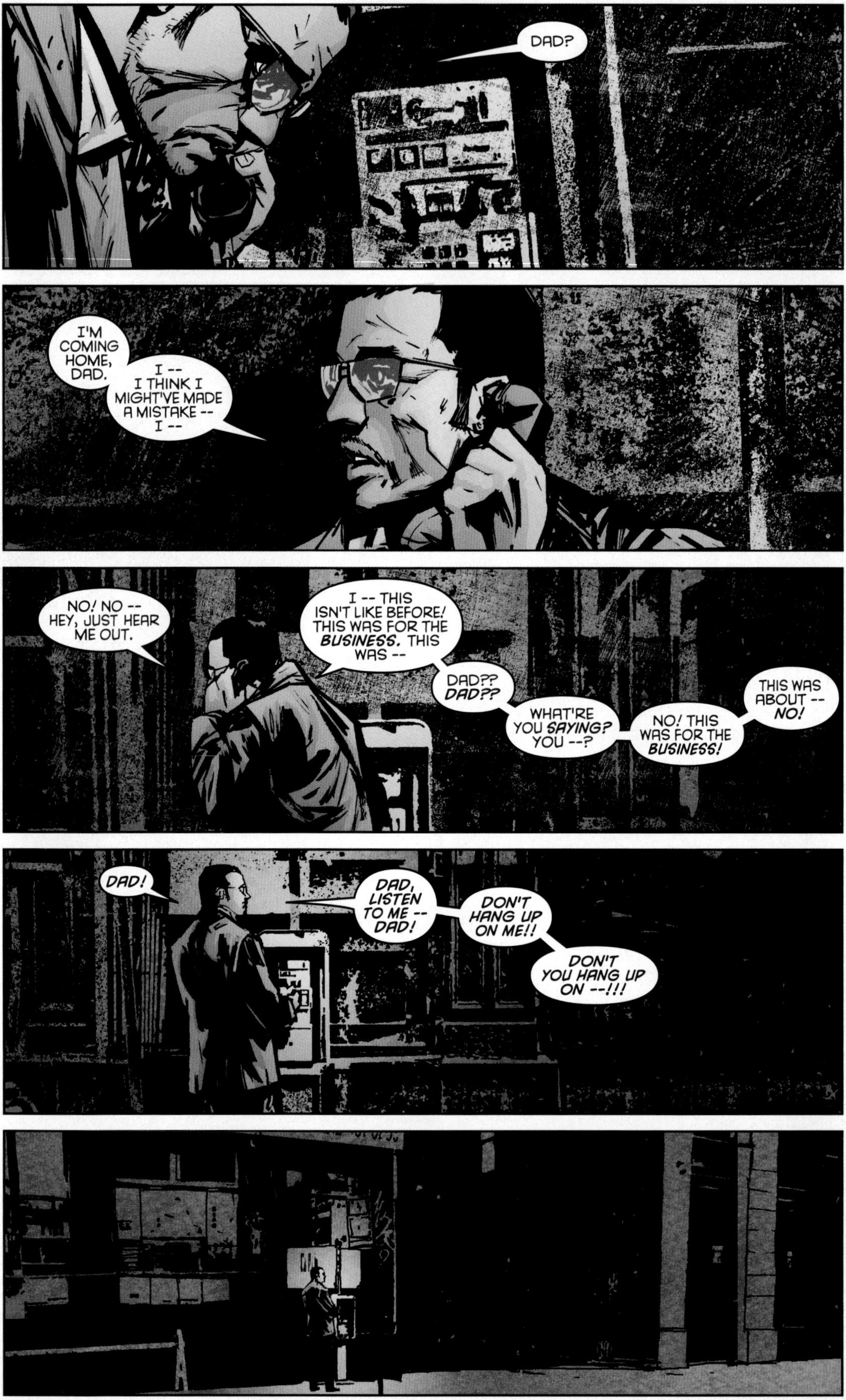
DAD?
I'M COMING HOME, DAD.
I -- I THINK I MIGHT'VE MADE A MISTAKE -- I --
NO! NO -- HEY, JUST HEAR ME OUT.
I -- THIS ISN'T LIKE BEFORE! THIS WAS FOR THE *BUSINESS.* THIS WAS --
DAD?? *DAD??*
WHAT'RE YOU *SAYING?* YOU --?
NO! THIS WAS FOR THE *BUSINESS!*
THIS WAS ABOUT -- *NO!*
DAD!
DAD, LISTEN TO ME -- DAD!
DON'T HANG UP ON ME!!
DON'T YOU HANG UP ON --!!!

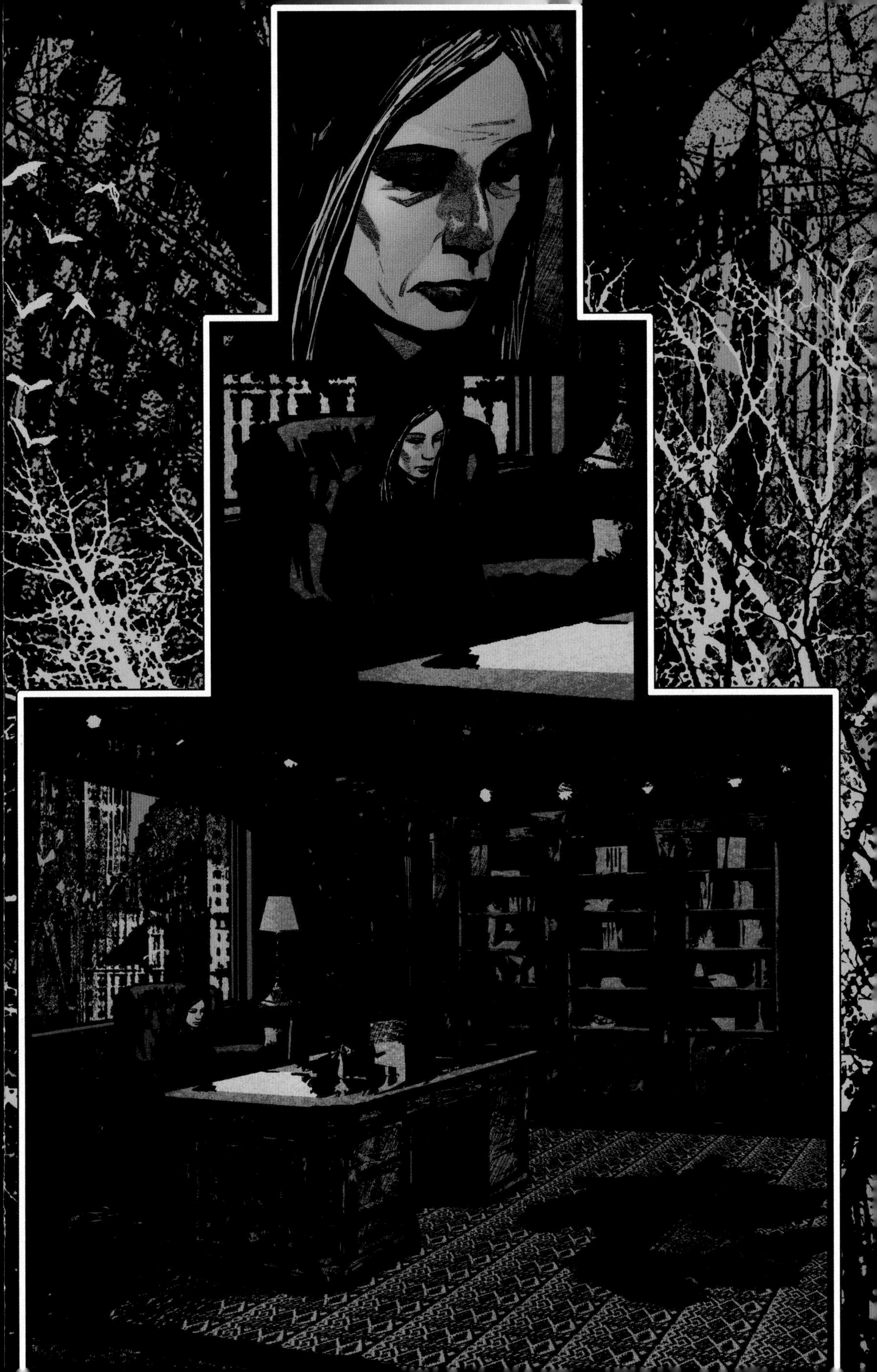

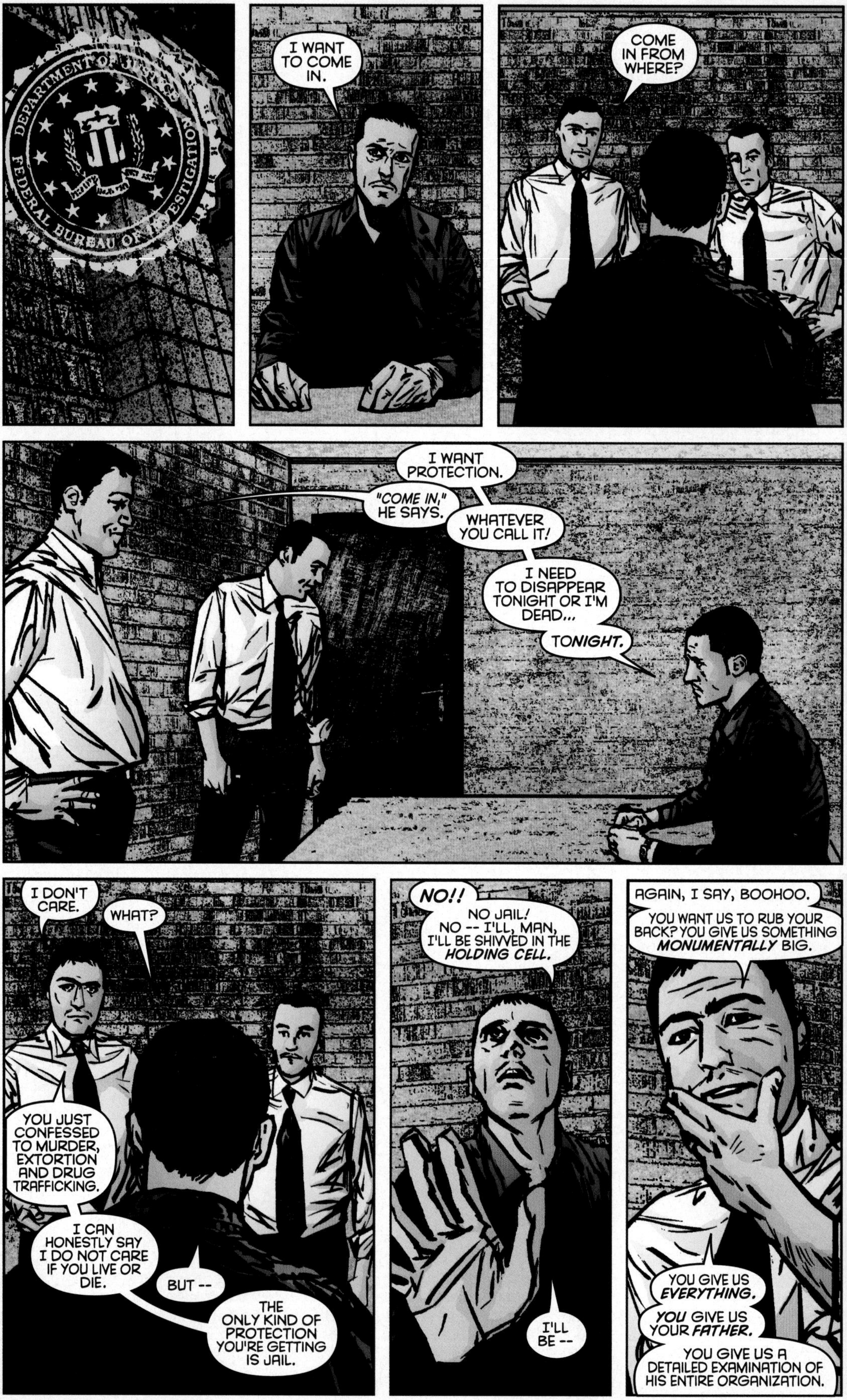
DEPARTMENT OF JUSTICE
FEDERAL BUREAU OF INVESTIGATION
I WANT TO COME IN.
COME IN FROM WHERE?
I WANT PROTECTION.
"COME IN," HE SAYS.
WHATEVER YOU CALL IT!
I NEED TO DISAPPEAR TONIGHT OR I'M DEAD...
TONIGHT.
I DON'T CARE.
WHAT?
YOU JUST CONFESSED TO MURDER, EXTORTION AND DRUG TRAFFICKING.
I CAN HONESTLY SAY I DO NOT CARE IF YOU LIVE OR DIE.
BUT --
THE ONLY KIND OF PROTECTION YOU'RE GETTING IS JAIL.
NO!!
NO JAIL! NO -- I'LL, MAN, I'LL BE SHIVVED IN THE HOLDING CELL.
I'LL BE --
AGAIN, I SAY, BOOHOO.
YOU WANT US TO RUB YOUR BACK? YOU GIVE US SOMETHING MONUMENTALLY BIG.
YOU GIVE US EVERYTHING.
YOU GIVE US YOUR FATHER.
YOU GIVE US A DETAILED EXAMINATION OF HIS ENTIRE ORGANIZATION.

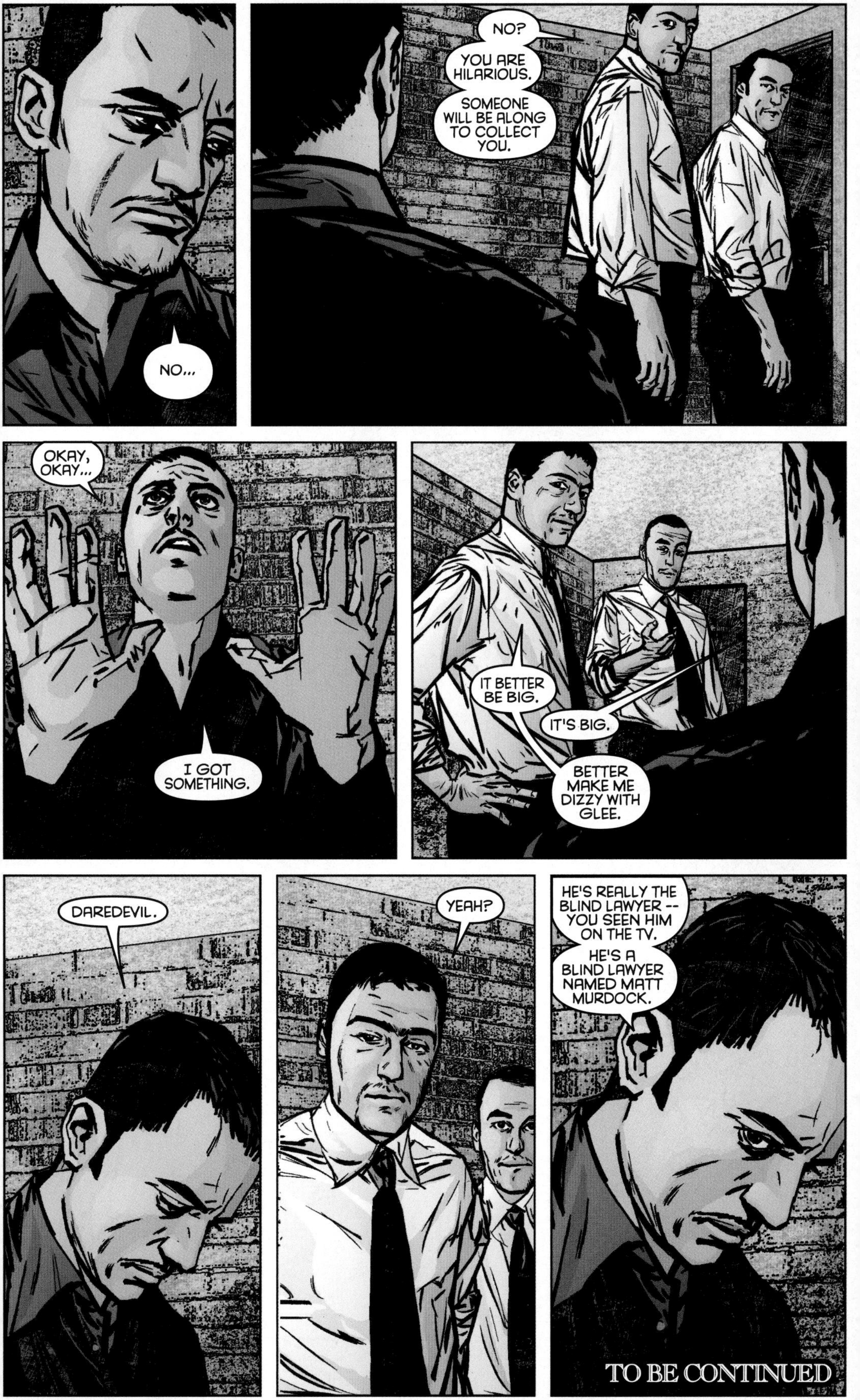
NO...
NO?
YOU ARE HILARIOUS.
SOMEONE WILL BE ALONG TO COLLECT YOU.
OKAY, OKAY...
I GOT SOMETHING.
IT BETTER BE BIG.
IT'S BIG.
BETTER MAKE ME DIZZY WITH GLEE.
DAREDEVIL.
YEAH?
HE'S REALLY THE BLIND LAWYER -- YOU SEEN HIM ON THE TV.
HE'S A BLIND LAWYER NAMED MATT MURDOCK.
TO BE CONTINUED

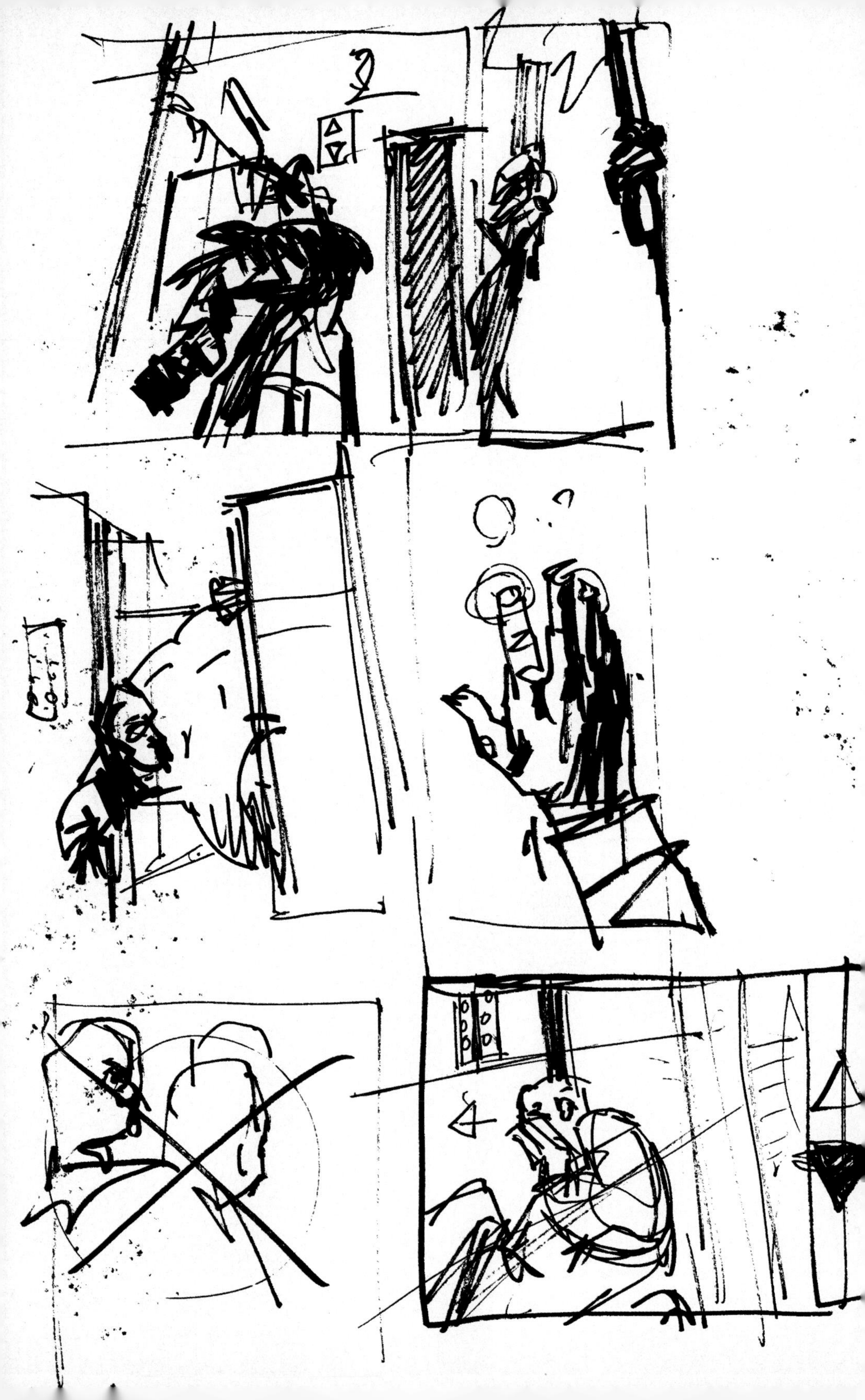

SHOOT.

SPX: BAM BAM BAM

4- HE DIVES INTO THE ELEVATOR LIKE HE IS SLIDING HOME.
BULLETS HITTING THE WALLS ABOVE HIS HEAD.

SPX: BAM BAM BAM

SPX' SPAK SPAK SPAK PING

5- SILKE'S HAND REACHING UP AND HITTING AN ELEVATOR BUTTON.

6- OVER THE SHOULDERS OF THE ASSASSINS AS THE ELEVATOR DOORS
START CLOSING.

7- INSIDE THE ELEVATOR- SILKE FREAKING OUT AS BULLETS JUST
MISS HIM. THE DOORS CLOSING.

8- SILKE SAFE IN THE ELEVATOR. ON HIS HANDS AND KNEES. HIS
GLASSES CROOKED. HIS MOUTH HANGING OPEN. HIS ENTIRE FACE
SAYS: HOLY ~~SHIT~~!

9- TIGHT ON THE ELEVATOR 'DOWN' ARROW LIT UP.

PAGE 20-

WE WILL REVEAL THAT THIS IS A QUIET CITY STREET. SILKE IS IN
A LIT PAYPHONE BOOTH ON A STREET CORNER. THE STREET IS PRETTY
MUCH DESERTED BUT THE WELL LIT PAYPHONE IS A PARGET - LIKE
WEARING A SPOTLIGHT.

SILKE IS ON THE PHONE- LOOKING ROUND FOR THE ENTIRE SCENE-
PANICKED, PARANOID, LOOKING FOR ANY KIND OF SIGN THAT HE IS

GLASSES CROOKED

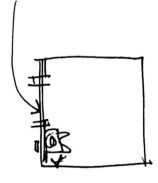

DEMONS →

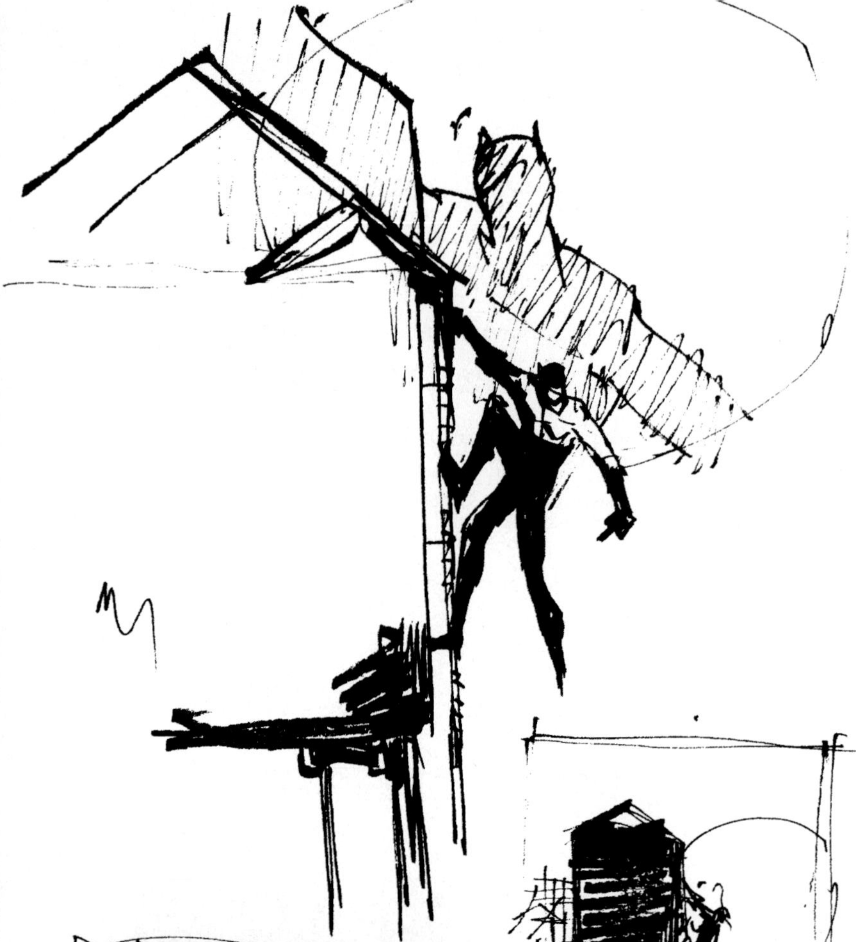

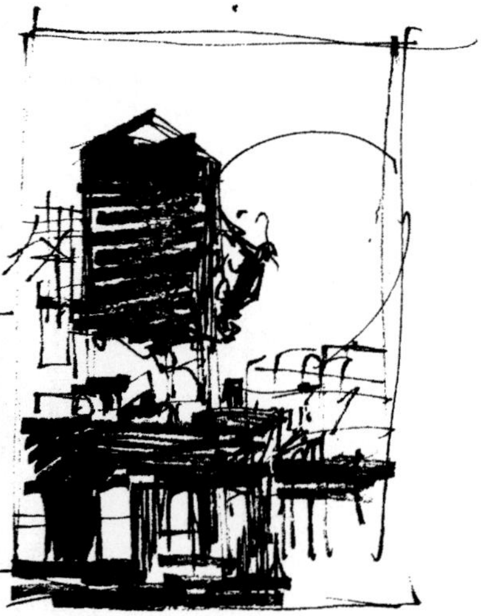

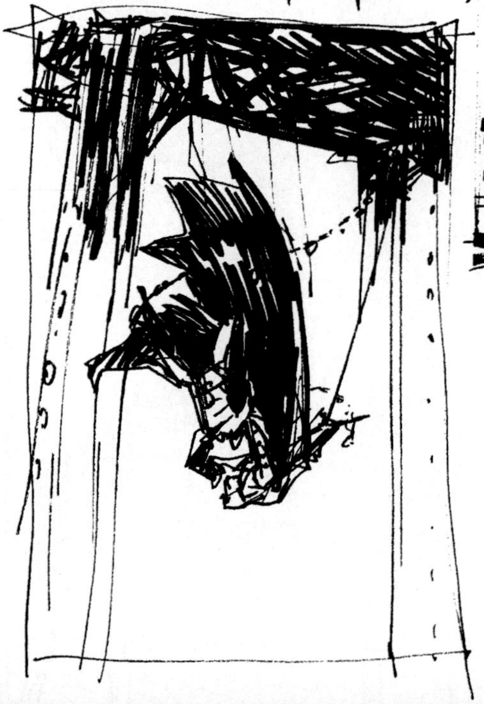

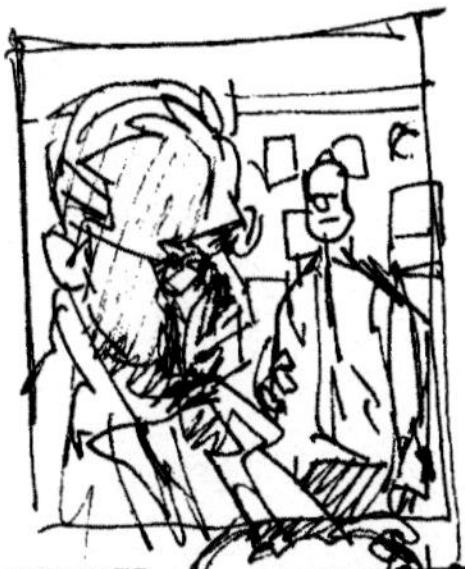

DIRECTOR DAVIS
YES- YEAH- JUST BOOK HIM.
ATTEMPTED MURDER, CONSPIRACY TO COMMIT MURDER, `RACKETEERING.
THROW THE DAMN BOOK AT HIM FOR EVERY STUPID THING HE CONFESSES TOO.
...BUT DO IT PRISTINE. LETS MAKE IT STICK FOREVER.

FBI AGENT DRIVER
SIR, HE GAVE US SOMETHING.

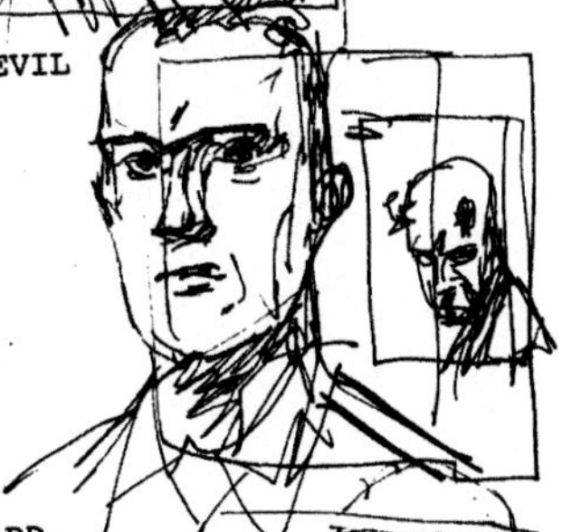

4- TIGHTER ON AGENT DRIVER- HE IS STANDING BY THE DAREDEVIL PHOTO ON THE BOARD.

FBI AGENT DRIVER (CONT'D)
HE OFFERED US SOMETHING IN EXCHANGE FOR PROTECTION.

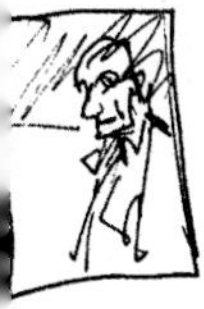

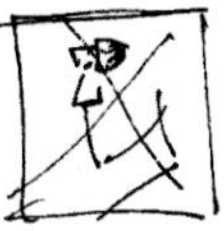

5- DIRECTOR DAVIS AT THE DOOR- CONFUSED.

DIRECTOR DAVIS
WHAT? HIS FATHER?

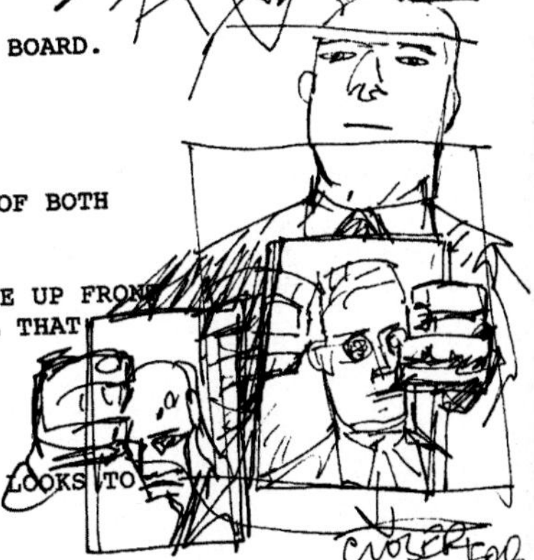

6- AGENT DRIVER TAKES THE DAREDEVIL PICTURE OFF THE BOARD.

FBI AGENT DRIVER
NO, SIR.

7- DIRECTOR DAVIS'S P.O.V. THE AGENT HANDS A 5 X 7 OF BOTH MATT MURDOCK AND DAREDEVIL.

THE DAREDEVIL PIC IS FROM A DIFFERENT ANGLE THAN THE UP FRONT PORTRAIT OF DAREDEVIL. IT SHOULDN'T BE CLEAR AT ALL THAT THESE ARE THE SAME PERSON.

PAGE 12-

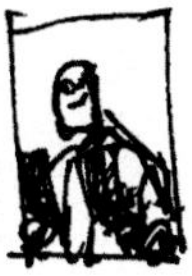

1- DIRECTOR DAVIS HOLDS BOTH. ONE IN EACH HAND AND LOOKS TO HIS AGENT.

DIRECTOR DAVIS
WHAT IS THIS?

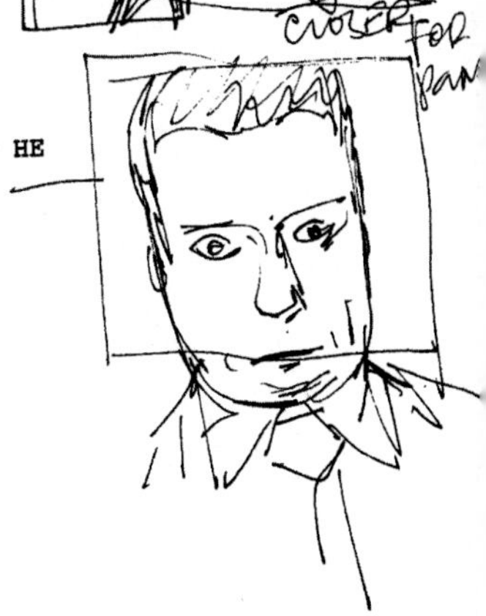
CLOSER FOR

2- TIGHT ON DRIVER, OUR TIGHTEST SHOT YET. WE SEE THAT HE BELIEVES WHAT HE IS SAYING IS TRUE.

FBI AGENT DRIVER
HE SAYS THAT THAT MAN, MATTHEW MURDOCK...

3- SAME AS ONE.

DIRECTOR DAVIS'
THE ATTORNEY- I KNOW HIM.
I'VE MET HIM.

4- SAME AS 2.

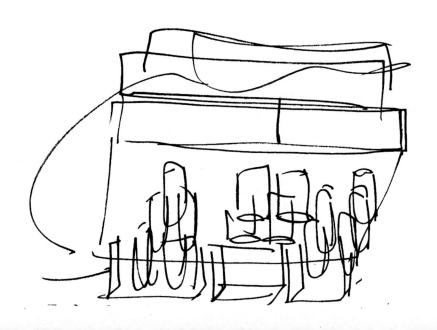

3- WIDER STILL. DOBBS LOOKS AROUND THE STREET AS HE TALKS ON THE PHONE.

AGENT DOBBS (CONT'D)
HI, ITS HENRY.
HEY, YEAH, LISTEN,
WE NEED TO TALK.
NO.
NO, IN PERSON.

RATS

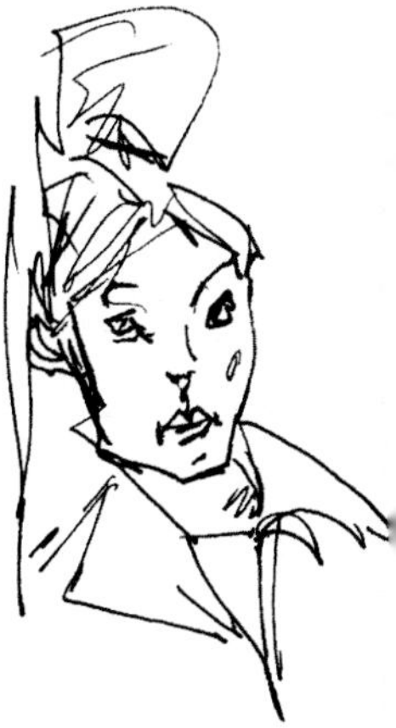

4- WIDER STILL. HE LOOKS AROUND AND LISTENS.

5- WIDER STILL. DOBBS LOOKS AROUND AS HE TALKS. PUTS HIS HAND OVER THE MOUTH PIECE.

AGENT DOBBS (CONT'D)
WELL, LET ME ASK YOU...
YOUR PAPER- IS YOUR PAPER STILL PAYING
FOR STUFF?
I MEAN- PAYING FOR A STORY?

6- WIDE OF STREET. SOMEWHERE ON THE UPPER WEST SIDE, A SMATTERING OF UNSUSPECTING NEW YORKERS WALK PST, A HUGGING COUPLE EMBRACE AND WALK.

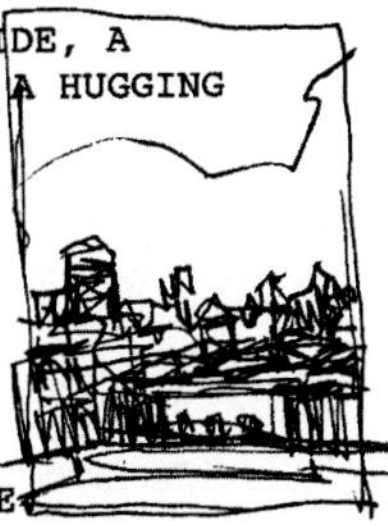

AGENT DOBBS (CONT'D)
WELL, YEAH.
ITS BIG.

PAGE 19-

1- INT. MATT MURDOCK'S BROWNSTONE- SAME AS BEFORE

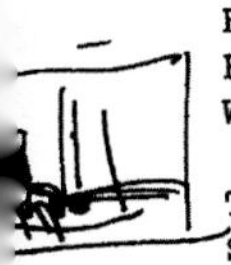

FOGGY'S P.O.V. OF A FULL FIGURE OF MATT, IN A T-SHIRT AND BOXERS, SITS, SHOULDERS SLUMPED, ON AN OTTOMAN IN HIS DARK WOOD DEN.

THE LIGHTS ARE VERY LOW. THE SHADES ARE ALL DRAWN. ITS BRIGHT SUNSHINE OUTSIDE, BUT YOU CAN'T TELL FROM LOOKING IN HERE.

ITS A HEAVY MOOD BETWEEN THE TWO. THE NEWSPAPER HEADLINE HANGS IN HIS HAND.

MATT MURDOCK
I'M AN IDIOT.

2- MATT'S P.O.V. FOGGY SITS ON A COUCH WITH HIS COFFEE HIS HANDS, HIS JACKET OFF, HIS TIE UNDONE, SLEEVES ROLLED UP.

FOGGY
HOW DOES THIS MAKE YOU AN IDIOT?

3- MATT HOLDS UP THE HEADLINE IN DEFEAT.

MATT MURDOCK
I JUST -
I NEVER EVEN IMAGINED THAT THIS COULD

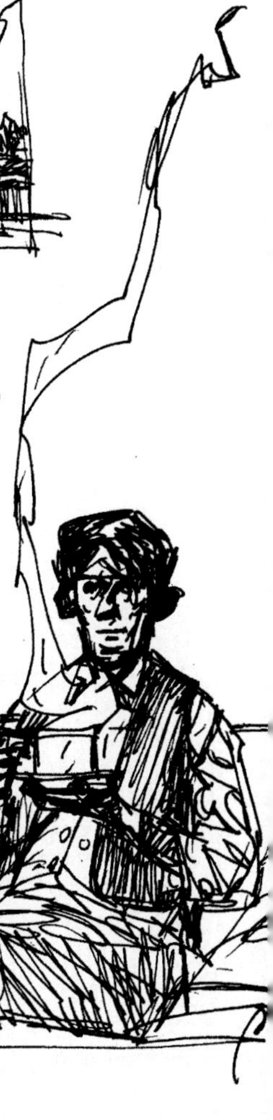

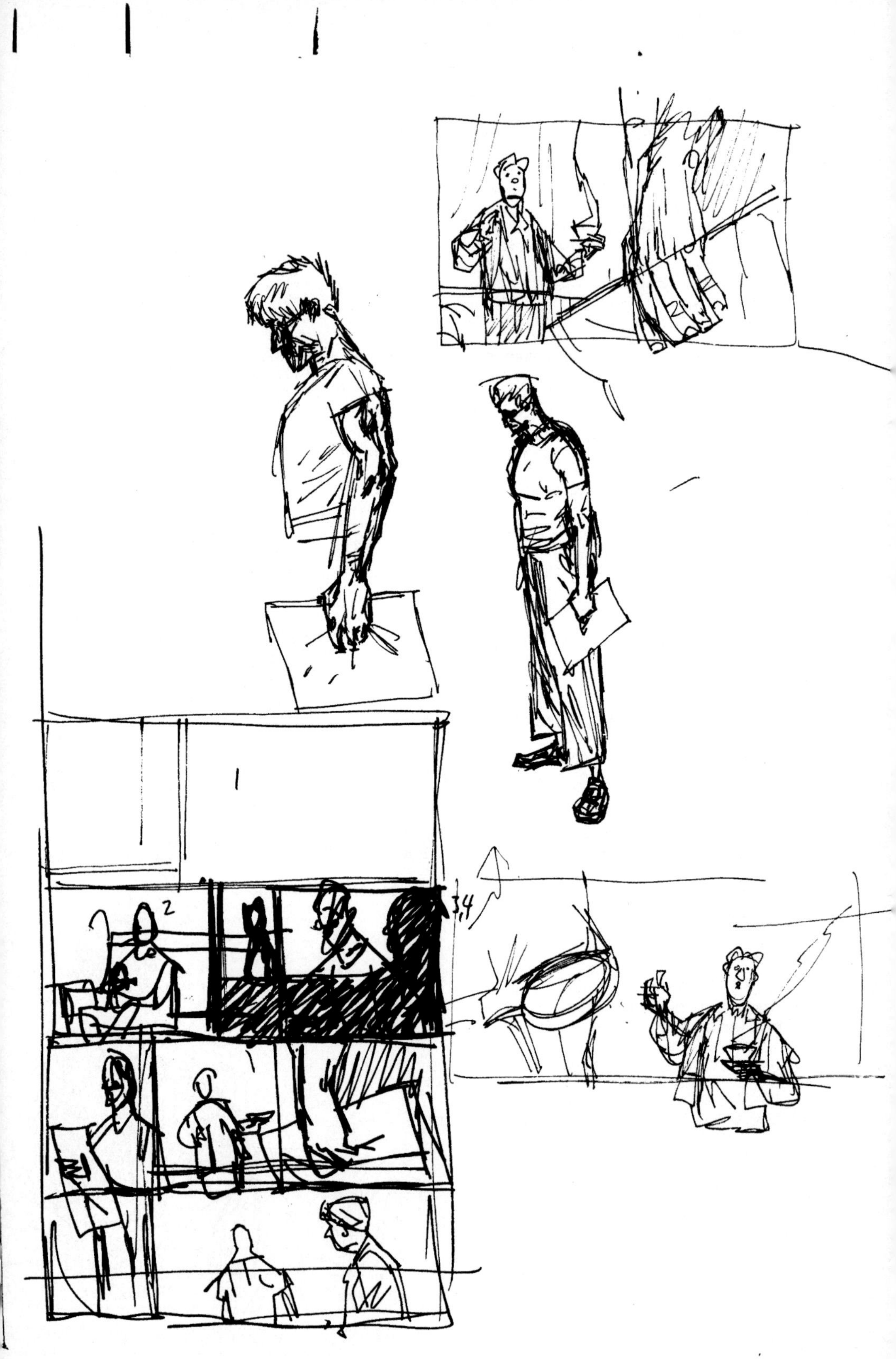
1
2
3,4

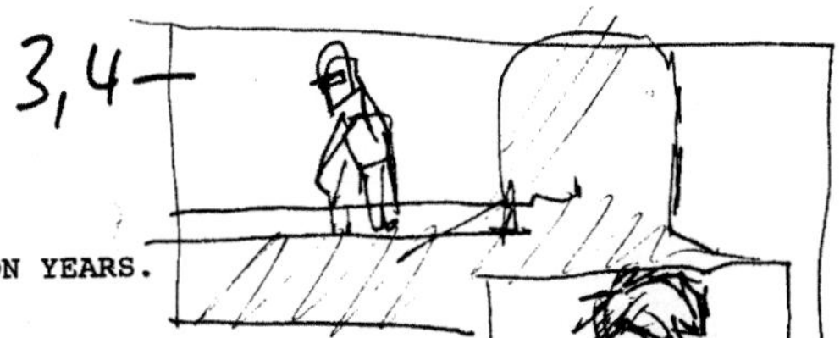
3,4-

HAPPEN.
NEVER IN A MILLION YEARS.

4- FOGGY, SHRUGS GENTLY.

FOGGY
WELL, IT WAS BOUND TO HAPPEN TO ONE OF
YOU GUYS ONE DAY.
RIGHT?

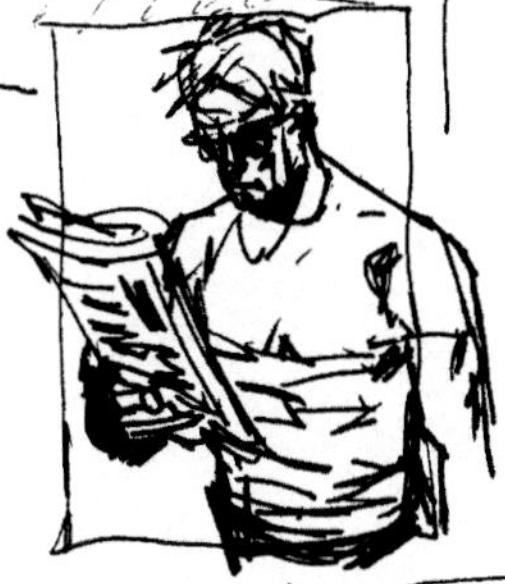

5- MATT LOOKS AT IT IN DISGUST.

MATT MURDOCK
JUST THOUGHT IT'D BE SPIDER-MAN.

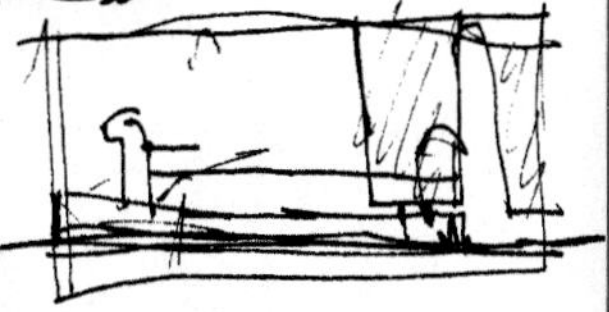

6- FOGGY SITS UP, ALMOST REGAL, PURPOSEFUL. SHAKING OFF THE DEFEAT OF IT AND BUILDING UP FOR THE FIGHT TO COME.

FOGGY
SO, WHAT ARE WE GOING TO DO?

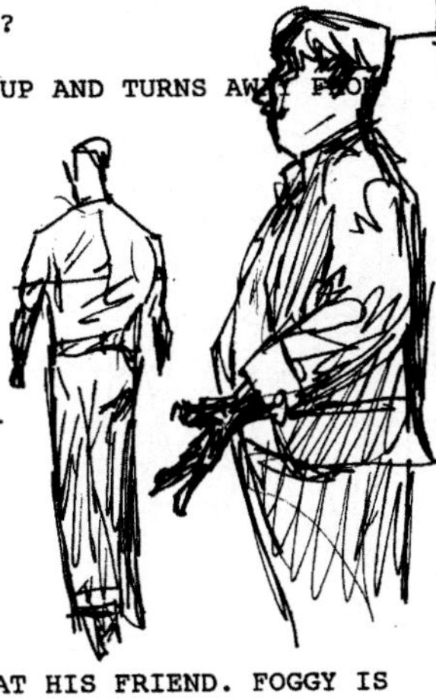

7- MID WIDE OF THE ROOM. MATT STANDS UP AND TURNS AWAY FROM FOGGY.

MATT MURDOCK
OH FOGGY, NO!

FOGGY
WHAT?

MATT MURDOCK
THIS - THIS IS MY CROSS TO-

FOGGY
OH NO.
NO NO NO.

PAGE 20-

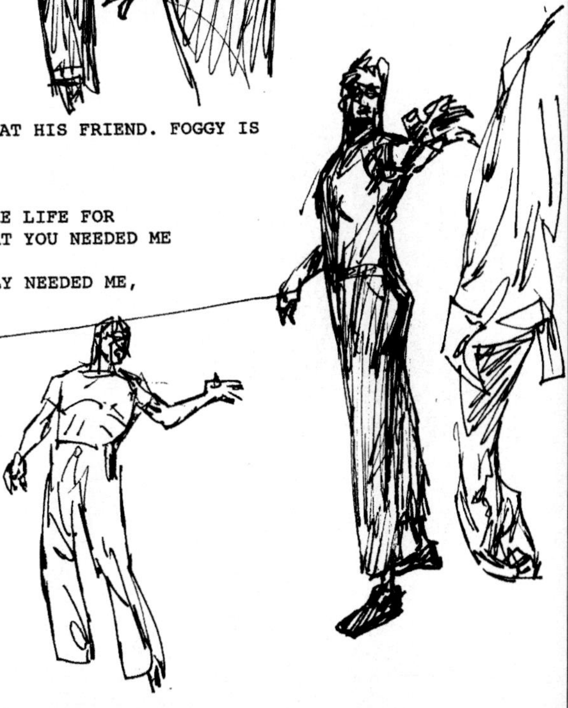

1- FROM BEHIND MATT, FOGGY GESTURES AT HIS FRIEND. FOGGY IS READY TO HELP.

FOGGY (CONT'D)
I'VE BEEN WAITING MY ENTIRE LIFE FOR
THIS. FOR THE ONE TIME THAT YOU NEEDED ME
MORE THAN I NEEDED YOU.
TO BE THERE WHEN YOU REALLY NEEDED ME,
I AM, SO, IN THIS.

2- TWO SHOT. MATT TURNS TO FOGGY.

MATT MURDOCK
FOGGY...

FOGGY
I'M IN.

MATT MURDOCK

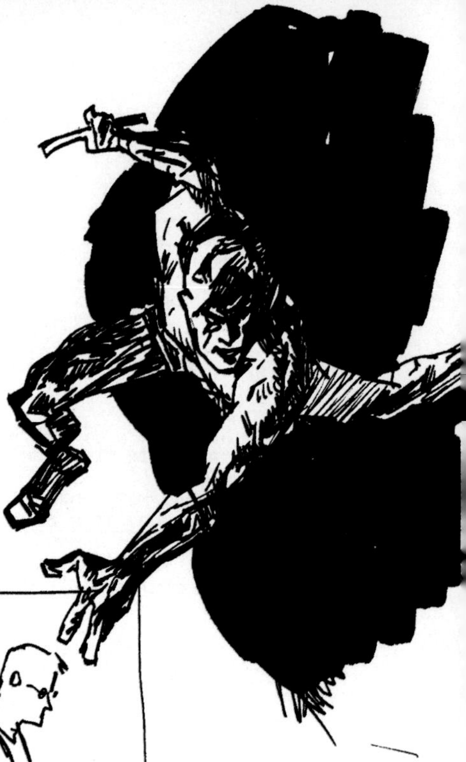

22

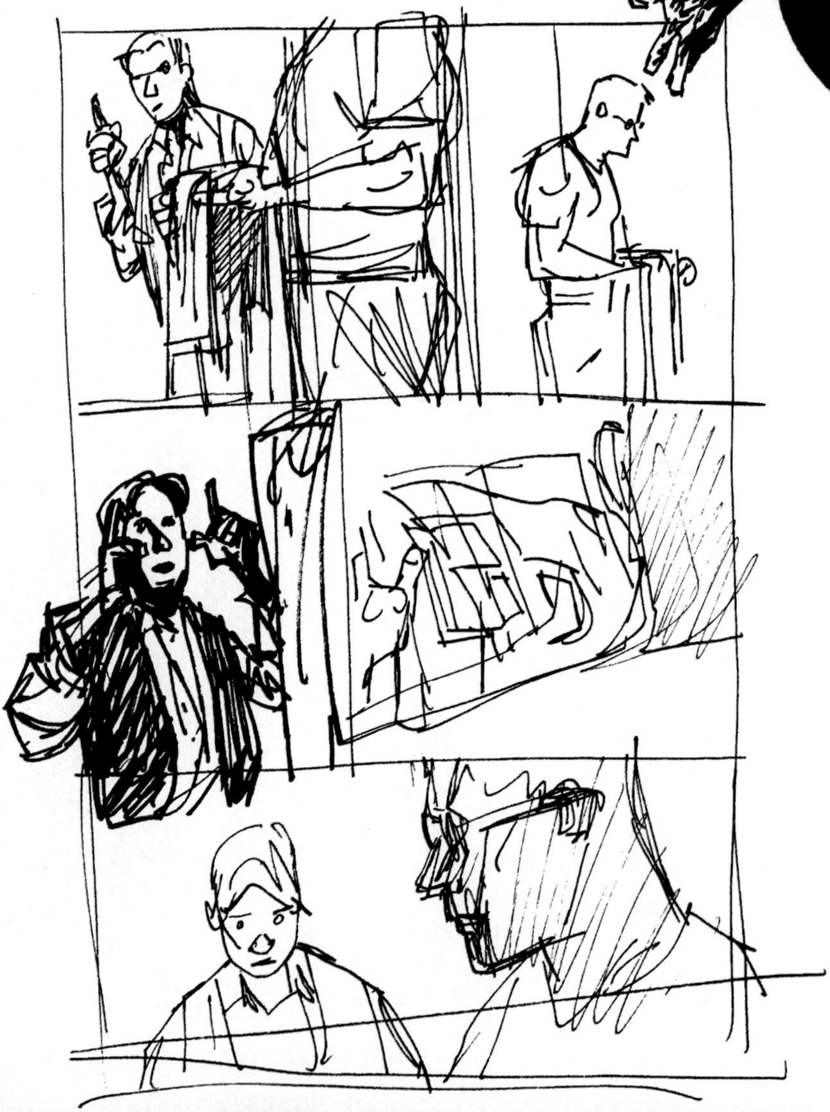

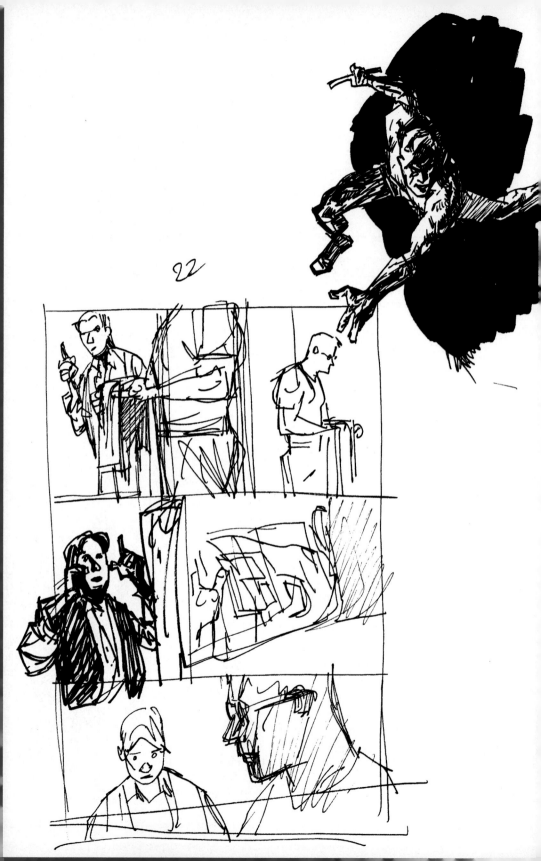

WHAT IS THIS? IS THIS NEWS? WHAT THEY
DID? NO.

3- MATT HUNCHES DOWN TO AN OLD TRUNK IN HIS DEN AND OPENS IT. HIS DAREDEVIL COSTUME FOLDED NEATLY.

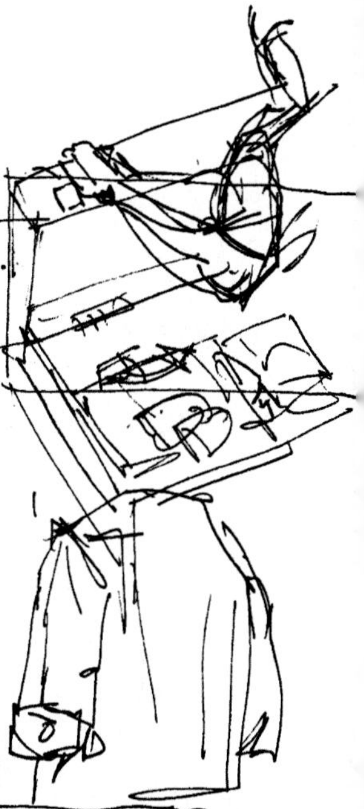

4- TIGHT ON MATT...

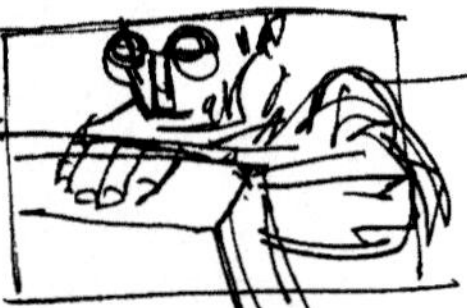

MATT MURDOCK
WHO DID THIS TO ME?

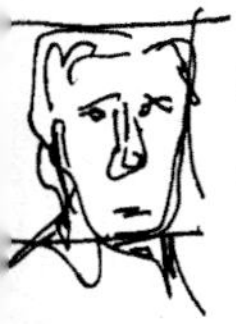

5- FOGGY HOLDS HIS TONGUE.

6- MATT STANDS HOLDING HIS COSTUME. FOGGY SMIRKS BEHIND HIM.

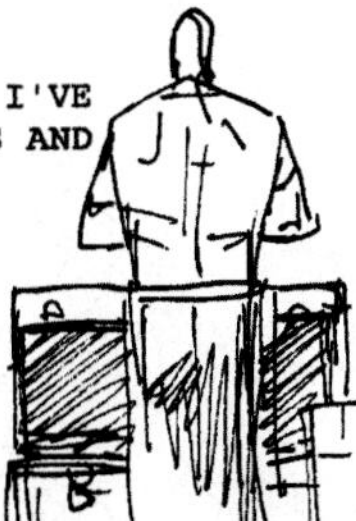

MATT MURDOCK (CONT'D)
THANK YOU FOR NOT TELLING ME THAT I'VE
BEEN VERY CARELESS WITH MY SECRETS AND
THAT IT COULD BE ANYONE.

FOGGY
YOU'RE WELCOME.
BUT YOU HAVE BEEN...
...AND IT COULD BE.

PAGE 22-

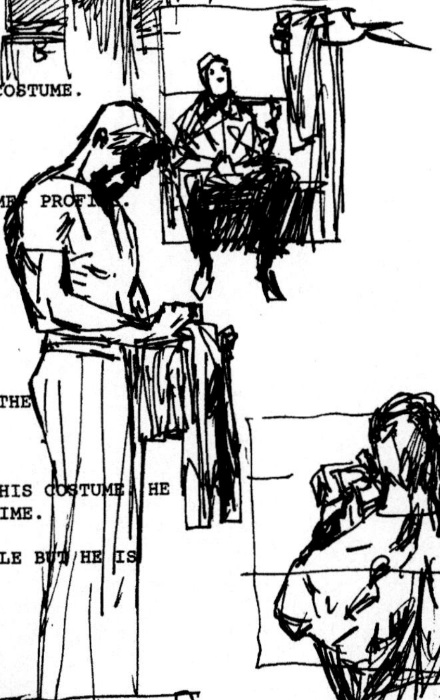

1- FOGGY LOOKS AT MATT'S HANDS HOLDING THE COSTUME.

MATT MURDOCK
BUT MAYBE- MAYBE THIS IS A SIGN.

2- FOGGY'S POV OF MATT LOOKING AT THE COSTUME- PROFILE.

MATT MURDOCK (CONT'D)
A SIGN?

3- FOGGY FRAMES HIS IMAGINARY SIGN.

FOGGY
A BIG FRICKIN' NEON SIGN.
AND IT SAYS ITS TIME TO JUST PUT THE
COSTUME AWAY ONCE AND FOR ALL.
YOU'RE DONE, DON'T YOU THINK?

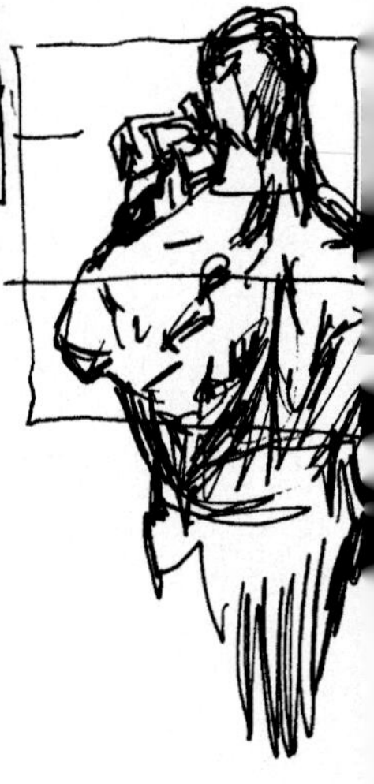

4- OVER MATT'S SHOULDER, THE DOUBLE D'S OF HIS COSTUME. HE TOUCHES THE EMBROIDERY LIKE ITS THE FIRST TIME.

5- MATT LOOKS AT FOGGY, FOGGY IS BEING GENTLE BUT HE IS SERIOUS.

FOGGY (CONT'D)
ITS TIME TO RETIRE.

TO BE CONTINUED

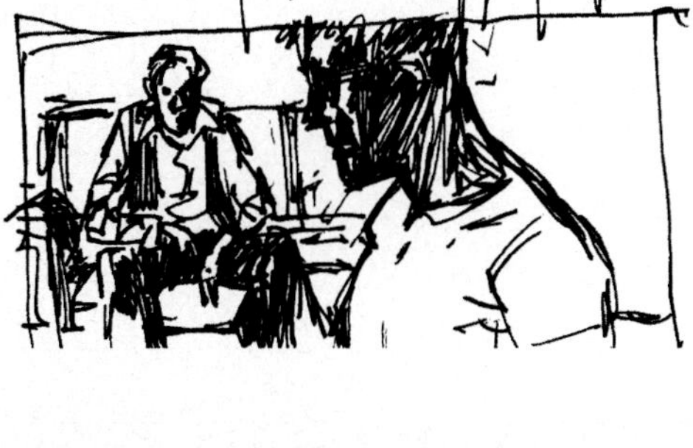

MCAUSS 5
ANSW 4

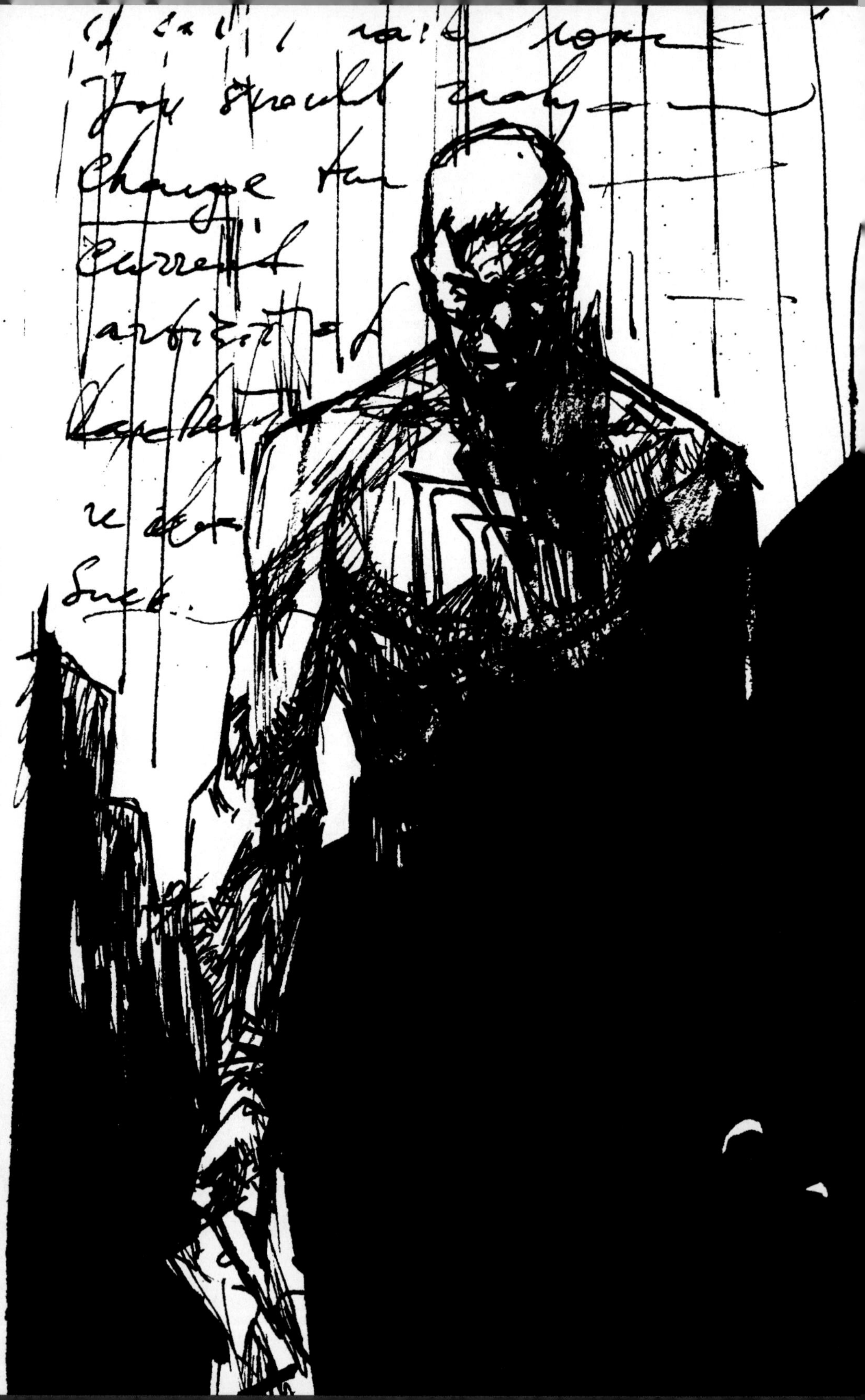
You should really
Change the
Current

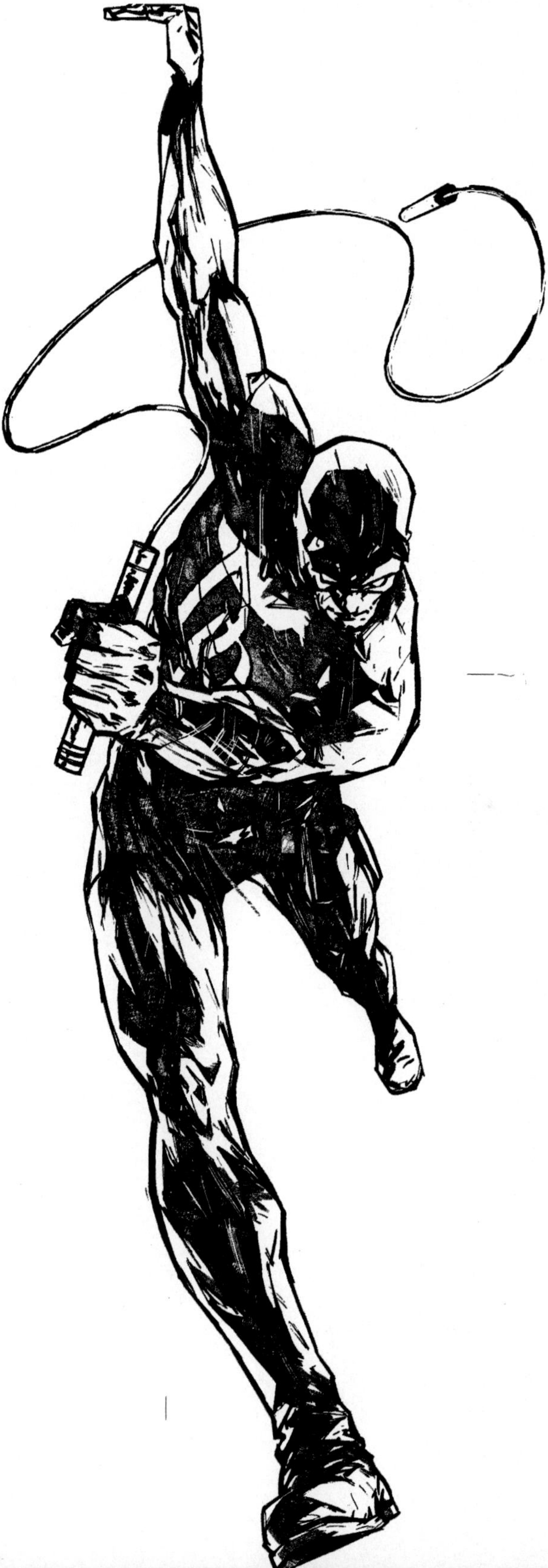

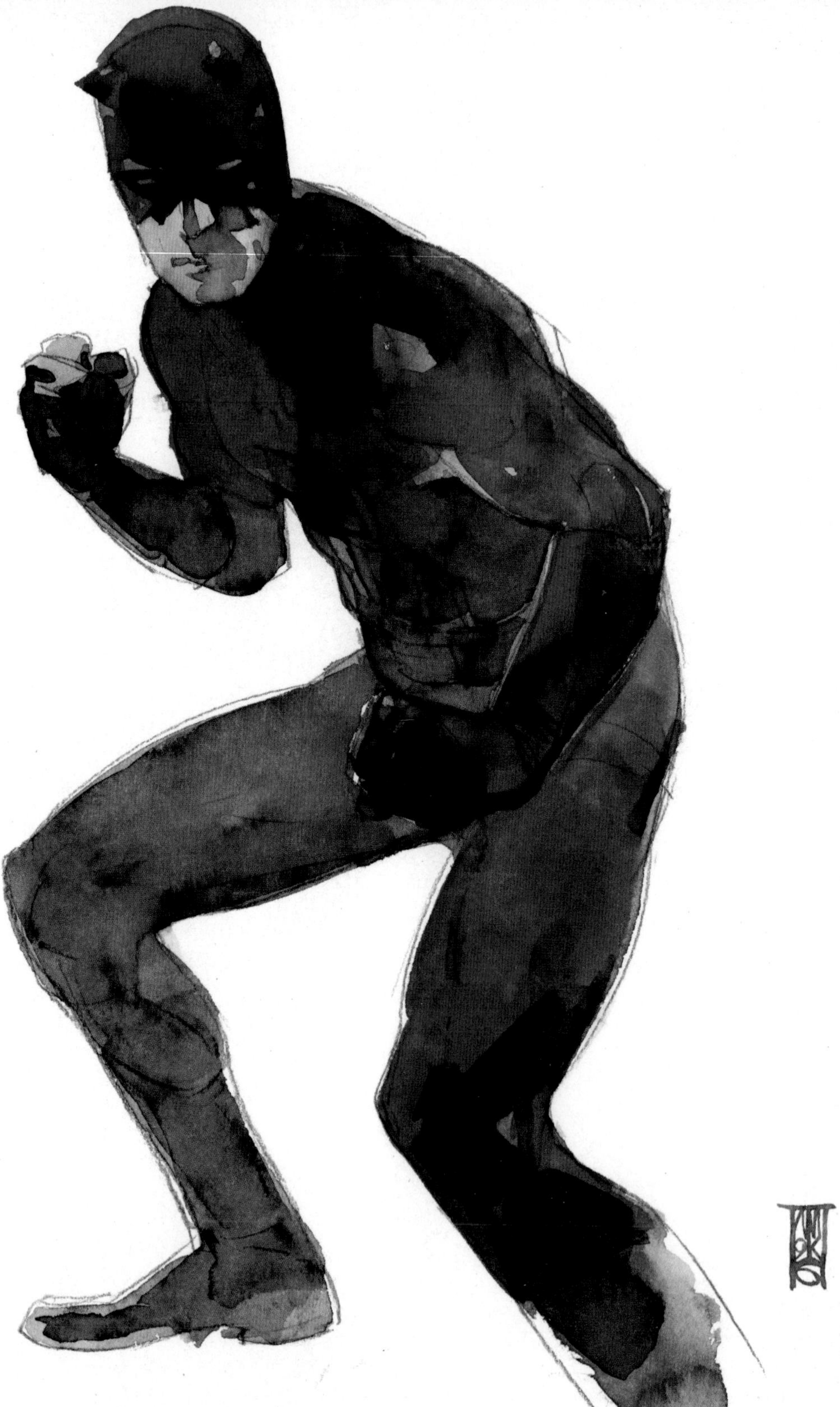